Mammoth Area Rock Climbs

The Climbing Guide to the Eastern Sierra—North

3rd Edition

Becky Hutto and Isabel Ledesma on the 3rd pitch of **Hair Raiser Buttress** 9***** at Granite Basin. ©*Kevin Calder Photo.*

See Page 237

MAMMOTH AREA ROCK CLIMBS

The Climbing Guide to the Eastern Sierra—North

BY MARTY LEWIS
AND JOHN MOYNIER
3RD EDITION

EASTERN SIERRA CLIMBING GUIDES VOL. 2

MAXIMVS PRESS

Mammoth Area Rock Climbs 3rd Edition

The Climbing Guide to the Eastern Sierra—North
by Marty Lewis and John Moynier
EASTERN SIERRA CLIMBING GUIDES VOL. 2

Maximus Press
P.O. Box 3952
Mammoth Lakes, CA 93546
Phone & Fax: 760-387-1013
E-mail: smlewis@qnet.com
http://maximuspress.com

Front Cover Photo: Theresa Morgan on the **Black Dihedral** 10b****. ©*Bill McChesney Photo.*
Left Back Cover Photo: Schatzi Sovich on **Pocket Pool** 10b**. ©*Greg Epperson Photo.*
Right Back Cover Photo: Nick Noel at the **Boy Scout Camp**. ©*Kevin Calder Photo.*

MAXIMVS PRESS

ACKNOWLEDGMENTS

This guide would have not been possible without the information and ideas provided by the following people: Craig Albright, Scott Ayers, John Bachar, Greg Barnes, Dimitri Barton, Dave Bengston, Kevin Calder, Vern Clevenger, Peter Croft, Claude Fiddler, Urmas Franosch, Steve Gerberding, Todd Graham, Alan Hirahara, Neil Hightower, Grant Hiskes, Barry Hutten, Malcolm Jolley, Kevin Leary, Bruce Lella, Lance Lewis, Dan McDevitt, Mike Melkonian, Doug Nidever, Dennis Phillips, Sean Plunkett, Dean Rosnau, Mick Ryan, Neil Satterfield, Steve Schneider, Eric Sorenson, Jim Stimson, Alan Swanson, George Swiggum, Bill Taylor, Dave Titus, Bill Trethewey, Ken Yager and Dave Yerian.

Thanks to all the photographers, their fantastic images make a giant contribution in capturing the fun and the feel of the climbing around Mammoth.

A Special thanks to Errett Allen and Alan Bartlett authors of: *"Sierra East Side Rock Climbs"* and Grant Hiskes author of: *"Sport Climbing Guide to Clark Canyon"*—valuable references and predecessors to our guide.

ABOUT CLIMBING GUIDES

The moment a climbing guide comes out, it begins a slow downward slide in accuracy; holds break, routes get added, routes get removed, bolts fail, government policies change, roads close, prices go up, business' close and acts of god occur. What you find in the real world takes precedent over anything found in a guidebook.

There are few facts in a guidebook. Climbing guides are simply collections of personal opinions. At best the information is based on a broad consensus, but the information can also be just the experience of the author or even hearsay.

While most art can easily be thrown away and forgotten, the art a first ascentionist creates on our public lands can last for generations. Because of this, it is important we have the freedom to critique these routes. In this great country the freedom to express these opinions is guaranteed—even if you ruffle some feathers.

Keep in mind guidebooks are a personal, subjective work of opinion, try not to take them too seriously. And if you want a guidebook that reflects your opinions perfectly, you'll have to write it yourself!

—Marty Lewis

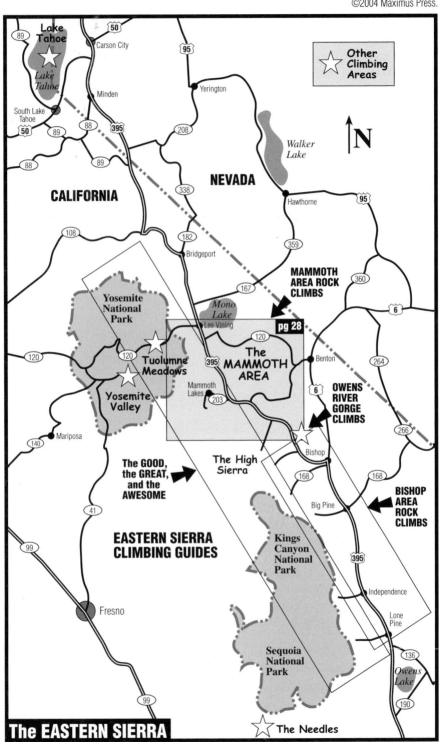

The EASTERN SIERRA

EASTERN SIERRA CLIMBING GUIDES

The Eastern Sierra is located on the edge of three major biogeographic regions: the Sierra Nevada Mountains, the Great Basin Desert and the Mojave Desert. Elevations in the Eastern Sierra range from 3,500 ft. to 14,500 ft., creating one of the most beautiful, diverse and dramatic landscapes imaginable. The area has tremendous contrasts. In the Owens Valley, Bishop is one of the driest cities in the country, with a short mild winter and a long hot summer—while 45 miles away in the High Sierra, Mammoth Lakes has a long cool winter averaging 25 feet of snow, and a short mild summer.

Within this region you will find world class bouldering, great traditional cragging, diverse sport climbing, long alpine rock climbs and quick access to Yosemite, making this area quite possibly one of the best rock climbing locations in the world. On the coldest days of winter you may be climbing on south facing volcanic boulders at 4,000 ft. or during the hottest days of summer you may be alpine cragging on north facing granite at 10,000 ft. Either way you can almost always find excellent conditions.

http://maximuspress.com

Vol. 1—
Owens River Gorge Climbs
by Marty Lewis
Featuring 600 fantastic climbs at California's premiere sport climbing area.

Vol. 3—
Bishop Area Rock Climbs
Currently Out of Print
A guidebook to the four season cragging and world class bouldering in the Bishop, California area.

Vol. 2—
Mammoth Area Rock Climbs
by Marty Lewis and John Moynier
Great summer cragging and bouldering in the cool Sierra around Mammoth Lakes, California.

Vol. 4—
The Good, the Great and the Awesome
by Peter Croft
The Guidebook to the top 40 High Sierra Rock Climbs.

MAXIMUS PRESS BOOKS

A deadly bolt more than 20 years old … one of several
thousand on popular climbs throughout the United States.

A new bolt rated to over 5,000 pounds. The ASCA
wants to replace the bad bolt above with one of these.

Bad Bolts Kill

We need YOUR help. The American Safe Climbing Association has helped replace more than
4,500 bolts throughout the country. We estimate that there are more than 20,000 bad bolts
remaining on popular climbs today. Your $50 donation will make at least one route safe . . . and
that one route could be the next one you climb. The ASCA would like to get there before you do.

The American Safe Climbing Association is a 501(c)3 organization and contributions are tax-deductible.

TABLE OF CONTENTS

Chapter 6

Chapter 7

Chapter 8

Chapter 9

Chapter 10

Chapter 11

FOREWORD

Backward: In the fall of 1980, I followed the example of a few good friends and fled my love/hate relationship with "The Ditch", driving east over Tioga Pass and landing in Mammoth. I found myself in the midst of what surely must be one of the most beautiful, spectacular and incredible places to live and recreate on this earth. I soon met some of the few local climbers, like Marty Lewis (there were probably no more than 50 active local climbers in the entire area at the time) and my companions and I began to survey this awesome realm.

Some vivid lasting memories: a mountain lion crossing Johnny Meadow, bald eagles floating in the wind over White Mountain, bobcat kittens running along the road near Clark Canyon, a sunrise at the Buttermilks lighting up Basin Mountain wreathed in golden clouds, that defies description, and, oh yes… there's the climbing.

Some great earlier pioneers like Fred Beckey, Doug Robinson, Dean Hobbs, Bob Harrington and others had already left us a legacy of amazing routes widely scattered across this immense landscape. We repeated many of these classics, but having survived the struggles, triumphs and failures of Yosemite walls, we were ready for more, and almost everywhere we looked were untouched crags in beautiful semi-wilderness settings. Kids in a candy store. Over the next several years we tried to tag every first ascent in the East Sierra. I believe I can safely claim that we scratched the surface.

One day, after watching the space shuttle blow up on live TV in the morning, we went out to the Benton Crags in a somber mood, did a new route and named it "Challenger". One day I watched one of my best friends pull a dishwasher sized block off while leading a new route, take a hideous fall and whack his melon when the rope stopped him. We spent the entire drive back to the Mammoth hospital trying to talk him out of his insistence on driving while the blood ran into his eyes (he recovered completely—no dumber than before). One day while looking for new routes at an area near Mammoth, we stumbled across a hidden defile full of ancient native paintings, reminding us who the real pioneers were.

Fast Forward: This is the great stuff, the stuff you will always remember even more than all the pristine clear blue days when everything was perfect—a common occurrence on the East Side. I've read some silly stuff over the years about the challenge, intellectual loftiness or "Zen" of climbing. Ultimately, in my humble opinion, climbing is pointless and stupid… and I've always loved it. The routes are out there for anyone willing to pull on a pair of sticky loafers. Make good memories. I sincerely hope that everyone who uses this volume will love, appreciate and enjoy the Eastern Sierra as much as I did. If you are reading this you are probably surrounded by treasure. Go spend it.

—Errett Allen
Estes Park, CO

Preface

The inspiration for this guidebook began many years ago. The locations of most of the crags in the area were a closely guarded secret and only a few climbers knew the whereabouts of even the most accessible crags. Many climbers agreed that eventually these areas should get the attention from the climbing community that they deserved, but the question was how.

In addition to the word-of-mouth "buzz" through the climbers' grapevine, the area was covered in the 1988 guidebook "Sierra East Side Rock Climbs", written by Errett Allen and Alan Bartlett. The book went out of print in the summer of 1992, however, and it is just about impossible to obtain. During the summer of 1990, Climbing magazine featured an article by John Sherman further expounding the incredible bouldering in the area, and there had been an article on Deadman bouldering many years before.

With the development of the Owens River Gorge into a world class climbing area many climbers were soon passing through the Mammoth Area. With an exceptional summer climate, climbers looked to this area as a way to beat the heat. The Deadman bouldering areas became recognized for its quality climbing and clean landings. However, this area was able to remain a bolt-free, highball and top-rope crag and so locals had to look elsewhere to satisfy their sport climbing jones.

Clark Canyon offered unique pocket climbing on steep bolt protected rock. This area had been overlooked previously and knowledge of the area was primarily word-of-mouth. What little was known concerned the uniquely featured boulders at the north end of the canyon, including the "Swiss Cheese Boulders" and the now popular "Potato Patch". As the area's potential became known, a loose-leaf, underground guide was produced by longtime local climber Grant Hiskes, but after he left the area this task was left to me.

By this time, the local climbing shop that I managed was being bombarded with climbers wanting information on the local routes. Trying to maintain Grant's little guide was taking too much effort (due to the immediate popularity and intense rapid route development of Clark Canyon), so Marty Lewis and I decided that it was time to publish a real guide. That was the fall of 1992 and after a heavy winter, we both looked forward to researching the areas found in this guide. After much deliberation, we decided to cover most of the areas within a reasonable drive from the Town of Mammoth Lakes.

Now in the 3rd edition, we have expanded the book to include the crags covered in the original "Sierra East Side" guidebook and added the most recent developments and discoveries. So here is our guide to the climbing found in the Mammoth Area. We hope you enjoy it!

—*John Moynier*

See Page 208

Colin Broadwater bouldering at the **Fault Line**. ©*Shawn Reeder Photo.*

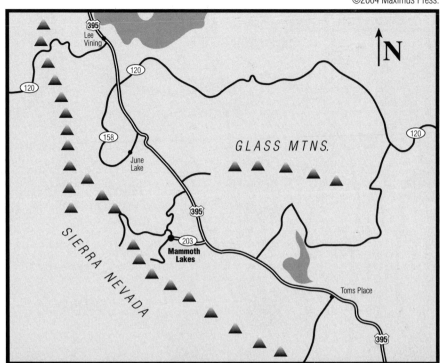

CHAPTER 1

INTRODUCTION

©2004 Maximus Press.

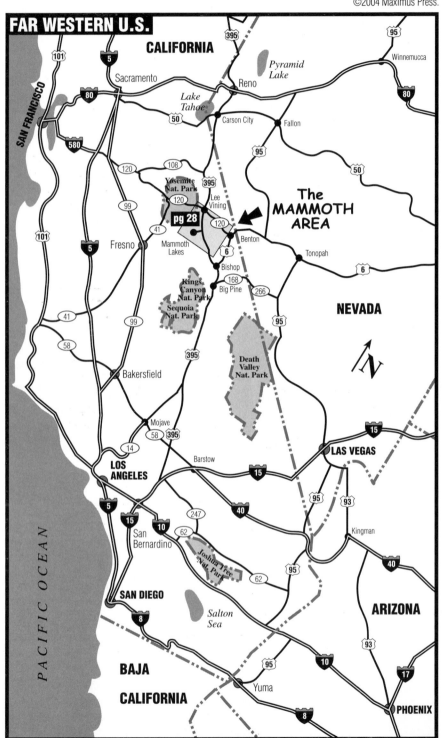

INTRODUCTION

C ongratulations! You are examining the latest edition of the first comprehensive guidebook devoted to the Mammoth Area. This book has been painstakingly researched for *your* enjoyment. This is the resource that all future guidebook authors will use as a reference. Please read the entire introduction.

This guidebook will help you find a variety of interesting crags amidst the worlds largest single-stand forest of sweet smelling Jeffrey Pines. Individually the crags in this book would be considered minor areas, but considered collectively the quantity and quality of these crags makes for an excellent climbing experience. Soon you can be pulling down on steep volcanic rock; either killer sport routes or bouldering. You can also climb on excellent granite; options include gear routes, sport climbs or bouldering.

Where is the Mammoth Area?

The Town of Mammoth Lakes is located in East-Central California, east of Yosemite National Park, high in the Sierra Nevada Mountains. Highway 395 provides access to the Eastern Sierra and the Town of Mammoth Lakes.

Driving Times (in hours):

Los Angeles 5.5	Yosemite Valley 2.5*	Tuolumne Meadows 1*
Reno 3	Salt Lake City 8	Joshua Tree 6.5
Las Vegas 5.5	Sacramento 5	Smith Rock 9.5

*Tioga Pass (Hwy. 120) is usually closed from November through May. This makes Yosemite Valley an epic 8 hour drive. Tuolumne Meadows becomes accessible only by ski touring.

Climate

The relatively high elevation of these crags (6,600 ft.—10,700 ft.) and the long snowy winters here combine to make these primarily late spring to fall climbing areas. Furthermore, many of these areas are accessed by dirt logging roads which are not plowed (or graded) and may not be passable due to snowdrifts until late May or June. Daytime temperatures in summer are generally in the high 70°s. Occasionally a pattern of afternoon thundershowers, complete with hail and lightning, can last for days. Nighttime temperatures are cool, and often dip below freezing. Fall usually starts with an Indian Summer (calm sunny days and crisp nights). Eventually there will be a snowstorm followed by cold weather. This signifies the beginning of winter. This can occur anywhere from early October to early December, bringing an end to the climbing season in the Mammoth Area.

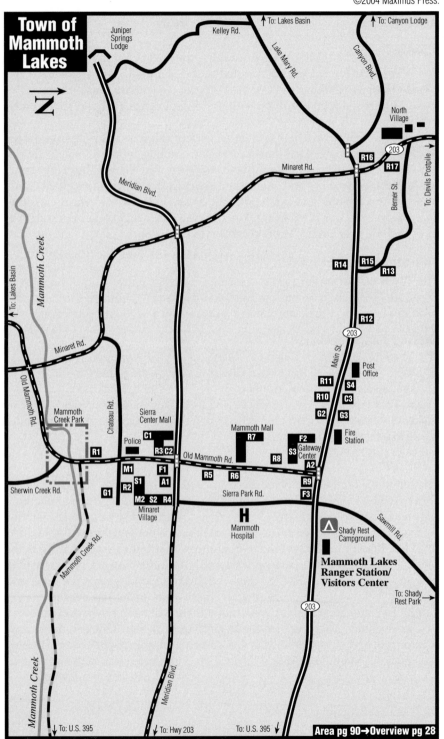

Amenities

ATM's/Banks
A1. Union Bank
A2. Bank of America

Coffee
C1. Sierra's Best Coffee
☎ 934-7408.
C2. Starbucks
C3. Looney Bean
☎ 934-1435.

Fast Food
F1. Carls Jr.
F2. Subway
F3. McDonalds

Gear/Gyms
G1. Body Shop
Weight lifting and climbing. ☎ 934-3700.
G2. Mammoth Mountaineering Supply
Awesome climbing shop. ☎ 934-4191.
www.MammothGear.com.
See advertisement on page 270.
G3. Kittredge Sports
General sport shop with climbing gear.
☎ 934-7566.

Movie Theaters
M1. Plaza Theater
☎ 934-3131.
M2. Minaret Cinemas
☎ 934-3131.

Restaurants
B=Breakfast, L=Lunch, D=Dinner.
R1. Stove (BLD)
Country Cookin'. ☎ 934-2821.
R2. Skadi (D)
Fine dining, great atmosphere and awesome views. ☎ 934-3902.
R3. Shogun (D)
Japanese cuisine, awesome sushi.
☎ 934-3970.

R4. Giovanni's (LD)
Gourmet pizza and Italian food.
☎ 934-7563.
R5. Grumpy's (LD)
Sports bar/ restaurant. ☎ 934-8587.
R6. Roberto's Cafe (LD)
Authentic Mexican food. ☎ 934-3667.
R7. Good Life (BL)
Wholesome, healthy food. ☎ 934-1734.
R8. Nik-n-Willies (LD)
Great sandwiches, pizza, takeout.
☎ 934-2012.
R9. Breakfast Club (BL)
Breakfast and bakery. ☎ 934-6944.
R10. Paul Schat's Bakery (BL)
Fresh baked goods. ☎ 934-6055.
R11. Base Camp Cafe (BLD)
Good food, reasonable prices, mountaineering decor. ☎ 934-3900.
R12. Angel's (LD)
Hearty homestyle cooking. ☎ 934-7427.
R13. Gomez's (LD)
Great Mexican food. ☎ 924-2693.
R14. Matsu (LD)
Asian cuisine, eat in or take out.
☎ 934-8277.
R15. Tommy Ho's (LD)
Pizza and sandwiches. ☎ 934-8140
R16. Whiskey Creek (D)
Steakhouse, bar and microbrews.
☎ 934-2555
R17. Bergers (LD)
Great burgers and sandwiches.
☎ 934-6622.

Shopping
S1. Vons
Large supermarket with pharmacy.
S2. Booky Joint
Books (excellent climbing section), Music, Video Rentals. ☎ 934-3240.
See advertisement on page 271.
S3. Rite-Aid
Pharmacy and general store.
S4. Napa Auto Parts
☎ 934-3375.

Access Information

Practically every crag in the Mammoth Area is located on public land administered by the Inyo National Forest. Granite Basin and the High Tension Boulders are located on land administered by the Bureau of Land Management. If you are a citizen of this great country—you own these lands.

Some of the bouldering located on the Sherwin Plateau is on private property owned by the Los Angeles Department of Water and Power. Historically the L.A.D.W.P. has allowed recreation on their land. We as climbers must use this land responsibly, and respect any rules that are imposed. If we don't, we could be denied access to these lands.

Recently, the Town of Mammoth Lakes and its environs have entered a phase of unprecedented development. The effects of this growth are rippling up and down the Eastern Sierra. As more and more people try to recreate on the same limited resources—Land Managers will find themselves between a rock and a hard place. It is almost inevitable that our freedoms will be restricted further. This may take the form of fee areas, mandatory shuttle buses, quotas, and certain dirt roads being closed to vehicles. Only the future knows.

Guidelines
- ☞ Be respectful and courteous to Land Managers.
- ☞ Follow all posted rules and regulations.
- ☞ Never drive off of established roads.
- ☞ Maintain a low profile.

Camping
There are a number of camping options. The area maps at the beginning of each chapter show the locations of various official campgrounds and some choices for primitive camping. Camping reservations: ☎ 877-444-677 or www.reserveusa.com.

Primitive Camping
Free dispersed camping is allowed almost anywhere away from paved roads and settlements, on public land, unless posted otherwise. Be discrete and pick hardened sites (previously used campsites). Check with the Forest Service office in Bishop, Mammoth Lakes or Lee Vining for more information.

- ☞ Do not camp in the parking areas of the crags. The Forest Service and Bureau of Land Management have made it quite clear that the parking areas are neither dispersed or discrete.
- ☞ Never camp on L.A.D.W.P. land.

Environmental Concerns

Please note that these are beautiful natural areas. Please remove all signs of your passing, including tape, litter and other trash. Try to stick to established trails. If you must answer the call to nature, please do so at least 100 feet from trails, routes and water sources. Never drive off of the established dirt roads.

Brief History

The Mammoth area has a rich history of climbing. The familiar alpine backdrop of the Minarets has inspired Sierra climbers from the days of John Muir, who made the first ascent of Mt. Ritter, the tallest summit in the area, in 1872. Charles Michael, one of California's earliest rock climbing pioneers, climbed perhaps the hardest route in the country when he ascended Michael's Minaret in 1923.

The Town of Mammoth Lakes has long been a haunt for Yosemite climbers looking for an escape from the Valley. The development of the resort community, in conjunction with the growth of the Mammoth Mountain Ski Area (and the winter jobs it offered), provided an attractive place to live outside of the claustrophobic confines of the Valley. Of course, most early climbers were primarily interested in climbing long routes, preferably crack systems on alpine granite. The popularity of nearby Tuolumne Meadows (at least in summer) added to the region's attraction, and many climbers put down roots (and routes) in the area.

With so much alpine rock around, it took awhile before these climbers turned their attention to the smaller volcanic crags hidden in the local forests. The glory was in run-out, multi-pitch routes, not forty foot tall boulders (no matter how steep or difficult) and the pocket-lined crags hidden in the forests around Mammoth were left to a select few who early-on had embraced the thrills and challenges of bouldering, not just as a means to train for longer routes, but as an end in itself.

Word of the amazing overhanging, pocketed cliffs offering a great pump and soft pumice landings began to circulate amongst climbers across the country. Although the location of these cliffs were a closely guarded secret, eventually enough climbers had heard of Deadman Summit to start sniffing around the maze of old logging roads in the Mammoth area for other crags.

The cat was out of the bag and climbers were soon coming to the Mammoth area just to play on the pumping top-rope and boulder problems of the Deadman's crags, Bachar Boulders and the Lion's Den.

By the late 1980s the nearby Owens River Gorge had begun to be developed as a sport climbing area, complete with eighty foot routes and closely spaced bolts. Wilting under the debilitating summer heat in the Gorge, however, climbers began searching the higher elevations and cool forests of the Mammoth area for leadable climbs. Eventually the accessible crags in Clark Canyon and the Bear Crag began to be developed as sport climbing crags. The fine welded tuff provides some of the most unique and enjoyable climbing in the Eastern Sierra.

Finally, the Mammoth area has come full circle as climbers have begun to turn their attention back to the granite cliffs. Armed with cordless drills, beefy bolts and sport climbing ethics, many of the crags once deemed "climbed out" now offer a wealth of excellent new routes. Foremost of these is the Dike Wall and Crystal Crag in the Mammoth Lakes Basin and the Gong Show Crag in Rock Creek Canyon. Enjoy!

John Bachar placing a bolt on the first ascent of **Stumpbuckets** 12b*** at the Stumps (1987). ©*Dimitri Barton Photo.*

See Page 151

First Ascent Ethics

Every crag in this book has a separate history and separate ethics. Please respect the history of the individual crags before arbitrarily bolting a new route.

Squeeze Jobs

Because of the nature of volcanic rock, just about any piece of rock can be climbed. Does this mean we should grid bolt all the formations? No! Squeeze jobs detract from the beauty of the original lines.

☞ If your proposed route would share numerous holds with a preexisting route it is a squeeze job.

☞ If a climber on your proposed route would interfere with a climber on an adjacent route it is a squeeze job.

☞ If bolts on your proposed route can easily be clipped from the adjacent route it is a squeeze job.

Anchors

Mussy Hook Anchor System.

With the exception of multi-pitch traditional climbs and bouldering areas, most easily accessible crags should have fixed anchors at the top. Usually, this is the environmentally responsible thing to do. This saves the delicate ecosystems above and to the sides of the crags from the heinous erosion caused by scores of climbers "walking off".

Sling wads, chains and coldshuts are no longer appropriate anchors. After years of experimentation there is an anchor system that is quickly becoming the standard for the Eastern Sierra. Most first ascentionists, CRAG and the ASCA have all agreed to use these anchors exclusively on Eastside crags. The anchor consists of a quick link and tow hook on a conventional bolt hanger. This system is known as a "Mussy Hook" and can be purchased from Fish Products (see advertisement on page 272) or from Maximus Press (see page 286).

First Ascent Guidelines

☞ On free climbs pitons should not be used, place a bolt if necessary.

☞ Keep the number of projects to a minimum.

☞ If you put up a route—you may get a bunch of high-fives from your bros—but from others you may be criticized. Try not to take it too personal, it's part of the game.

Climbing in the Mammoth Area

Conduct

Your style of climbing is your own business. However, please operate within these simple rules when in the Mammoth Area:

☞ If you retreat off a route before the anchors, please leave a carabiner behind. Leaving a retreat sling is ugly, dangerous, and considered bad style.

☞ Please don't leave chalk graffiti on the crags. This includes giant tick marks, arrows, X's and words.

Is this really necessary? Clark Canyon hieroglyphics.

☞ Rather than clipping a bolt and hypocritically spraying that you could have gotten a piece of gear in, it would be way prouder to actually carry gear and place it.

☞ Because of the large investment of time, energy and money involved, please don't attempt to redpoint other people's projects (these are usually marked with a red tag on the first bolt or a fixed rope).

The Rock

Most of the climbing in the Mammoth area is on welded volcanic tuff, similar in some respects to both the Owens River Gorge and Smith Rock. The best of the welded tuff has a dark, smooth patina, with numerous pockets. At its worst, the rock is very flaky and rotten to the core. Sometimes the differences may be just a few feet away on the same outcrop.

Granite is the other type of rock predominately found here, it can vary from perfect glacier polish to grainy and crumbly.

Equipment

The following is a list of suggestions for the different types of climbing:

Gear Climbs: Bring a standard rack—cams, nuts and runners.

Sport Climbs: 14 quickdraws and a long rope (60m or more).

Top-roping: Long runners and some gear may be required.

Bouldering: A bouldering pad. Top-roping gear can come in handy for the many tall problems.

Fixed Anchors

The anchors in the Mammoth Area take a tremendous beating. To help reduce wear and tear, use quickdraws at the anchors; especially for extended top-roping sessions. Donations for anchor replacement can be made to the local organization CRAG at Wilson's Eastside Sports (see advertisement on page 271) or at the Rubber Room (see advertisement on page 273). A portion of the profits from this guidebook are spent on route maintenance.

Safety Concerns
Climbing is dangerous, think safety!

Prevention
The top four ways to get seriously injured or killed are:

#1. Climber dropped by belayer. Many of the routes in the Mammoth Area are rope stretchers. Get in a habit of tying a knot in the end of the rope. Communicate with your belayer when getting lowered. The belayer should watch for the end of the rope.

#2. Climber failed to tie in properly. Get in the habit of checking your knot before you step off the ground, when the climbing gets tough, and before lowering.

#3. Dropping loose rock. Even on popular routes holds will occasionally break. Don't hang out under climbers.

#4. Falling off of tall boulders. Be careful on highball boulder problems, if you don't feel solid try to down-climb.

Objective Hazards
Weather: Be ready for thunderstorms and lightning to come in fast and violently, especially on hot summer afternoons.

Ticks: Bloodthirsty ticks are often found lurking in the brush on the approaches to most of the volcanic crags (ticks are especially partial to Clark Canyon).

Wildlife: Mountain Lions, Bears and Coyotes inhabit all of these areas. Sightings are extremely rare, but you should still keep a close eye on your children and dogs.

In Case of an Accident
In the event of a serious injury, you should telephone for emergency help by dialing 911.

Medical Care is available at:
Mammoth Hospital
85 Sierra Park Rd.
Mammoth Lakes
☎ 760-934-3311.

To get there, drive U.S. 395 until reaching the Mammoth Lakes (Hwy. 203) exit. Drive west on Hwy. 203 for 2 miles. Turn left on Sierra Park Rd. (McDonalds is on the corner). After less than a mile the hospital will be seen on the left.

How to Use This Guide

U.S. 395 is the major route both to the Mammoth Area and connecting the various crags. The crags in this guide are orientated from south to north, beginning with the Rock Creek Area and ending with Lee Vining Canyon.

Roads

Many of the crags in this book are accessed via dirt roads. A vast majority of these can be negotiated in any standard car. Some of the roads are narrow and lined with sagebrush, if you drive a giant vehicle, it will most certainly get scratched up.

Maps

This book features a number of exploding maps. The first is an Overview Map (page 28) which shows the general layout of the Mammoth Region and the individual areas. The Area Maps will help you find the individual crags and assist you in driving to them. Approach Maps show the final driving directions as well as the hike to the crags. Make sure to set and use your odometer, there are many more single lane dirt roads than the maps show.

After this more complex crags may have Crag Maps and Cliff Maps. The page numbers listed with the maps will allow you to zoom in and out as necessary.

Approach Instructions

The approach instructions will be found at the beginning of each individual crag's introduction. Referencing the Area Map (at the beginning of each chapter) and the Approach Map should get you where your going. The directions for each crag begin at the junction of Hwy. 203 and U.S. 395 (the

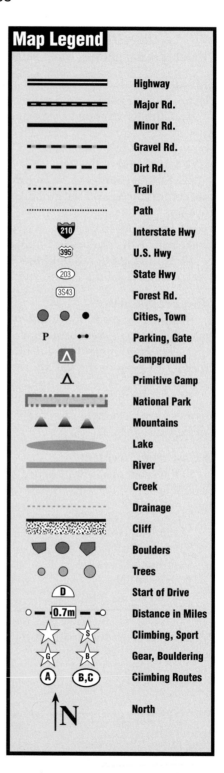

Map Legend

═══════	Highway
━ ━ ━ ━	Major Rd.
━━━━━━	Minor Rd.
▬ ▬ ▬ ▬	Gravel Rd.
▬ ▬ ▬ ▬	Dirt Rd.
··············	Trail
··················	Path
210	Interstate Hwy
395	U.S. Hwy
203	State Hwy
3S43	Forest Rd.
● ● ●	Cities, Town
P ●●	Parking, Gate
⛺	Campground
△	Primitive Camp
▬▬▬▬	National Park
▲ ▲ ▲	Mountains
⬭	Lake
━━━━━	River
━━━━━	Creek
·············	Drainage
▒▒▒▒▒	Cliff
▽ ● ▽	Boulders
○ ○ ○	Trees
D	Start of Drive
○━0.7m━○	Distance in Miles
☆ ☆	Climbing, Sport
☆ ☆	Gear, Bouldering
Ⓐ Ⓑ,Ⓒ	Climbing Routes
↑N	North

offramp for Mammoth Lakes). For the Mammoth Lakes Area (Chapter 5) all approach instructions begin at the junction of Hwy. 203 (Main St.) and Old Mammoth Rd. in the Town of Mammoth Lakes.

> *Important Note*—Difficulty Ratings and Quality Ratings are not facts. These systems are subjective and based on a consensus of opinions.

Difficulty Ratings

Pitches have been rated according to the Yosemite Decimal System. Difficulty ratings should be comparable to routes found in the Owens River Gorge and Tuolumne Meadows. The 5th class prefix has been dropped for simplicity. Boulder problems have been rated on the V-scale.

Quality Ratings

Quality ratings have been assigned based on the following factors: the amount of sustained climbing, the aesthetics of the moves, pump factor, exposure, location and rock quality. Squeeze jobs, contrived lines, and poorly equipped routes subtract from the quality rating.

*****	Mammoth Area Classic
****	Awesome
***	Great
**	Good
*	Mediocre
•	Poor

Ratings

YDS	Verm
5.8	V0-
5.9	V0
10a	
10b	V0+
10c	V1
10d	
11a	V2
11b	
11c	V3
11d	
12a	V4
12b	V5
12c	
12d	V6
13a	V7
13b	V8
13c	
13d	V9
14a	V10
14b	V11
14c	V12

Following the quality rating an (r) indicates a runout route.

Route Descriptions

Following the name and route rating is a description of the gear that is required. First, is the number of bolts, if any, followed by any gear that may be required, if any. Next is a brief description of the route. Pitches longer than 25 meters / 80 feet, and then the descent information are then noted. Finally listed is the first ascent information (if known). The first climber listed completed the first redpoint of each route. Subsequent climbers contributed to the route in some fashion.

Bouldering Descriptions

This book is not a comprehensive bouldering guide, the bouldering descriptions are vague at best. The directions will get you there and give you an idea of the quality and size of the area. Beyond that, you'll have to explore and boulder what inspires you. That's how its been done around here for the last thirty years.

Warning: Many of the boulder problems in the Mammoth Area can be quite tall—some border on free soloing—be extra careful!

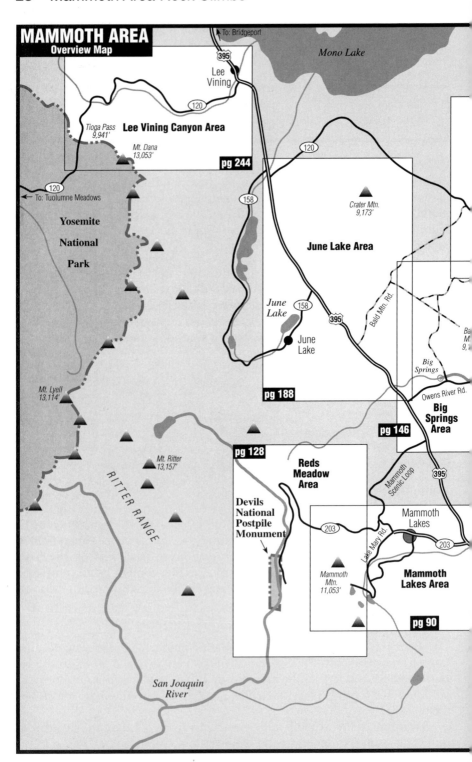

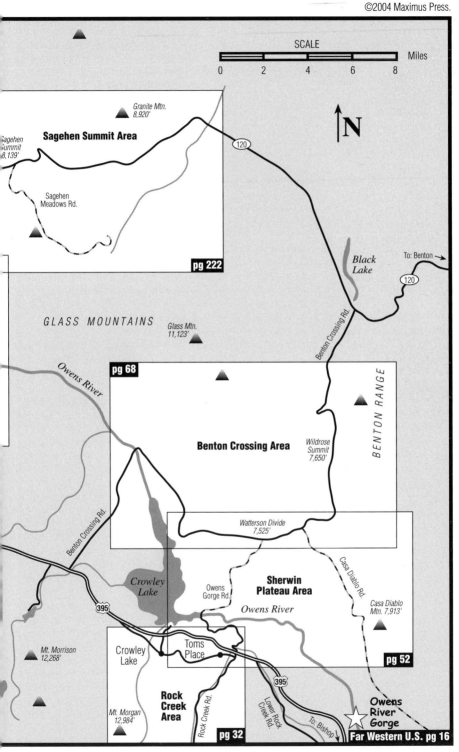

SCALE

Miles

0   2   4   6   8

N

Granite Mtn.
8,920'

Sagehen Summit Area

Sagehen
Summit
8,139'

Sagehen
Meadows Rd.

pg 222

Black
Lake

To: Benton →

120

120

GLASS MOUNTAINS   Glass Mtn.
11,123'

Owens River

pg 68

BENTON RANGE

Benton Crossing Rd.

Benton Crossing Area   Wildrose
Summit
7,650'

Watterson Divide
7,525'

Casa Diablo Rd

*Crowley
Lake*   Owens
Gorge Rd.   **Sherwin
Plateau Area**   Casa Diablo
Mtn. 7,913'

Benton Crossing Rd.   *Owens River*

pg 52

395

Mt. Morrison
12,268'   Crowley
Lake   Toms
Place

395

Lower Rock
Creek Rd.   *Owens
River
Gorge*

**Rock
Creek
Area**   Rock Creek Rd.   To: Bishop ↓

Mt. Morgan
12,984'   **pg 32**   **Far Western U.S. pg 16**

See Page 41 Steve Bullock on **Wages of Skin** 10c**** at the Gong Show Crag. ©*Andy Selters Photo.*

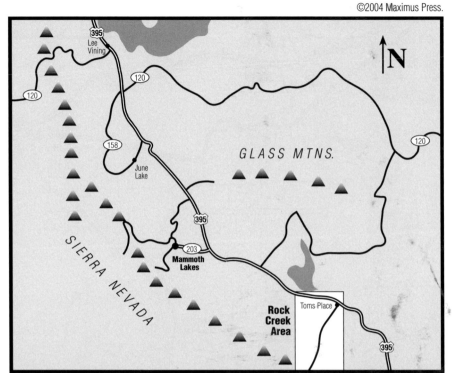

CHAPTER 2

ROCK CREEK AREA

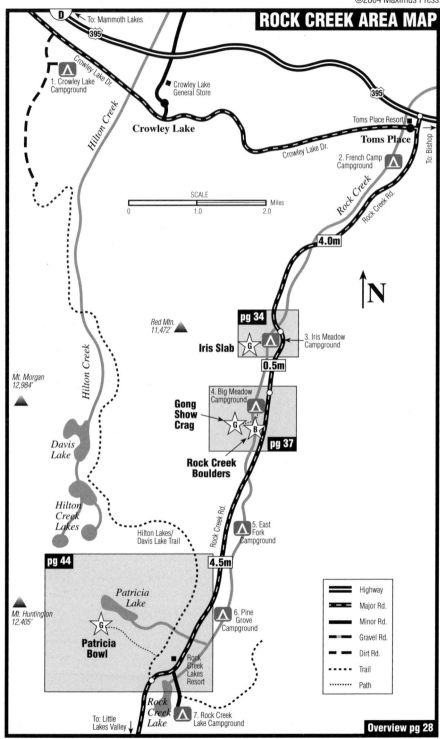

©2004 Maximus Press.

ROCK CREEK AREA MAP

ROCK CREEK AREA BASICS

The Rock Creek Area is located in a beautiful alpine canyon draining the 13,000 ft. peaks of the Bear Creek Spire region. As one drives south up the canyon there are many cliffs on the right (west) side. The rock is granite varying from perfect to grainy and scaly. The routes included in this guide are the best of what the area offers. South of the Gong Show Crag there are tons of obscure routes scattered above hideous scree and brush slopes.

Because the cliffs receive generous morning sun and the road is plowed in winter, the climbing season can start in early spring and extends into late fall. Crossing Rock Creek in late spring and early summer can be challenging.

Getting There

The Rock Creek Area is located 15 miles south of Mammoth off of U.S. 395. Turn right at the Rock Creek Rd./ Tom's Place turnoff. Head south up the steep canyon.

Amenities

Tom's Place Resort
Lodging, restaurant and bar as well as a small grocery section. ☎ 760-935-4239.

Rock Creek Lakes Resort
Lodging, limited groceries and a restaurant (great sandwiches and chili, as well as dreamy pies).
☎ 760-935-4311.

Crowley Lake General Store
Groceries, fresh baked goods and gas.
☎ 760-935-4666.

Camping

1. Crowley Lake Campground
Open April through October, **there is no fee**. Picnic tables, no potable water, vault toilets, elev. 6,800 ft.
☎ 760-872-4881.

2. French Camp Campground
Open mid April through October, the fee is $15. Picnic tables, piped water, flush toilets, elev. 7,500 ft. ☎ 760-873-2500.

3. Iris Meadow Campground
Open June through mid September, the fee is $16. Picnic tables, piped water, flush toilets, elev. 8,400 ft.
☎ 760-873-2500.

4. Big Meadow Campground
Open June through mid September, the fee is $16. Picnic tables, piped water, flush toilets, elev. 8,600 ft.
☎ 760-873-2500.

5. East Fork Campground
Open mid May through October, the fee is $15. Picnic tables, piped water, flush toilets, elev. 9,000 ft. ☎ 760-873-2500.

6. Pine Grove Campground
Open June through October, the fee is $15. Picnic tables, piped water, flush toilets, elev. 9,300 ft. ☎ 760-873-2500.

7. Rock Creek Lake Campground
Open June through October, the fee is $15. Picnic tables, piped water, flush toilets, elev. 9,600 ft. ☎ 760-873-2500.

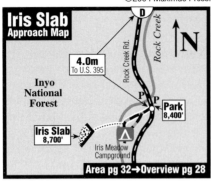

©2004 Maximus Press.

Iris Slab Approach Map

4.0m To U.S. 395

Rock Creek Rd.

Rock Creek

N

Inyo National Forest

Iris Slab 8,700'

P P Park 8,400'

Iris Meadow Campground

Area pg 32→Overview pg 28

Iris Slab Details

Environment: Juniper forest.
Elevation: 8,700 ft.
Season: May to October.
Exposure: Southeast facing, morning sun.
Rock Type: Granite.
Gear Climbs: 9 routes, 5.5 to 10c.
Top-roping: Bolt anchors.
Drive From Mammoth: 25 minutes.
Approach: 10 minutes, walk on a dirt road, then scramble; 300 ft. gain.
Special Concerns: Do not park in the campground.

Iris Slab

The Iris Slab is a quality granite crag, with a short approach. It has long been a popular area with the local guide services, and a great place for beginning climbers.

TCU's and tiny wireds come in handy when leading the thin cracks and seams found here. For top-roping go around the crag to the right. Bolted anchors will be found along the top. All routes are less than 25m/80' long.

©2004 Maximus Press. *John Moynier Photo.*

Iris Slab

Descent

XX
XX

B

F

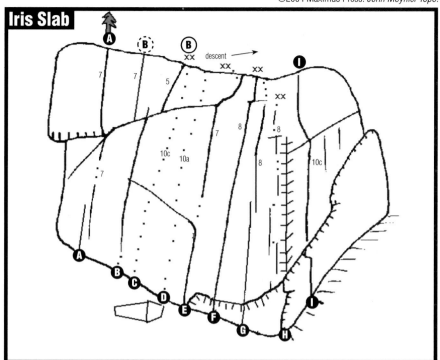

The Approach: From the U.S. 395/203 junction head south on U.S. 395 for 15 miles then turn right at the Rock Creek Lake/Toms Place exit. Head south up the canyon on Rock Creek Rd. After 4 miles park outside the Iris Meadow Campground.

Walk into the campground and take the right fork in the road. You will be able to see the Iris Slab quite clearly from here. Before campsite #1 cross Rock Creek on a rickety log or hop across four large boulders. Then scramble up a steep trail to the crag.

History: Developed in the '70s.

Iris Slab

A. Concrete Jungle 7**
Gear to 2". Twin cracks lead to a seam, then more crack. Tree anchor, walk off right.

B. Easy Skankin' 5**
Gear to 2.5". Climb the crack then step right into another crack. Lower off.
Variation: 7**. Gear to 2.5". Climb the crack, then step left into a headwall crack. Gear Anchor, walk off right.

C. Crazy Bald Head 10c*(r)
Gear to 1". Nebulous slab. Lower off.

D. Exodus 10a*(r)
Gear to 1". Nebulous slab. Lower off.

E. Get Up, Stand Up 7****
Gear to 1". Discontinuous thin crack. Lower off.

F. Welcome to the Iris Slab 8****
Gear to 2". Thin crack. Lower off.

G. Sting 8****
Gear to 1.5". Thin crack to mantle. Lower off.

H. Groovin' 8***(r)
Gear to 1". Discontinuous cracks. Lower off.

I. Powered by Ganja 10c**(tr)
Face/thin crack. Gear anchor, walk off right.

Rio Rose bouldering at the **Rock Creek Boulders**. ©*Shawn Reeder Photo.*

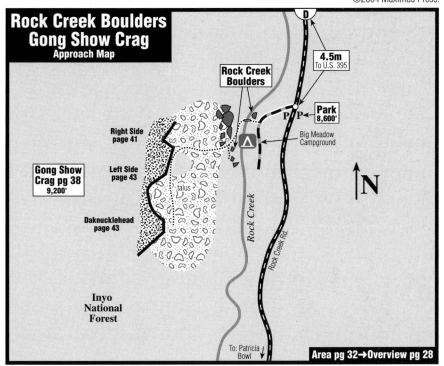

Rock Creek Boulders

This small bouldering area lies in a shady forest along Rock Creek. The boulders tend to be quality angular granite reminiscent of the bouldering found in Yosemite Valley.

The Approach: From the U.S. 395/203 junction head south on U.S. 395 for 15 miles then turn right at the Rock Creek Lake/Toms Place exit. Head south up the canyon on Rock Creek Rd. After 4.5 miles park outside the Big Meadow Campground.

Walk into the campground, upon reaching campsite #2, a large granite erratic (with excellent boulder problems) will be seen on the right. More bouldering will be found across the creek towards the left (south) in the forest.

Rock Creek Boulders

Environment: Deciduous forest.
Elevation: 8,600 ft.
Season: May to October.
Exposure: Varied, shady forest.
Rock Type: Granite.
Bouldering: ★★, 25 problems.
Drive From Mammoth: 25 minutes.
Approach: 5 minute walk.
Special Concerns: Do not park in the campground.

Gong Show Crag
A. Gong Show 11d***
B. Main Attraction 8**
C. Overexposure 9**
D. Wages of Skin 10c****

Right Side pg 41

Descent

Descent

Left Side pg 43

A

B

C   D

Approach Map pg 37

Gong Show Crag

The Gong Show Crag offers some of the finest granite climbing in the Mammoth Area. The rock is usually just under vertical, with many edges, cracks, seams and flakes, and it is of exceptional quality.

The Approach: Map page 37. From the U.S. 395/203 junction head south on U.S. 395 for 15 miles then turn right at the Rock Creek Lake/Toms Place exit. Head south up the canyon on Rock Creek Rd. After 4.5 miles park outside the Big Meadow Campground.

Walk into the campground, upon reaching campsite #2, a large granite

Gong Show Crag Details

Environment: Alpine talus slope with scattered aspens.
Elevation: 9,200 ft.
Season: May to October.
Exposure: East facing, morning sun.
Rock Type: Granite.
Gear Climbs: 16 routes, 5.8 to 11d.
Sport Climbs: 12 routes, 5.9 to 12c.
Drive From Mammoth: 25 minutes.
Approach: 20 minute talus scramble with a 600 ft. gain.
Special Concerns: Do not park in the campground.

erratic (with excellent boulder problems) will be seen on the right, cross Rock Creek here. Turn left (south) on a faint trail and go about 50 ft., then head west straight up strenuous talus blocks. Stay to the right on firm talus until close to the crag.

History: A few traditional climbs were done during the '80s, most notable of these is Kevin Leary's *Gong Show* (11d). During the early '90s Scott Ayers and company put up some brilliant sport climbs. In a controversial move they placed some bolts next to potential gear placements. While they ruffled a few feathers, most climbers have enjoyed and accepted these fantastic climbs.

See Page 41

Brian Ketron on **He She** 10b*****. ©*Shawn Reeder Photo.*

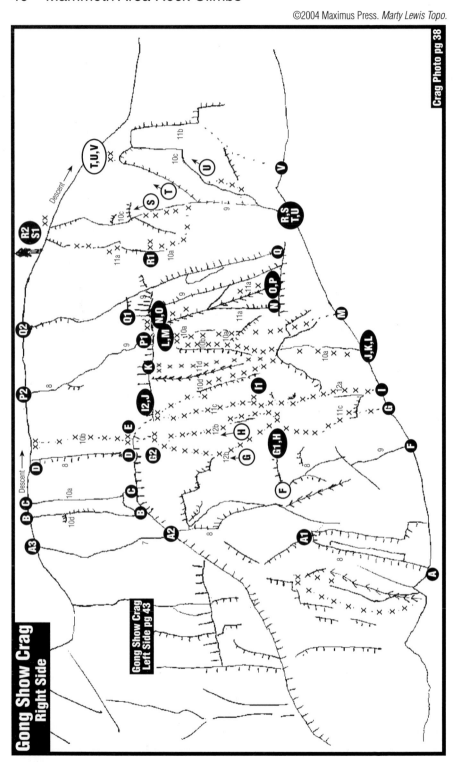

Crag Photo pg 38

Gong Show Crag
Right Side

Gong Show Crag
Left Side pg 43

Gong Show Crag - Right Side

Intro: Page 38. For all routes that top-out, traverse right (north) across blocky ledges or do three 25m/80' rappels starting at the top of *Freakshow*.

A. Main Attraction 8**
Pitch 1: 8** . Gear to 3.5' . Dihedral with bushes. Belay on ledge, gear anchor.
Pitch 2: 8** . Gear to 3.5' . Step down and left and right to a finger crack, then head up and left around a roof. Gear anchor.
Pitch 3: 7** . Gear to 3.5' . Go up crack on the left. Or traverse right on ledges and finish via routes B-E.
Descent: Walk off right.

B. Social Climber 10d**
Gear to 5". Offwidth through small roof. Gear anchor.

C. D.M.Z. 10a***
Gear to 3". Excellent finger crack. Gear anchor.
☞ The best finish for the *Main Attraction*.
FA: Jim Stimson, 1980s.

D. Schlitzy 8*
Gear to 3". Dihedral with loose blocks. Gear anchor.

E. Freakshow 10b**
5 bolts. Face. Bolt anchor.
FA: Scott Ayers, Paul Linaweaver, 1992.

F. Carney Trash 9*
Gear to 3". Discontinuous cracks. Lower off.

G. Never Say Never 12b****
Pitch 1: 11c*** . 8 bolts. Difficult bulge to slab. 20m/60'.
Pitch 2: 12b**** . 11 bolts. Wild technical face. 25m/80'.
Can be linked as 1 pitch.
FA: Scott Ayers, Paul Linaweaver, Mike Strassman, Henry Means, Austin Hearst, 1992.

H. Man Overboard 12b****
10 bolts. Excellent right hand variation of *Never Say Never*. 25m/80'. Can be linked as 1 pitch.
FA: Scott Ayers, Henry Means, 1992.

I. Anything Goes 12a*****
Pitch 1: 12a**** . 11 bolts. Seams to thin face. 20m/65'.
Pitch 2: 11c****** . 7 bolts. Killer arete. 15m/50'. Can be linked as one 35m/115' pitch. The first pitch of *Never Say Never* can also be linked into the 2nd pitch of *Anything Goes*.
FA: Scott Ayers, John Fowler, Cameron Guthrie, 1992, TD.

J. Switch Hitter 10d******
14 bolts. Start in a mini-dihedral then go left to ramp. 35m/115' rappel down *Anything Goes*.
FA: Paul Linaweaver, Scott Ayers, Mike Strassman, Henry Means, 1992, TD.

K. Radioactive Man 11d***
12 bolts. Sustained and wild face. 40m/130' rappel.
FA: Chris MacNamara, Sarah Felchin, Greg Barnes, 2001, TD.

L. He She 10b******
14 bolts, opt. gear: 0.75" piece. Same start as *Switch Hitter* then go right up a dihedral. 40m/130'. 20m/60' rappel to ledge.
☞ Almost a sport climb, use the gear to protect a strange runout in the middle of the pitch. ➤ Photo page 39.

M. Sideshow 10a*****
9 bolts, opt. gear to 3" (sporty without the gear). Face climb to a hand crack, then go up a slippery ramp to a seam/crack. 30m/100' lower off or a 20m/60' rappel to ledge.

N. Last Exit 11a***
2 bolts, gear to 2.5' . Start in a dihedral, then rattly fingers lead to an arete. Lower off.
FA: Dale Bard, Tony Puppo, 1980s.

O. Hey! 11a**
4 bolts, gear: 1" piece. Arete, a little contrived. Lower off.
FA: Paul Linaweaver, Scott Ayers, 1990, GU.

P. Overexposure 9**
Pitch 1: 9*** . Gear to 3.5' . Fun dihedral to a fixed belay. Lower off or climb 2nd pitch.
Pitch 2: 9** . Gear to 3.5' . Pass the roofs, then climb a wide crack.

Q. Alpine Fracture Clinic 9*
Pitch 1: 9* . Gear to 3' . Climb a crack to a corner then up through a strenuous roof.
Pitch 2: 7** . Gear to 3" . Crack.
FA: Mike Strassman, Scott Ayers, 1992.

R. Show Me the Monkey 11a**
Pitch 1: 10a** . 5 bolts, gear to 2.5' . Start up *Brush Up*, then clip bolt and traverse left and then up to belay. Lower off or climb 2nd pitch.
Pitch 2: 11a** . 4 bolts, gear to 2.5' . Dihedral to bulge to blunt arete. Gear anchor.
FA: Scott Ayers, Henry Means, 7/1998.

S. Eavesdropping 10c****
5 bolts, gear to 3.5' . Start *Brush Up*, then clip bolt and go straight up a bolted seam to a steep dihedral. 50m/165'. bolt anchors. ☞ Thinking he was doing a first ascent, Scott Ayers placed all 5 bolts on this climb. ➤ Photo page 258.
FA: Andy Selters, Bobby Knight, 7/1996. Retrobolts: Scott Ayers.

T. Brush Up 9.
Gear to 6". Climb a dihedral to a chimney behind a huge flake. 30m/100'. lower off.
FA: Alan Bartlett, Tony Puppo, 1980s.

U. Wages of Skin 10c****
3 bolts, gear to 3". Climb a dihedral, cross an offwidth then face climb to a beautiful splitter. 30m/100' lower off.
➤ Photo page 30.
FA: Todd Vogel, Doug Robinson, 1993.

V. Air Conditioner 11b**(r)
Gear. Sporty face to dihedral. 30m/100' lower off.
FA: Bobby Knight, Andy Selters, 7/1996.

Kevin Leary on the first ascent of the **Gong Show** 11d*** (1980). ©*Jim Stimson Photo.*

Gong Show Crag
Left Side

Gong Show Crag
Right Side pg 41

Daknucklehead

scramble

Approach Map pg 37

Gong Show Crag - Left Side
Intro: Page 38.

A. Unknown 11a**
2 bolts, gear to 2". Steep crack to seams. Lower off.
FA: Kelly Cordner, 1999.

B. Unknown 11b***
8 bolts. Shallow dihedral on a blunt arete. Lower off.
FA: Kelly Cordner, 1999.

For routes C-E scramble up a 4th class gully that is left of the routes. Bring gear to 0.5" for the bottom belay stances.

C. Gong Show 11d***
Gear to 3.5". A wide crack out a big roof. Lower off.
☞ An early Eastside testpiece. ➤ Photo facing page.
FA: Kevin Leary, Art Hanon, 1980.

D. Jonny Mon 12c****
7 bolts. Overhanging arete. Lower off.
FA: Brian Ketron, 7/2002, TD.

E. Tripping Old Birds 10b****
14 bolts. Climb the long orange face. 40m/130' rappel.
FA: James Lombard, 7/2002, TD.

F. Grab a Handful 9**
6 bolts. Golden face. Lower off.

G. Self-Contained Unit 10b**
7 bolts. Golden face. Lower off.

Daknucklehead
Gong Show Crag Intro: Page 38. To get to this cliff start at *Self-Contained Unit* and traverse left horizontally across an unstable scree slope until reaching a small buttress. *Omaha Stylee* is located at the toe of the buttress.
Daknucklehead is up and around to the left about 100 ft.

Omaha Stylee 11c**
4 bolts. Tricky seams lead to a knobby roof. Lower off.
FA: Kevin Calder, Marty Lewis, 8/1994, TD.

Daknucklehead 10d**
Gear to 2.5". A clean dihedral that leans and jogs left. Gear anchor, scramble left 100 ft. to a 10m/30' rappel off a detached block. ☞ Fixed anchors on top would have made this a three star climb.
FA: Mike Strassman, Paul Linaweaver, 1980s.

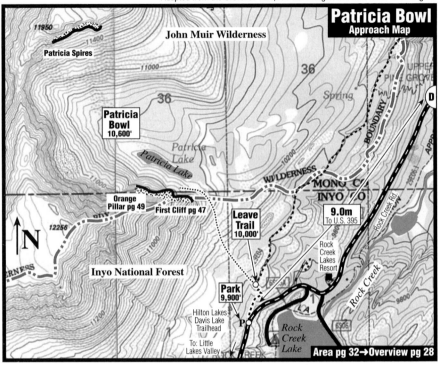
Adapted from the U.S.G.S. 1:24,000 Mt. Morgan and Mt. Abbot Quadrangles.

Patricia Bowl

This high altitude crag is located in a beautiful alpine cirque with tons of granite. The cliffs covered in this book are the first ones reached on the south side of the cirque. Beyond this, towards the west and the north there are huge expanses of cliffs and towers many of which were climbed back in the 80s. The towers on the north side of the bowl are called the Patricia Spires. On the second tower in, there is a stellar 10a right facing corner. A half dozen other routes also exist on either side. The wilderness setting of Patricia Bowl makes it a very special place, it's hard to believe it's only a mile from Rock Creek Rd.

Patricia Bowl Details

Environment: Scree and talus slope.
Elevation: 10,600 ft.
Season: July to September.
Exposure: North facing.
Rock Type: Granite.
Gear Climbs: 26 routes, 8 to 11c.
Sport Climbs: 3 routes, 10a to 10b.
Drive From Mammoth: 35 minutes.
Approach: 35 minutes. Short trail then X-country hiking and a talus scramble. 700 ft. gain.
Special Concerns: Patricia Bowl is in the John Muir Wilderness. Motorized drills are prohibited.

The Approach: From the U.S. 395/203 junction head south on U.S. 395 for 15 miles and turn right at the Rock Creek Lake/Toms Place exit. Head south up the canyon on Rock Creek Rd. After 9 miles park at the Hilton Lakes/Davis Lake Trailhead.

©2004 Maximus Press. *Todd Graham Photo.*

Patricia Bowl

First Cliff pg 47

Orange Pillar pg 49

Hike north on this trail about 5 minutes until reaching some switchbacks. After the 4th turn a path heads west into the woods. Follow this path northwest. A steep scrubby section leads to a talus field. The cliff is just ahead, skirt around to the right on scree.

History: Various local climbers have played in the bowl, but Ken Yager probably was most active—soloing many of the obvious moderate lines on the Patricia Spires. Local guides climbed the long wishbone shaped arete in the center of the bowl. The ubiquitous Galen Rowell first tapped the potential of the south side. Gary Slate climbed many lines on the First Cliff. Recently climbers have redeveloped this cliff with fixed anchors and added some great new lines.

©2004 Maximus Press. *John Moynier Photo.*

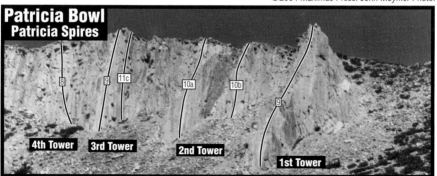

Patricia Bowl
Patricia Spires

8   9   11c   10a   10b   9

4th Tower   3rd Tower   2nd Tower   1st Tower

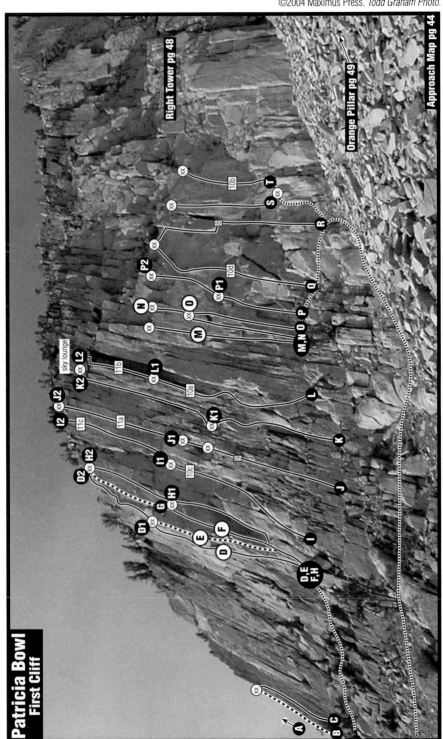

Patricia Bowl
First Cliff

Patricia Bowl - First Cliff

Intro: Page 44.

A. Heliotropic 10b**
10 bolts. Face. Lower off.
FA: Eric Sorenson, Urmas Franosch, 9/2003.

B. Stoic Tree Arete 10a***
8 bolts. Climb the orange arete. Lower off.
FA: Todd Graham, Bruce Lella, Mike Pope, 7/2002, TD.

C. The Rock on Her Left Hand Pays the Bills 10b**
Gear to 3". Climb the crack right of *Stoic Tree Arete*, traverse left to a gold block and climb the left crack. Lower off.
FA: Barry Oswick, Eric Sorenson, 7/2003, GU.

D. Patricia Lake Crack 9***
Pitch 1: 8**. Gear to 2.5". Large left facing dihedral.
Pitch 2: 9***. Gear to 2.5", opt. 5" piece. Climb up chimney then traverse right to anchor on *Breathless Arete*.
FA: Eric Sorenson, Barry Oswick, Peter Schultz, 9/2003.

E. Project 12a?
Arete.
P: Todd Graham

F. Sons of Liberty 10d*****
5 bolts, gear to 2". Climb up short pillar past one bolt, then move up and right to a dihedral, climb past 4 bolts to a killer hand crack. Lower off.
FA: Todd Graham, Brian Carkeet, 6/2002, TD.

G. Breathless Arete 10a***
5 bolts. Arete. Lower off.
FA: Todd Graham, 7/2002, TD.

H. Pie in the Sky 11b*****
Pitch 1: 10b**. 6 bolts, gear to 3.5". Climb up short pillar past one bolt then traverse right to a left facing book, pass 5 bolts then climb a roof to a hand crack.
FA: Todd Graham, Brian Carkeet, 7/2002, TD.

Pitch 2: 11b*****. Gear to 3.5". Step right from anchors and continue up the long, airy, sustained crack to a ledge.
FA: Todd Graham, Joel St. Marie, 8/2002, TD.
Descent: Two 25m/80' rappels.

I. Turning Point 11c***
Pitch 1: 10c***. Gear to 2". Start at a small pine tree on a ledge right of *Pie in the Sky*. Climb easy cracks to a big left facing corner, climb this pass a bulge and belay under the 2nd roof. Bolt anchor.
Pitch 2: 11c***. Gear to 3.5". Move right out of corner to a splitter fingers and hands crack on the face.
Descent: Rappel *Whiz Bang*.
FA: Brian Postlethwait, Matt Theilen, 7/2003, GU.

J. Whiz Bang 11a***
Pitch 1: 9**. Gear to 2". Climb the crack and belay at 2nd pair of belay bolts encountered.
Pitch 2: 9***. Gear to 3.5". Off the left side of the ledge climb the fingers to hands crack. Lower off.
Descent: Rappel 30m/100', then rappel 6m/20', then rappel 30m/100'.
FA: Brian Postlethwait, Barry Oswick, 7/2003, GU.

K. Bone Saw 10c**
Pitch 1: 10c**. Gear to 3". Climb blocks to a small left facing corner with finger crack. Lower off or climb 2nd pitch.
Pitch 2: 9**. Gear to 4". Wide crack in left facing corner.
Descent: Two 27.5m/90' rappels.
FA: Brian Postlethwait, Eric Sorenson, 8/2003, GU.

L. The Shaft 11b***
Pitch 1: 10a**. Gear to 3". Climb up and left to the large right facing corner. Bolt anchor.
Pitch 2: 11b***. Gear to 3.5". A finger crack in a corner, widens to fists, then turn a 5' roof.
Descent: Rappel *Bone Saw*.
FA: Brian Postlethwait, Barry Oswick, 7/2003, GU.

M. Forces of Nature 10d***
Gear to 4". Start just left of *Modern Trad* then follow the left crack system, mostly fingers. 30m/100', lower off.
FA: Brian Postlethwait, Barry Oswick. 8/2003, GU.

N. Modern Trad 10a***
3 bolts, gear to 3". Pass 3 bolts then move right into a vertical hand crack, pass a roof, then continue up finger and hand cracks. 30m/100' lower off.
FA: Todd Graham, Brian Carkeet, TD.

O. Freedom Fighter 11a*****
1 bolt, gear to 3.5". Climb the crack to a jug, clip bolt, then climb a corner to a roof. Lower off.
FA: Todd Graham, 7/2002, TD.

P. Columbine 10d***
Pitch 1: 10d***. 2 bolts, gear to 3". Interesting roofs. Lower off.
Pitch 2: 10c**. Gear to 3". Crack. Lower off.
FA: Urmas Franosch, Eric Sorenson, 9/2003.

Q. Satin Rose 10d***
Gear to 2.5". Hand crack to thin crack to right facing corner. 35m/115' lower off.
FA: Urmas Franosch, Barry Oswick, Matt Ciancio, 9/2003.

R. Living the Dream 8**
Gear to 3.5". Climb the dihedral, hands to wide fists. Rappel 35m/115' lower off.
FA: Brian Postlethwait, Barry Oswick, 7/2003, GU.

S. Golden Flake 10b***
Gear to 3". Climb up and left to ledge, then straight up a flake. 30m/100' lower off.
FA: Brian Postlethwait, Barry Oswick, 7/2003, GU.

T. Flyin' High 10b*
Gear to 2". Nice straight in fingers to hands. Lower off.
FA: Brian Postlethwait, Barry Oswick, 7/2003, GU.

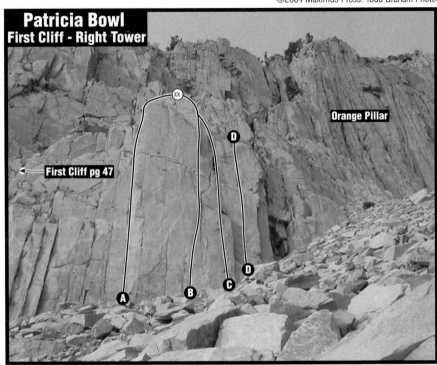

Patricia Bowl
First Cliff - Right Tower

Orange Pillar

First Cliff pg 47

Ken Yager at **Patricia Bowl** (early 1980s). ©*Errett Allen Photo.*

Patricia Bowl -
First Cliff - Right Tower

Intro: Page 44.

A. Dirty Girl 9**
Gear to 4". Crack. Lower off.
FA: Eric Sorenson, Jody Martin, 9/2003.

B. What'shisface 10d***
Gear to 4". Crack. Lower off.
FA: Urmas Franosch, Barry Oswick, Eric Sorenson, 8/2003.

C. I Had a Dream 10b**
Gear to 4". Crack. Lower off.
FA: Eric Sorenson, Barry Oswick, 8/2003.

D. What'sherface 10a**
Gear to 2.5". Dihedral. Walk off right.
FA: Barry Oswick, Eric Sorenson, 8/2003.

Orange Pillar

Crag Photo pg 45

Orange Pillar

Patricia Bowl Intro: Page 44. Traverse right across scree about ten minutes past the First Cliff to get here.

A. Unknown 10b**
Gear. Dihedral. Rappel *Boi-oi-oi-ing.*
FA: Todd Graham, Barry Oswick, Urmas Franosch, 8/2003.

B. Boi-oi-oi-ing! 10a****
Pitch 1: 10a****. Gear to 3.5". Climb past wedged orange block, tight hands. 25m/85' lower off.
Pitch 2: 10a****. Gear to 3.5". Climb continuous hand crack to ledge. Long pitch.
Pitch 3: 9*. Gear to 3". Climb up ramp, angling left, then up loose face/cracks.
Descent: 30m/100' rappel, then a short rappel to top of *Do I Make You Horny,* keeping the rappel rope out of the crack.
FA: Barry Oswick, Urmas Franosch, Eric Sorenson, 9/2003.

C. Do I Make You Horny? 10b***
Gear to 4". Climb thin cracks to a 3.5" crack near the arete. 30m/100' lower off or rappel, keeping the rope out of the crack, then rappel the 1st pitch of *Boi-oi-oi-ing!*
FA: Urmas Franosch, Dustin Clark, 9/2003.

D. High Expectations 10d***
Gear to 2.5". Right facing corner to left facing corner to thin crack crux. 30m/100' lower off.
FA: Todd Graham, Barry Oswick, 7/2002, TD.

E. Tommy Boy 10a***
Gear to 2". Hand crack in a corner. Lower off.
FA: John Moynier, Vilis Ozolins, 1987.

F. Housekeeping 10c**
Gear to 4". Crack. Lower off.
FA: Brian Postlethwait, Eric Sorenson, 9/2003.

See Page 55

Josh Huckaby bouldering at **Spot X**. ©*Kevin Calder Photo.*

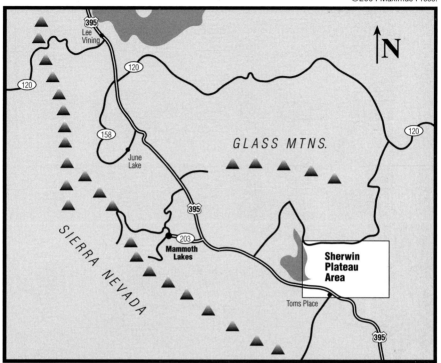

CHAPTER 3

SHERWIN PLATEAU

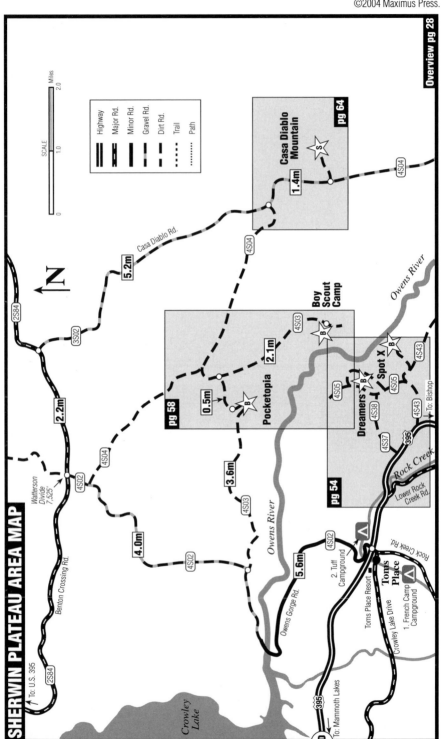

SHERWIN PLATEAU AREA MAP

Overview pg 28

SCALE

Miles

Highway
Major Rd.
Minor Rd.
Gravel Rd.
Dirt Rd.
Trail
Path

Casa Diablo Mountain

pg 64

1.4m

4S04

Casa Diablo Rd.

5.2m

Owens River

Boy Scout Camp

4S03

2.1m

Pocketopia

pg 58

0.5m

4S04

Watterson Divide 7,525'

4S02

4S04

2.2m

3S02

2S84

N

To: U.S. 395

2S84

Benton Crossing Rd.

4.0m

4S02

3.6m

4S03

Owens River

Spot X

Dreamers

4S05

4S38

4S05

4S43

4S43

4S37

395

Rock Creek

pg 54

Lower Rock Creek Rd.

To: Bishop

5.6m

Owens Gorge Rd.

4S02

2. Tuff Campground

Toms Place Resort

Toms Place

Rock Creek Rd.

1. French Camp Campground

Crowley Lake Drive

Crowley Lake

395

To: Mammoth Lakes

SHERWIN PLATEAU AREA BASICS

Driving along U.S. 395 in the vicinity of Sherwin summit, there appears to be a wealth of enticing looking cliffs and boulders. Unfortunately, climbers expecting to find the well-bonded tuff of the Deadman Summit Boulders will be disappointed—most of the rock is pretty chossy. However, if you head back through the forest to the rim of the Owens River Gorge, you will discover that there are small pockets of quality bouldering.

The Sherwin Plateau is a beautiful place to explore. Here you will find dense Jeffrey pine forests with sweeping views of the Sierra Nevada and the White Mountains, on the edge of a deep gorge. Climbers that enjoy adventure bouldering, off the beaten track will love it out here.

Getting There

The Sherwin Plateau Area is located 15 miles south of Mammoth off of U.S. 395. Turn left at the Owens Gorge Rd. turnoff (4S02). Wind around and through a residential area. Ahead is the Crowley Lake Dam and the north end of the Owens River Gorge. The boulders are scattered about in this forest.

Amenities

Tom's Place Resort
Lodging, restaurant and bar as well as a small grocery section. ☎ 760-935-4239.

Camping

1. French Camp Campground
Open May through October, the fee is $15. Picnic tables, piped water, flush toilets, elev. 7,500 ft. ☎ 760-873-2500.

2. Tuff Campground
Open May through mid October, the fee is $15. Picnic tables, piped water, flush toilets, elev. 7,000 ft. ☎ 760-873-2500.

Primitive Camping

In this area it is possible to discretely camp for free, almost anywhere north of U.S. 395, away from paved roads, as long as you are not on land owned by the Los Angeles Department of Water and Power or other private property. Check with the Forest Service in Bishop for more information.

Adapted from the U.S.G.S. 1:24,000 Toms Place and Casa Diablo Mtn. Quadrangles.

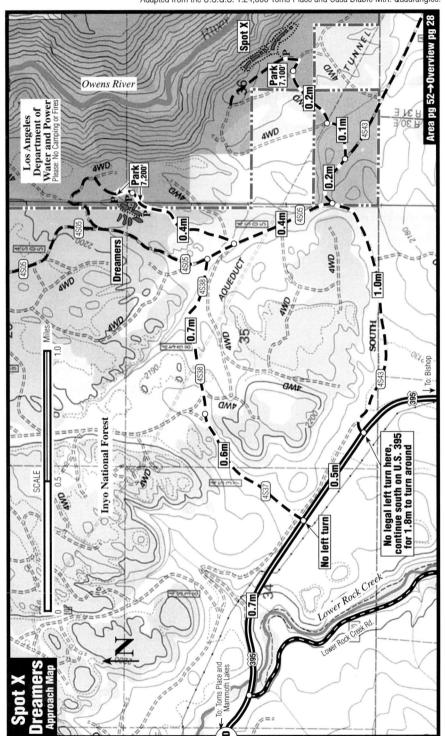

Spot X

Located on the rim on the Owens River Gorge, Spot X features spectacular views and some really well bonded pocketed rock. The adventurous problems can be tall and are spread out over a long cliff band, requiring a bit of exploration to find the best stuff.
➤ Photo pages 50, 56.

The Approach: From the U.S. 395/203 junction head south for 17 miles and look for the Lower Rock Creek turnoff. 1.2 miles beyond this is a dirt road on the left (4S43). Do not turn left here! Continue south on U.S. 395 for 1.8 miles to a legal turn around. Go back north on US. 395 1.8 miles and turn right on road 4S43. Take this road 1.2 miles to a junction, turn left here, leaving road 4S43 at a 4S43 sign. Follow this 0.1 miles, when the road curves left look for a right turn up a steep hill. Take this for 0.2 miles to a flat area, turn right, then left and park on the rim of the Owens Gorge.

From here walk along the rim in either direction and descend where convenient to access the bouldering.

History: Kevin Calder and Josh Huckaby seem to have developed most of the problems around 2001.

Spot X Details

Environment: Jeffrey pine forest.
Elevation: 7,100 ft.
Season: April to November.
Exposure: Northeast facing.
Rock Type: Volcanic tuff.
Bouldering: ★, 50 problems.
Drive From Mammoth: 30 minutes.
Approach: 5 to 10 minute walk.

Dreamers

The most popular of the Sherwin Plateau bouldering areas is the Dreamers, probably because it's the easiest one to get to. You will get a good idea of the Sherwin Plateau atmosphere here—warmer temperatures, solitude and beautiful views. ➤ Photo page 57.

The Approach: From the U.S. 395/203 junction head south for 17 miles and look for the Lower Rock Creek turnoff. 1.2 miles beyond this is a dirt road on the left (4S43). Do not turn left here! Continue south on U.S. 395 for 1.8 miles to a legal turn around. Go back north on US. 395 1.8 miles and turn right on road 4S43. Take this road 1.0 miles to a junction. Turn left here and follow this road 4S05 for 0.4 miles. From here turn right and drive up a hill, after 0.4 miles there will be a parking spot on the left. From here you walk to the north to find the boulders. Or you can continue a little farther as the road gets rougher, park, and then walk west to the boulders.

History: Developed in the spring of 2000 by Rick Cashner and company.

Dreamers Details

Environment: Jeffrey pine forest.
Elevation: 7,200 ft.
Season: April to November.
Exposure: Varied, sun and shade.
Rock Type: Volcanic tuff.
Bouldering: ★★, 25 problems.
Drive From Mammoth: 30 minutes.
Approach: 1 minute walk.

See Page 55

Josh Huckaby bouldering at **Spot X**. ©*Kevin Calder Photo.*

See Page 55

Russ Walling bouldering at the **Dreamers**. ©*Kevin Calder Photo.*

Adapted from the U.S.G.S. 1:24,000 Casa Diablo Mtn. and Toms Place Quadrangles.

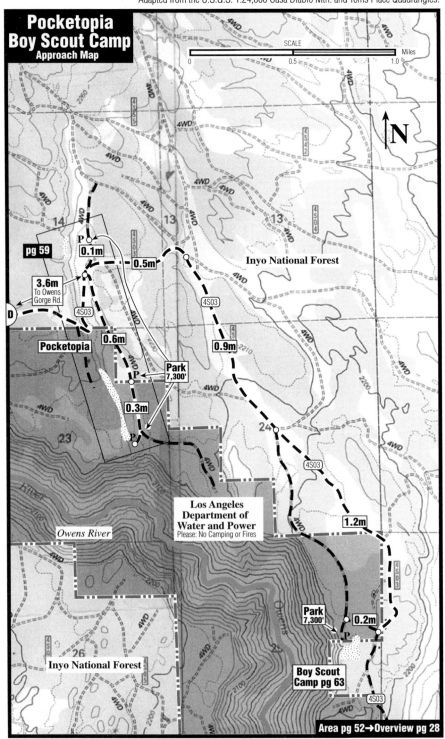

**Pocketopia
Boy Scout Camp**
Approach Map

SCALE

0   0.5   1.0   Miles

N

pg 59

P
0.1m

0.5m

3.6m
To Owens
Gorge Rd.

4S03

D

Pocketopia

0.6m

Inyo National Forest

4S03

0.9m

P

**Park
7,300'**

0.3m

P

23

**Los Angeles
Department of
Water and Power**
Please: No Camping or Fires

1.2m

Owens River

Inyo National Forest

26

**Park
7,300'**

0.2m

P

**Boy Scout
Camp pg 63**

4S03

Area pg 52→Overview pg 28

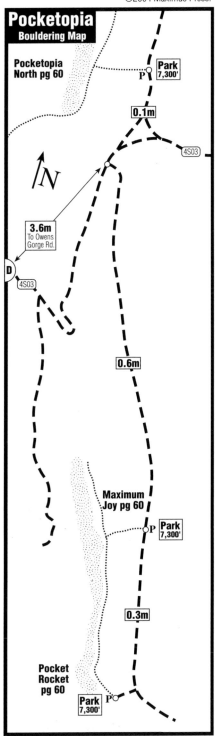

Pocketopia Details

Environment: Jeffrey pine forest.
Elevation: 7,300 ft.
Season: April to November
Exposure: East facing, morning sun.
Rock Type: Volcanic tuff.
Bouldering: ★★★, 100 problems.
Drive From Mammoth: 35 minutes.
Approach: 1 minute walk.

Pocketopia

The long east facing cliff band of Pocketopia is the largest bouldering area on the Sherwin Plateau. The highest concentration of quality problems lie on the Wedge and on boulders directly behind it in the Maximum Joy sector.

The Approach: From the U.S. 395/203 junction drive south 15 miles. Turn left at the Owens Gorge Rd. turn-off (4S02). Wind around and through a residential area, pass the Crowley Lake Dam and at 5.6 miles from U.S. 395 turn right at a sign that says "CASA DIABLO MTN. 10 →" on road 4S03. Follow this road until it drops and makes a sharp left into a valley at 3.6 miles. From here turn right and head south down the valley to reach Pocketopia South. The first parking area is at 0.6 miles for the Maximum Joy sector, 0.2 miles beyond this is the Pocket Rocket sector. Or continue on 4S03 to the first left turn which leads to Pocketopia North.

History: John Bachar was probably the first person to tap the vast potential of this area, climbing many early classics. Later on Kevin Calder was also a key player in the development.

Pocketopia
North

Bouldering Map pg 59

Pocketopia
Maximum Joy

The Wedge

Pocketopia
Pocket Rocket

Colin Broadwater bouldering at **Pocketopia**. ©*Kevin Calder Photo.*

Josh Huckaby bouldering at **Pocketopia**. ©*Kevin Calder Photo.*

Kevin Calder bouldering at the **Boy Scout Camp**. ©*Kevin Calder Collection.*

Boy Scout Camp

Ironically the Boy Scout Camp was the first Sherwin Plateau spot to be developed and the most remote. There are a number of fine pocketed problems found here.

The Approach: Map page 58. From the U.S. 395/203 junction drive south 15 miles. Turn left at the Owens Gorge Rd. turnoff (4S02). Wind around and through a residential area, pass the Crowley Lake Dam and at 5.6 miles from U.S. 395 turn right at a sign that says "CASA DIABLO MTN. 10 →" on road 4S03. Follow this road as it winds through the forest for 4.1 miles. Turn right and at a "Y" go right again, a subtle sign will indicate that you are still on 4S03, continue for 0.9 miles to a fork in the road. Take the left branch (still on 4S03) and drive 1.2 miles. Turn right here and wind through some boulders for 0.2 miles until reaching a "T". Turn left here after 0.1 miles there is a loop parking area.

From here walk south on a path to a beautiful overhanging arete. Much of the bouldering is behind this boulder up a slot to the left, there is also bouldering to the right on the rim of the Owens Gorge.

History: This was the site of an old Boy Scout camp. Most of the remnants have long since been removed. Doug Robinson was here in the 1970s and John Bachar bouldered here in the early 1990s. As is often the case in the Eastside scene, a new crew recently rediscovered and renamed the area, calling it the "Catacombs".

Boy Scout Camp Details

Environment: Jeffrey pine forest.
Elevation: 7,300 ft.
Season: April to November.
Exposure: Varied.
Rock Type: Volcanic tuff.
Bouldering: ★★, 50 problems.
Drive From Mammoth: 45 minutes.
Approach: 1 minute walk.

Boy Scout Camp

Approach Map pg 58

Adapted from the U.S.G.S. 1:24,000 Casa Diablo Mtn. Quadrangle.

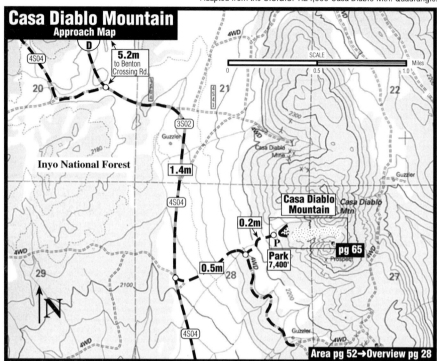

Casa Diablo Mountain

Casa Diablo Mountain is one of the coolest places to explore in the Mammoth Area. Surrounded by the Sierra Nevada, the White Mountains and the Glass Mountains, this spot offers incomparable vistas on the rocky slopes of a desert peak.

While there are just a few climbs, the bouldering potential seems unlimited—could this be the next great Eastside discovery? And hey, it sure is easier to get to than Hampi, India!

The Approach: From the U.S.

Casa Diablo Mountain
Environment: Pinyon pine forest.
Elevation: 7,400 ft.
Season: March to December.
Exposure: Varied.
Rock Type: Grainy granite.
Sport Climbs: 5 routes 5.7 to 11b.
Gear Climbs: 1 route 5.7.
Bouldering: ★, tons of potential.
Drive From Mammoth: 40 minutes.
Approach: 1 minute walk.

395/203 junction head south on U.S. 395 for 5.5 miles, then turn left on Benton Crossing Rd. Drive 18 miles, and turn right at a sign that says "CASA DIABLO→/BISHOP→" on a dirt road (3S02). From here drive south for 5.2 miles, pass the junction of road 4S04 and continue 1.4 miles. Turn left here and head east up a slope, after 0.5 miles continue straight past a road that branches right. Just beyond up a hill is a loop parking area right below the crag.

History: Kelly Cordner bolted this crag.

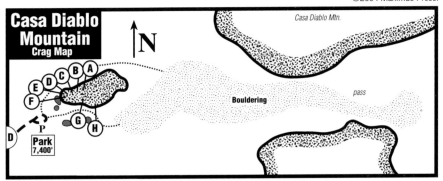

Casa Diablo Mountain

A. Project ?
Bolts. Face.
P: Phil Carl.

B. Unknown 7*
Gear. Dihedral. Lower off.

C. Unknown 8**
Bolts. Face. Lower off.
FA: Kelly Cordner.

D. Unknown 9**
Bolts. Face. Lower off.
FA: Kelly Cordner.

E. Unknown 9**
Bolts. Start in a cave, face and crack. Lower off.
FA: Kelly Cordner.

F. Unknown 7**
Bolts. Slab, mantle crux. Lower off. ☞ Kevin Calder free soloed this one in his five-tennies before it was bolted.
FA: Kevin Calder. Retrobolts: Kelly Cordner.

G. Unknown 11b**
Bolts. Climb the water groove around to the right on the south face. Lower off.
FA: Kelly Cordner.

H. Unknown ?·
Bolts. Funky line.

Becky Hutto on **Welcome to Planet M.F.** 10a**** at the Benton Crags. ©*Kevin Calder Photo.*

See Page 86

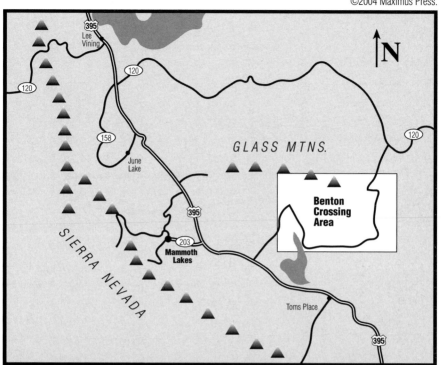

CHAPTER 4

BENTON CROSSING

©2004 Maximus Press.

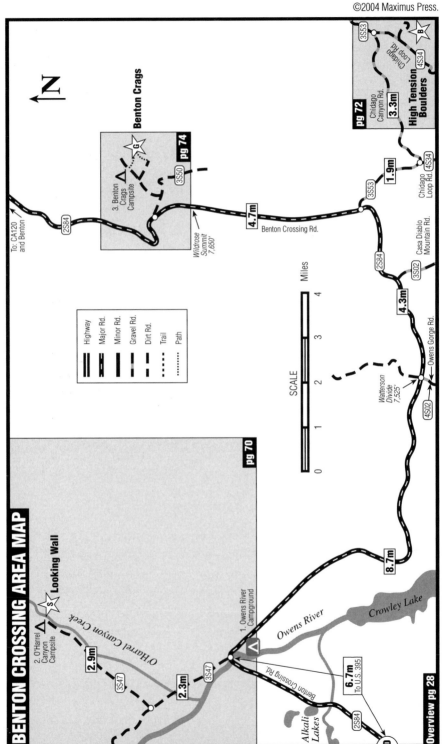

N

Benton Crags

pg 74

3. Benton Crags Campsite

3S50

Wildrose Summit 7,650'

2S84

To: CA120 and Benton

3S53

4.7m

Benton Crossing Rd.

High Tension Boulders

B

3S53

4S34

Chidago Loop Rd.

pg 72

Chidago Canyon Rd.

3.3m

1.9m

Chidago Loop Rd. (4S34)

Casa Diablo Mountain Rd.

2S84

3S02

4.3m

Watterson Divide 7,525'

4S02

Owens Gorge Rd.

Highway
Major Rd.
Minor Rd.
Gravel Rd.
Dirt Rd.
Trail
Path

Miles

SCALE

0   1   2   3   4

pg 70

BENTON CROSSING AREA MAP

Looking Wall

S

2. O'Harrel Canyon Campsite

O'Harrel Canyon Creek

2.9m

3S47

2.3m

3S47

8.7m

Crowley Lake

Owens River

1. Owens River Campground

Benton Crossing Rd.

6.7m
To U.S. 395

Alkali Lakes

2S84

D

Overview pg 28

BENTON CROSSING AREA BASICS

Benton Crossing is a paved road that connects the towns of Mammoth Lakes and Benton. It is also a shortcut for travelers wanting to head east on U.S. 6 into Nevada. This is the land of open range, hot springs and beautiful Sierra Nevada vistas.

Getting There

Start at the junction of Hwy. 203 and U.S. 395. Drive south on U.S. 395 for 5.5 miles until reaching Benton Crossing Rd. (there is a local landmark here "the little green church"). Turn left here and follow this road around the back side of Crowley Lake.

Amenities

For the most part this area is out in the middle of nowhere, but there is a small general store and cafe at the Owens River Campground.

Camping

1. Owens River Campground

Open May through October, the fee is $18. Picnic tables, piped water, pit toilets, showers, elev. 6,800 ft. ☎ 760-872-6911.

Primitive Camping

In this area it is possible to discretely camp for free, almost anywhere north of U.S. 395, away from paved roads, as long as you are not on land owned by the Los Angeles Department of Water and Power or other private property. Check with the Forest Service in Bishop for more information.

2. O'Harrel Canyon Campsite

Primitive camping within walking distance of the Looking Wall. Creek water, elev. 7,500 ft.

3. Benton Crags Campsite

Primitive camping within walking distance of the Benton Crags. No water, elev. 7,800 ft.

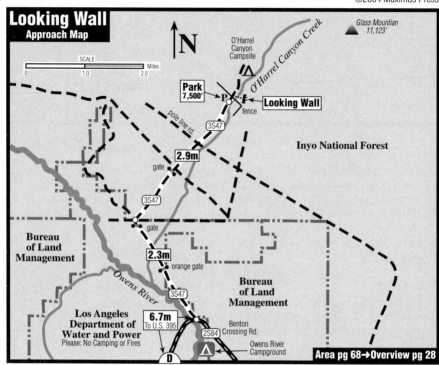

Looking Wall

The Looking Wall is located at the base of Glass Mountain. The crag offers short sport climbs on killer rock in a beautiful secluded canyon.

The Approach: From the U.S. 395/203 junction head south on U.S. 395 for 5.5 miles, then turn left on Benton Crossing Rd. Drive 6.7 miles, cross the Owens River and turn left on a dirt road (3S47). Drive this 2.3 miles through two gates and turn right just after the second gate (still on 3S47). Follow this road 2.9 miles and park on the left before a fence line.

Looking Wall Details

Environment: Aspen and pinyon forest on a creek.
Elevation: 7,500 ft.
Season: April to November.
Exposure: West facing, afternoon sun.
Rock Type: Quality granite.
Sport Climbs: 9 routes, 5.9 to 12b.
Top-roping: Bolt anchors.
Drive From Mammoth: 35 minutes.
Approach: 1 minute walk.

Cross the fence line and walk on a path to the east, cross the creek and you will find this crag.

History: Climbers had checked this cliff out in the late 1980s, but its potential wasn't tapped until the spring of 2001.

Looking Wall

For top-roping go around the crag on either side. Bolted anchors will be found along the top. All routes are less than 25m/80' long.

A. Pluto 10b*
4 bolts. Face. Lower off. Located about 100 ft. left of the other routes.
FA: Sean Jones, Blair Dixson, 5/2001, TD.

B. Mighty Earth 11a***
6 bolts. Gently overhanging face. Lower off.
FA: Blair Dixson, Sean Jones, 5/2001, TD.

C. The Sun 12a**
5 bolts. Face climb to a brutal roof. Lower off.
FA: Blair Dixson, Sean Jones, 5/2001, TD.

D. The Moon 9***
5 bolts. Stemming dihedral. Lower off.
FA: Blair Dixson, Sean Jones, 5/2001, TD.

E. Thunder Underground 10d**
6 bolts. Face climbing with seams. Lower off.
FA: Sean Jones, Blair Dixson, 5/2001, TD.

F. Distance of Man 11a***
6 bolts. Climb a mini dihedral to a steep arete. Lower off.
FA: Sean Jones, Blair Dixson, 5/2001, TD.

G. The Tribe 11a**
7 bolts. A huge dihedral leads to a steep face. Lower off.
FA: Blair Dixson, Sean Jones, 5/2001, TD.

H. Firewater 10a*
4 bolts. Blocky ledges lead to a short face. Lower off.
FA: Sean Jones, Blair Dixson, 5/2001, TD.

I. Vista Grande 11d*
4 bolts. Scramble up to a roof crack, then hard face climbing. Lower off.
FA: Sean Jones, Blair Dixson, 5/2001, TD.

Adapted from the U.S.G.S. 1:24,000 Banner Ridge Quadrangle.

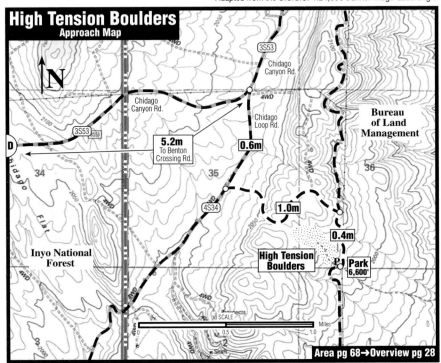

High Tension Boulders

Another one of the many hidden bouldering sites of the Eastern Sierra. Although some of the problems are worth the effort, this areas appeal lies mostly in its setting, its remoteness and that it is climbable during the winter months.

The Approach: From the U.S. 395/203 junction head south on U.S. 395 for 5.5 miles. Turn left on Benton Crossing Rd. and follow this road 20 miles, during which you will go

High Tension Boulders

Environment: High desert, below crackling power lines.
Elevation: 6,600 ft.
Season: Year round.
Exposure: Varied.
Rock Type: Granite.
Bouldering: ★.
Drive From Mammoth: 45 minutes.
Approach: 1 minute walk.

around the back side of Crowley Lake, and over the Watterson Divide. Turn right on Chidago Canyon Rd. (3S53), follow this 1.9 miles pass Chidago Loop Rd. (4S34), then drive another 3.3 miles to the other end of Chidago Loop Rd. Turn right on Chidago Loop Rd. (4S34) and drive 0.6 miles. Turn left here and drive 1 mile up a steep hill and over a ridgeline coming to a power transmission line. Turn right here and drive 0.4 miles to a drainage gully and park. The boulders are scattered about in the gully and on the hillside to the north.

High Tension Boulders

History: This spot was developed during the 1980s as the "High Tension Boulders". During the 1990s it was rediscovered and featured in an article in the Mammoth Times with another name (although we can't remember it). By the early 2000s it was rediscovered and renamed again, this time it was the "Megawatt Boulders". Here is an actual e-mail conversation between Errett Allen and Russ Walling illustrating the nefarious nature of Eastern Sierra bouldering history:

Errett: "Megawatt" granite bouldering area??? Hmmmm... if this is an area out in the Benton Range north of Bishop that has some major power lines running through it, a bunch of Mammoth low-lifes were bouldering there waaaaayyyyy back in the early 80s. We called it the "High Tension" area. Ask Marty Lewis or Kevin Calder -- I have photos of them on some of the problems we did.

Russ: Yep, it is the same area. I just re-named it and did all the "Madonna" ascents.... they were "like a virgin" to me. That is the joy of all the old guys never naming or laying claim to the secret areas.... file it under the heading of if you don't plant the flag, you don't get to name the peak. It's all hype anyway. I think the Buttermilks are getting renamed in the next edition of some exploitive topo guide. I even heard the going rate is a 12 pack to

rename a classic. Shameful!!!!!! I'll ask those old guys Marty and Kevin.... but senility is such a cruel mistress.... not sure they will remember. (Marty actually lives next door to me, and Kevin seems to find lots of things to watch on TV while on my couch.....)

Errett: Of course we didn't name or rate any of the problems we did -- back then V2 was just some Nazi method for visiting London and you hoped you never saw a maxi pad at the boulders.

Russ: Correcto! Especially the MaxiPad part.....

Errett: Its kinda cool how the power lines buzz in the background as you destroy your tendons.

Russ: I always thought that sound was coming out of my back..... adios, Russ

Adapted from the U.S.G.S. 1:24,000 Banner Ridge Quadrangle.

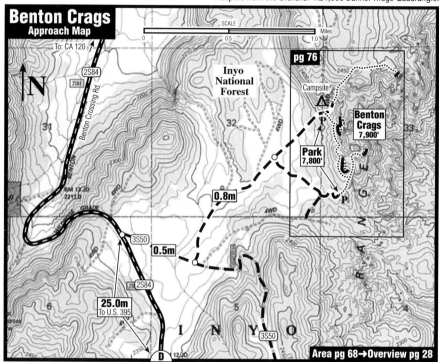

Benton Crags

The Benton Crags are a group of cliffs in the high desert east of Mammoth. A little slice of Joshua Tree transplanted into the Eastern Sierra. The rock is similar to J-tree (grainy quartz monzonite) and offers a wide range of traditional routes and a few sport climbs. There also seems to be a lot of untapped bouldering potential. More than just a climbing area, this is a great place to explore, offering excellent views and surprising geological sites.

It is a good area for experienced climbers looking for moderate adventure routes. Beginners should be aware that anchors and descents can be difficult and sometimes dangerous to find.

Benton Crags Details

Environment: Pinyon forest.
Elevation: 7,900 ft.
Season: April to mid December
Exposure: Varied, mostly east facing.
Rock Type: Grainy granite.
Gear Climbs: 59 routes, 5.4 to 11c.
Sport Climbs: 19 routes, 5.8 to 12c.
Bouldering: ★, tons of potential.
Drive From Mammoth: 40 minutes.
Approach: 5 to 20 minute scrambles with a 100 ft. gain.

The Approach: From the U.S. 395/203 junction head south on U.S. 395 for 5.5 miles. Turn left on Benton Crossing Rd. and follow this road a while, during which you will go around the back side of Crowley Lake, over the Watterson Divide and Wildrose Summit. At 25 miles the Benton Crags will be seen on the right. Turn right on a dirt road (3S50), follow this for a 0.5 miles then turn left and follow another dirt road for 0.8 miles. From here continue straight to a turnout for the northern half of the Benton Crags. Or turn right and follow this dirt road to a turnout for the southern half of the Benton Crags.

From both parking areas the first cliffs are about five minutes away.

History: Developed in the early 1980s by a group of Yosemite traditionalists who had moved to Mammoth. After a 20 year lull, activists are finding new lines.

This crag has always been popular with the local guides, especially as it is accessible for much of the year and does not share the extreme weather of the Sierra crest.

Marty Lewis on **Tough Muffin** 9** (1985). ©*Scott Cole Photo.*

See Page 77

Crocodile Rock pg 85

Junk Food Rock pg 80

Psycho Killer Rock pg 79

Benton Crags

Locals Only Rock pg 77

©2004 Maximus Press.

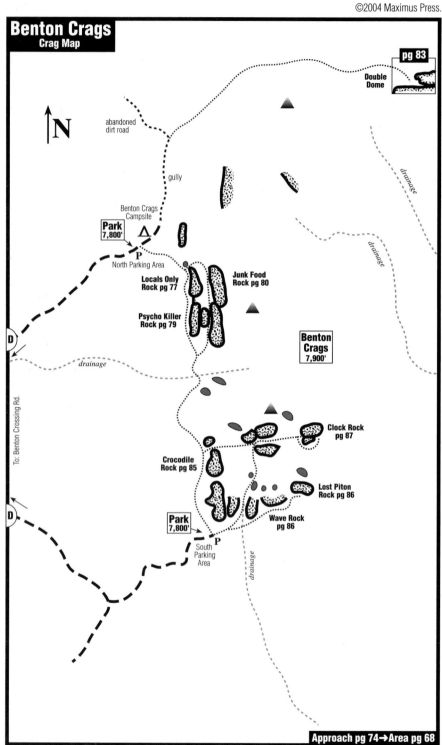

Benton Crags
Crag Map

pg 83

Double
Dome

N

abandoned
dirt road

gully

Benton Crags
Campsite

Park
7,800'

P
North Parking Area

Locals Only
Rock pg 77

Junk Food
Rock pg 80

Psycho Killer
Rock pg 79

Benton
Crags
7,900'

D

drainage

drainage

drainage

To: Benton Crossing Rd.

Clock Rock
pg 87

Crocodile
Rock pg 85

Lost Piton
Rock pg 86

Park
7,800'

D

P
South
Parking
Area

Wave Rock
pg 86

drainage

©2004 Maximus Press. *John Moynier Topo.*

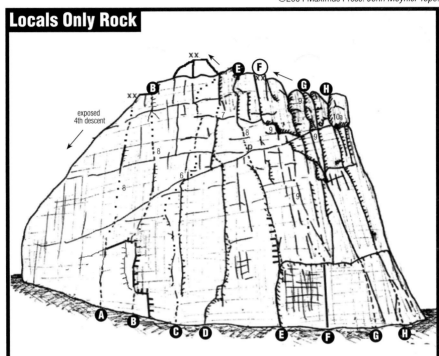

Locals Only Rock

Locals Only Rock

Benton Crags Intro: Page 74. A great introduction—Locals Only Rock is just 5 minutes from the car and has some of the highest quality rock found at the Benton Crags. Descend by a 35m/115' rappel off of the top of *Locals Only* or a 25m/80' rappel off of the *Tube* or continue left (north) via a short rappel and a 4th class scramble to the ground.

A. Tube 8**
Gear to 2.5". Discontinuous cracks. Lower off.
FA: Jon-Mark Baker, Sean Plunkett, 1983.

B. Pipeline 8***(r)
Gear to 3". Discontinuous cracks. Gear anchor.
FA: Sean Plunkett, Errett Allen, Scott Cole, 5/1983.

C. Locals Only 6****
Gear 3.5". Right facing flake to discontinuous cracks. 35m/115' lower off.
FA: Scott Cole, Errett Allen, Stan VanMarbod, 5/1983.

D. Get Lost 7****
Gear to 3". Climb blocky ledges to a crack, follow this then step left to a crack then back right. 35m/115' lower off.
FA: Errett Allen, Scott Cole, Stan VanMarbod, 5/1983.

E. No Trespassing 8***
Gear. A hand crack leads to a right facing dihedral then face climb past a piton then continue up a crack. Gear anchor.
FA: Errett Allen, Steve Kabala, 6/1983.

F. Surfin' Safari 9****
Gear to 3". A finger crack leads to a ledge, from here climb seams, then traverse left under a roof and finish up a dihedral. 35m/115' lower off.
FA: Scott Cole, Errett Allen, Stan VanMarbod, 5/1983.

G. Tough Muffin 9**
Gear. Crack. Gear anchor. ➤ Photo page 75.
FA: Scott Cole, Errett Allen, 6/1983.

H. Low Cal 10a*
Gear. Wide crack. Gear anchor.
FA: Ken Yager, Errett Allen, 1983.

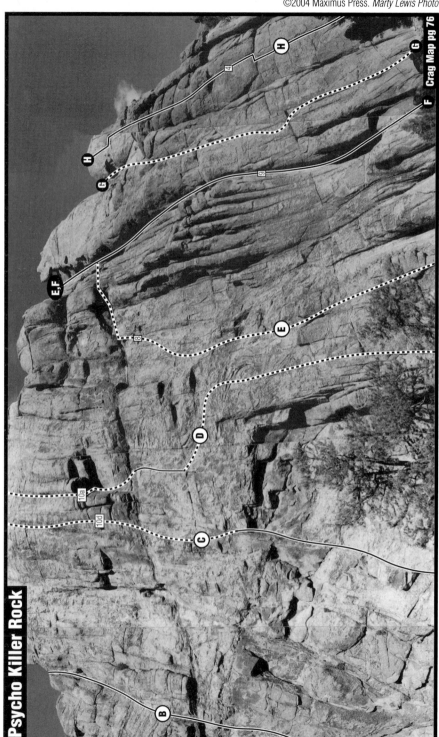

Psycho Killer Rock

Crag Map pg 76

Errett Allen on the first ascent of **Lucky Charms** 8*** (1983). ©*Scott Cole Photo.*

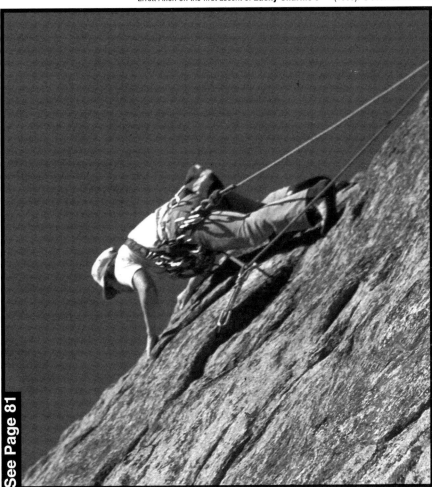

See Page 81

Psycho Killer Rock

Benton Crags Intro: Page 74. From the summit descend straight back (east), then scramble around the right (south) side of the formation, 3rd class.

A. Jimmy Jones 9 •
Gear. Chimney. Gear anchor.
FA: Fred Feldman, Errett Allen, 1983?

B. Caligula 9*
Gear. Crack. Gear anchor.
FA: Fred Feldman, Errett Allen, 1983?

C. Grain Damaged 10d**(tr)
Climb a right facing dihedral pass a roof, then up a vertical seam.
FTR: Marty Lewis, Kevin Calder, 8/2003.

D. Psycho Killer 10a***(r)
1 bolt, gear to 4". Climb the ramp to a bolt, then traverse left to a dihedral, climb this to an optional belay ledge. Move left and pass a roof then climb a slab. Gear anchor.
FA: Kevin Calder, Marty Lewis, 1983.

E. Psycho Chicken 8*
2 bolts, gear. Face to crack. Gear anchor.

F. Mayhem 9*
Gear to 5". Crack. Gear anchor.

G. Hannibal the Cannibal 8*
Gear. Discontinuous cracks. Gear anchor, 15m/50' fixed rappel off back of tower.
FA: Alan Bartlett, Allan Pietrasanta, 5/1999.

H. Hillside Strangler 4**
Gear. Crack. Gear anchor, 15m/50' fixed rappel off back of tower.
FA: Jim Yost, Errett Allen, 6/1983.

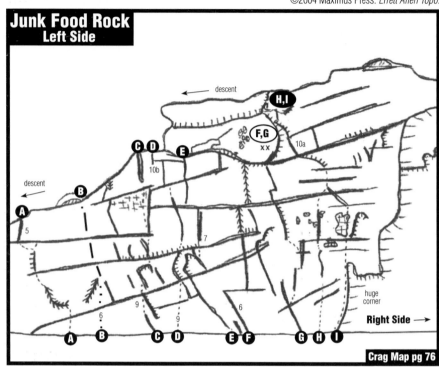

Junk Food Rock
Left Side

Crag Map pg 76

Junk Food Rock - Left Side

Benton Crags Intro: Page 74. Go around to the left of Locals Only Rock and then back right to find Junk Food Rock. Descend to the left, 3rd class.

A. M.D.R. 5*
Gear. Discontinuous cracks. Gear anchor.
FA: Grant Hiskes, 6/1983.

B. Golden Arch 6*
Gear. Face to cracks. Gear anchor.
FA: Alan Bartlett, Kim Walker, 6/1999.

C. Scrambled Eggs 8*
Gear to 4". Crack. Gear anchor.
FA: Jim Yost, Errett Allen, 11/1983.

D. Bit o' Honey 10b**
Gear to 3.5". Climb cracks to a bulge with a horizontal crack. Gear anchor.
FA: Errett Allen, Marty Lewis, Kevin Calder, 1984.

E. Post Toasties 7***
Gear. Cracks. Gear anchor.
FA: Scott Cole, 6/1983.

F. Wheaties 6**
Gear. Cracks. 35m/115' lower off.
FA: Scott Cole, 6/1983.

G. High Weed Glutin 8**
Gear. Cracks. 35m/115' lower off.
FA: Bob Finn, Scott Burke, 6/1983.

H. Granola Crunch 10a**
Gear. Cracks lead to a lieback corner. Gear anchor.
FA: Scott Burke, Bob McLaughlin, 6/1983.

I. Frosted Flakes 10a**
Gear. Dihedral to cracks to lieback corner of *Granola Crunch*. Gear anchor.
FA: Errett Allen, Scott Cole, Scott Burke, 6/1983.

©2004 Maximus Press. *Errett Allen Topo.*

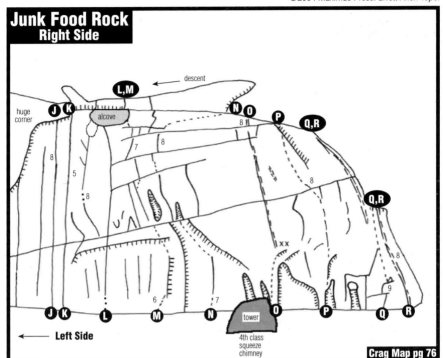

Junk Food Rock - Right Side

Benton Crags Intro: Page 74. Descend to the left, 3rd class. The following routes start in a narrow corridor right of a huge dihedral.

J. Pops 8*
Gear. Cracks. Gear Anchor.
FA: Errett Allen, Stan VanMarbod, 6/1983.

K. Kix 5*
Gear. Cracks. Gear Anchor.
FA: Errett Allen, Stan VanMarbod, 6/1983.

L. Twinkie Defense 8*
Gear. Cracks. Gear Anchor.
FA: Mike Strassman, Wendy Borgerd, 1987.

M. Wheateena 7*
Gear. Climb a dihedral, past a block on the left, then discontinuous cracks. Gear Anchor.
FA: Mark Yingst, Errett Allen, 1983.

N. Grape Nuts 8*
Gear. Climb a crack, pass a flake on the left, then up discontinuous cracks to a long traverse right. Gear Anchor.
FA: Mark Yingst, Errett Allen, 1983.

Climb down a narrow chimney to access these routes or approach around the right (south) side of Psycho Killer Rock.

O. Cream of Wheat 8***(r)
Gear. Climb the left side of a tower pass a belay, then follow a dike through a bulge. Gear Anchor.
FA: Fred Feldman, Errett Allen, 7/1983.

P. Hearts, Moons, Clovers 8*
Gear. Faint black streak. Gear Anchor.
FA: Mike Strassman, Scott Ayers, 1985.

Q. Magically Delicious 9*(r)
Gear. Platey face. Gear Anchor.
FA: Scott Cole, Connie , Errett Allen, 6/1983.

R. Lucky Charms 8**(r)
Gear. Dike. Gear Anchor. ➤ Photo page 79.
FA: Errett Allen, Scott Cole, 5/1983.

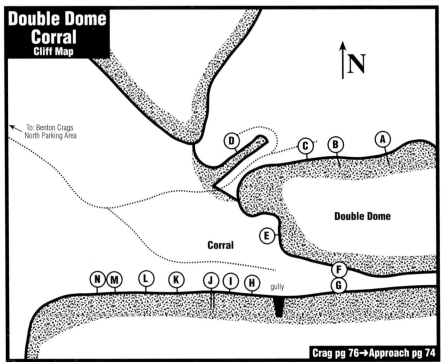

Double Dome Corral
Cliff Map

N

To: Benton Crags
North Parking Area

Double Dome

Corral

gully

Crag pg 76→Approach pg 74

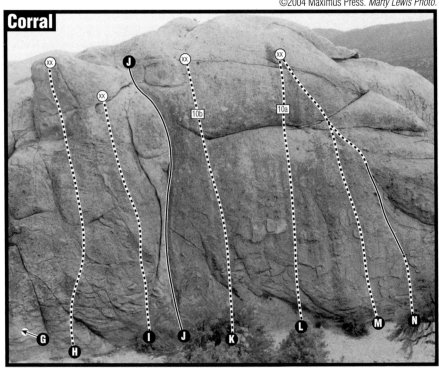

Corral

Double Dome

Benton Crags Intro: Page 74. This is the most remote cliff at the Benton Crags. Those who make the trek will find a fun selection of short moderate routes, in a beautiful setting with great views. From the North Parking Area head north up a gully and follow a faint trail marked with cairns. Pass some cliff bands then turn right (east) and wander through boulders and pinyon pines. After 15 minutes look for a gully/ledge on the right that leads to a grotto.

A. Double Trouble 9*
Gear. Climb the crack just right of a big cave. Gear anchor, walk off west.

B. Double Dealing 10a**
1 bolt, gear to 2.5". A hand crack that turns into a dike at the top. Lower off.
FA: Errett Allen, early 1980s.

C. The Bleeder 8***
6 bolts. Start at some huecos, then climb the slab. Lower off.
FA: Steve Gomez, 2001

D. Straineous 11b**
4 bolts. Climbs out a roof. Lower off.
FA: Neil Hightower, 2001.

Corral

E. Red 10a*
3 bolts. Face climb just left of a seam, then pass a horizontal crack. Lower off.
FA: Neil Hightower, 2001.

F. Grit 10b*
2 bolts. A chute in the corridor. Lower off.
FA: Neil Hightower, 2001.

G. Dike Hike 7*
3 bolts. A face in the corridor. Lower off.
FA: Neil Hightower, 2001.

H. Sugar Land 8**
4 bolts. Face to a bulge. Lower off.
FA: Neil Hightower, 2001.

I. Under Pressure 8**
4 bolts. A bouldery start leads to face. Lower off.
FA: Neil Hightower, 2001.

J. Pachyderm 8*
Gear. Double crack. Gear anchor, walk off right.

K. Green Street 10b***
5 bolts. Face. Lower off.
FA: Neil Hightower, Steve Gomez, 2001.

L. Haze 10a***
4 bolts. Face. Lower off. ➤ Photo this page.
FA: Neil Hightower, Steve Gomez, 2001.

M. Justice 9**
4 bolts. Face. Lower off.
FA: Neil Hightower, 2001.

N. Penner 10b*
Gear to 1". Crack. Lower off.
FA: Neil Hightower, 2001.

Christy Hightower on **Haze** 10a***. ©*Neil Hightower Photo.*

Ken Yager on **King Snake Flakes** 10c**** (1983). ©*Errett Allen Photo.*

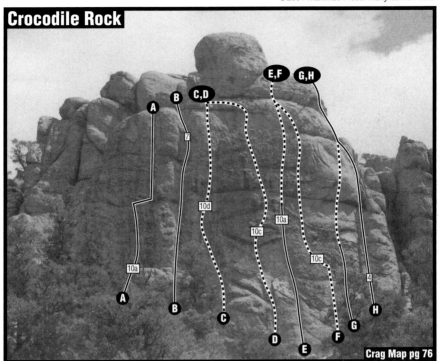

Crocodile Rock

Benton Crags Intro: Page 74. From the South Parking Area skirt left and to the north to reach this quality piece of rock. Bring some thin gear, especially RPs for the face climbs.

A. Slither 10a*
Gear. Crack. Gear anchor.
FA: Fred Feldman, Errett Allen, 1983.

B. Bush Family 7*
Gear. Climb a crack past bushes. Gear anchor.
FA: Bruce Hawkins, Alan Bartlett, 8/1999.

C. Poacher 10d**
1 bolt, gear. Pillar to Face. Gear anchor.
FA: Steve Schneider, Kevin Calder, 1/1986.

D. Challenger 10c***
1 bolt, gear. Face. Gear anchor.
FA: Steve Schneider, Kevin Calder, Errett Allen, 1/1986.

E. Competitive Edge 10a****
Gear. Crack to plates. Gear anchor.
FA: Grant Hiskes, Ken Yager, Sean Plunkett, 6/1983.

F. King Snake Flakes 10c****
1 bolt, gear. Face to seam to plates, a little sporty. Gear anchor. ➤ Photo facing page.
FA: Errett Allen, Ken Yager, 10/1983.

G. Running Scared 10b·(r)
Gear. Climb a thin crack, then go left to a knob, then right under an arch, then up the face. Gear anchor.
FA: Tom Herbert, Alan Bartlett, 10/1987.

H. Lizard 4**
Gear. Crack. Gear anchor.
FA: Fred Feldman, Errett Allen, 1983.

These two routes are found on a tower 300 ft. right. Scramble up to a ledge system to start these climbs.

I. Fun Fingers 10a**
Gear to 1". Pass a horizontal then enter a finger crack. Lower off.

J. The Flakes 9**(r)
3 bolts. Face. Lower off.

©2004 Maximus Press. *Marty Lewis Photo.*

Lost Piton Rock

Crag Map pg 76

Wave Rock

Benton Crags Intro: Page 74. From the South Parking Area head east on a faint trail, cross a gully and skirt this south facing cliff. Routes are listed left to right.

A. Heroes 11c**
6 bolts. The left most route. Climb a face between two right leaning cracks, crossing horizontals. Lower off.
FA: Neil Hightower, Eric Sorenson, 2001.

B. China Girl 9**
1 bolt, gear to 3". Start *Aladdin Sane*, then go left up flakes, pass horizontals, turn a roof on the left. Lower off.
FA: Eric Sorenson, 4/2004.

C. Aladdin Sane 8**
Gear. Climb a dihedral. Lower off.
FA: Neil Hightower, Eric Sorenson, 2001.

D. Sweet Tits 10b**
5 bolts. Fun roof. Lower off.
FA: Neil Hightower, 3/2004.

E. Stardust 10a***
6 bolts. Climb a broken dihedral to a roof. Lower off.
FA: Neil Hightower, 3/2004.

Continue east, then go up and left towards Lost Piton Rock for this climb.

F. Golden Years 12c*
3 bolts. East facing arete. Lower off.
FA: Neil Hightower, 2001.

Lost Piton Rock

This sizable piece of south facing cliff is located a couple minutes past Wave Rock. It features the best sport climbing found at the Benton Crags.

G. Young Americans 8*
Located up and left in a corridor.
3 bolts. Face. Lower off.
FA: Neil Hightower, Eric Sorenson, 2001.

H. Welcome to Planet M.F. (Mother F*cker) 10a****
8 bolts, gear: 2" piece. Climb a dike to thin face, then finish up a 5.8 hand crack. 30m/100' lower off.
☞ What's the deal with bitter old dudes and their offensive route names? ➤ Photo page 66.
FA: Marty Lewis, Kevin Calder, 8/2003, TD.

I. Mercury Landing 10c***
8 bolts. Technical face to juggy roof. Lower off.
FA: Neil Hightower, Eric Sorenson, Steve Gomez, 3/2004.

J. Rebel Rebel 8***
6 bolts. Climb plates. Lower off.
FA: Neil Hightower, Eric Sorenson, Steve Gomez, 3/2004.

K. Spiders From Mars 10b****
9 bolts. Start at a fixed bashie, then climb beautiful plates to a juggy roof. 30m/100' lower off.
FA: Neil Hightower, Eric Sorenson, 2001.

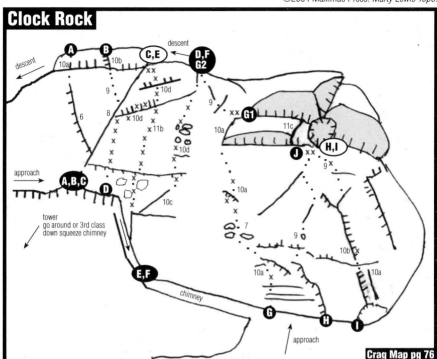

Clock Rock

Crag Map pg 76

Clock Rock

Benton Crags Intro: Page 74. Unlike most of the Benton Crags this cliff faces southeast, so it's sunny in the morning.

A. Analog 10a •
Gear to 4". Flake to reachy gritty roof. Gear anchor.
FA: Greg Barnes, Barry Hutten, Denice Hutten, 4/2000, GU.

B. Countdown 10b**
Gear to 2". Sporty dike to face to roof slot. Gear anchor.
FA: Greg Barnes, Barry Hutten, Denice Hutten, 4/2000, GU.

C. Quartz Digital 8**(r)
Gear to 3". A dike with tricky pro. Lower off.
FA: Ken Yager, 1983.

D. Clockwise 10d***
8 bolts, gear to 1". Climb face then traverse right along a roof, continue right in a crack. 3" to 4" gear anchor.
FA: Greg Barnes, Barry Hutten, 4/2000, TD.
Variation: 10d****. 10 bolts, lower off. Climb *Clockwise* but go straight up after roof traverse. Lower off.

E. Precision 11b***
11 bolts, gear to 3". Crack to jugs to sustained technical face. Lower off.
FA: Todd Snyder, Rachel Nelson, Greg Barnes, 9/2000, TD.

F. Synchronous 10d***
5 bolts, gear to 4". Start *Precision* then go right on a diagonaling thin crack, then up a cool face. Gear anchor.
FA: Greg Barnes, Barry Hutten, 4/2000, TD.

G. Rock Around the Clock 10a****
Pitch 1: 10a****. 4 bolts, gear to 2". Face climb past a bolt, then go left up easy sporty jugs, continue past 3 bolts, then enter a crack on the left side of a roof. 30m/100', lower off or climb 2nd pitch.
FA: Greg Barnes, John Aughinbaugh, Barry Hutten, 4/2000, GU.
Pitch 2: 9**. Gear to 2". Traverse left, then go up cracks and flakes. 3"-4" gear anchor.
FA: Greg Barnes, Denice Hutten, 4/2000, GU.

H. 9 to 5 9*
Gear to 3". Ledges and flakes lead to face climbing. 25m/80', lower off.

I. Here's to the Good Stuff 10b****
2 bolts, gear to 2.5". Scramble up to a hand crack, then climb a difficult dihedral, move right and finish via face climbing. 25m/80', lower off.
FA: Greg Barnes, Barry Hutten, 4/2000, GU.

J. Overtime 11c**
Gear to 2". Climb the roof crack then traverse left on a ledge. Lower off.
FA: Greg Barnes, Barry Hutten, 4/2000, GU.

See Page 115

Bird Lew on **Black Lassie** 10d**** at the Dike Wall. ©*Andy Selters Photo.*

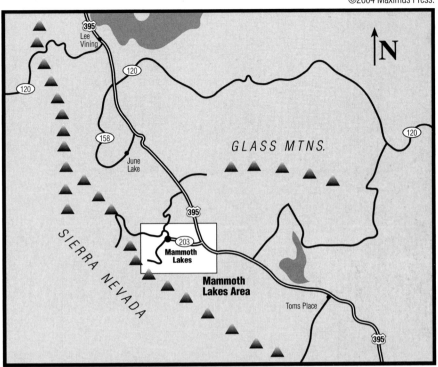

CHAPTER 5

MAMMOTH LAKES

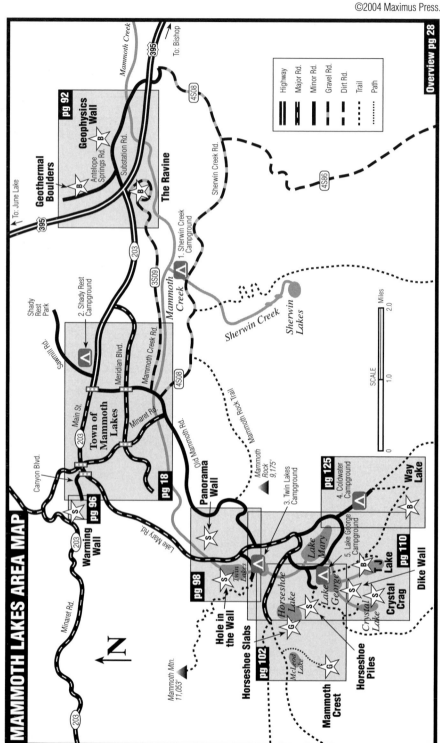

MAMMOTH LAKES AREA MAP

Overview pg 28

Legend:
- Highway
- Major Rd.
- Minor Rd.
- Gravel Rd.
- Dirt Rd.
- Trail
- Path

To: Bishop

Mammoth Creek

395

4S08

Sherwin Creek Rd.

4S86

pg 92

Geophysics Wall

Geothermal Boulders

Antelope Springs Rd.

Substation Rd.

The Ravine

To: June Lake

395

203

3S09

1. Sherwin Creek Campground

Mammoth Creek

Sherwin Creek

Sherwin Lakes

SCALE
0   1.0   2.0
Miles

Shady Rest Park

Sawmill Rd.

2. Shady Rest Campground

Meridian Blvd.

Mammoth Creek Rd.

4S08

Town of Mammoth Lakes

Main St.

Minaret Rd.

203

pg 18

Mammoth Rock Trail

Mammoth Rock 9,175'

Panorama Wall

Old Mammoth Rd.

3. Twin Lakes Campground

pg 125

4. Coldwater Campground

Way Lake

Canyon Blvd.

pg 96

Warming Wall

203

Lake Mary Rd.

pg 98

Hole in the Wall

Twin Lakes

Horseshoe Lake

Lake Mary

Lake George

5. Lake George Campground

Crystal Lake

T.J.

pg 110

Dike Wall

Crystal Crag

Minaret Rd.

N

Mammoth Mtn. 11,053'

Horseshoe Slabs

pg 102

McLeod Lake

Horseshoe Piles

Mammoth Crest

MAMMOTH LAKES AREA BASICS

The Mammoth Lakes Area offers great climbing only minutes from the Town of Mammoth Lakes. The boulders near U.S. 395 are climbable spring through fall. The rest of the climbing is located in the Mammoth Lakes Basin, which receives heavy winter snowfall, so these crags are best in summer and fall. The Lakes Basin is a very popular destination for tourists and all kinds of recreational users. During the peak season (July through Labor Day) the area is quite congested and parking can be a problem.

Mammoth Rock, one of the most obvious formations actually has little climbing potential. Aside from the alpine crags of Mammoth Crest and Crystal Crag, most of the climbing is found on small outcrops hidden in the forest.

Of course Mammoth is better known for its winter skiing than climbing, and it was skiing that drew climbers to the area. In the '70s a number of Yosemite climbers would winter in Mammoth, waiting for spring and the valley season to return. Many ended up staying and developing local crags, even starting a local guide service. Aside from the obvious cliffs of the Mammoth Crest, these climbers ferreted out the smaller crags ringing the lakes of the upper basin.

Getting There

From the U.S. 395/203 junction, drive west on Hwy. 203 for 2.7 miles to reach the Town of Mammoth Lakes.

Amenities

The Lakes Basin has a number of general stores and lodges. A detailed description of amenities and a map of the Town of Mammoth Lakes will be found on pages 18-19.

Camping

1. Sherwin Creek Campground

Open May through mid-September the fee is $13. Picnic tables, piped water, flush toilets, elev. 7,600 ft. ☎ 760-924-5500.

2. Shady Rest Campground

Open mid May through October, the fee is $13. Picnic tables, piped water, flush toilets, elev. 7,800 ft. ☎ 760-924-5500.

3. Twin Lakes Campground

Open late June to October, the fee is $14. Picnic tables, piped water, flush toilets, elev. 8,600 ft. ☎ 760-924-5500.

4. Coldwater Campground

Open mid June to mid September, the fee is $14. Picnic tables, piped water, flush toilets, elev. 8,900 ft. ☎ 760-924-5500.

5. Lake George Campground

Open mid June to mid September, the fee is $14. Picnic tables, piped water, flush toilets, elev. 9,000 ft. ☎ 760-924-5500.

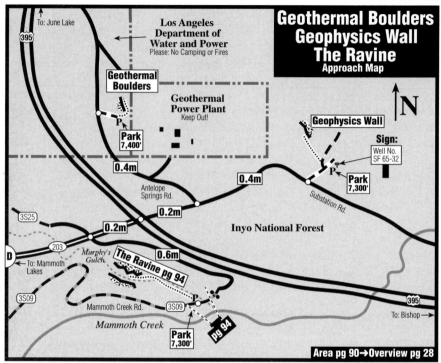

Geothermal Boulders

This bouldering area's main attraction is that it is only a five minute drive from Mammoth. The boulders are snow free most of the year. The problems are fun but limited, with marginal landings. The height of these problems adds adventure to a relatively undeveloped area.

The Approach: From the Town of Mammoth Lakes head east on Hwy. 203, cross under U.S. 395 and make the first left on Antelope Springs Rd. After 0.4 miles, the back side of the boulders will be seen on the right. A steep dirt road leads within 100 ft. of the boulders.

From the parking area walk east to the right of the first boulder seen. The cliff is just left around the corner.

History: Developed in the 1980s.

Geothermal Boulders

Environment: Jeffrey pine forest, near a noisy Geothermal Power Plant.
Elevation: 7,400 ft.
Seaon: April to November
Exposure: East facing, morning sun.
Rock Type: Polished volcanic tuff.
Bouldering: ★, 20 problems.
Drive From Mammoth: 5 minutes.
Approach: 1 minute walk.

Geophysics Wall

Geophysics Wall

The Geophysics Wall features a quick approach, with short and steep moderate problems in a concentrated area. It is just east of the Geothermal Plant.

The Approach: From the Town of Mammoth Lakes head east on Hwy. 203, cross under U.S. 395 and drive 0.6 miles further. Turn left on a dirt road, climb a short hill and a sign will be seen that says "Well No. SF 65-32", park here.

From the parking area walk northwest on a faint path, the wall is on the right.

History: Intrigued by the Geothermal Boulders, a couple of climbers who worked for the USGS began hunting around the area for another outcrop. They were quite surprised to find this band of excellent rock so close to the road and town.

Geophysics Wall Details

Environment: Jeffrey pine forest, near a noisy Geothermal Power Plant.
Elevation: 7,300 ft.
Season: April to November.
Exposure: Southwest facing, afternoon sun.
Rock Type: Polished volcanic tuff.
Bouldering: ★★, 35 problems.
Drive From Mammoth: 5 minutes.
Approach: 1 minute walk.

The Ravine

The Ravine features extensive walls of short boulder problems, with many dihedrals, aretes and cracks. There is an excellent long traverse problem halfway up the Ravine on the right.

The Approach: Map page 92. From the Town of Mammoth Lakes head east on Hwy. 203, just before reaching U.S. 395 is a paved road on the right (3S09). Take this road which parallels U.S. 395 for a while, it then doubles back and turns to dirt. A Forest Service gate is then passed. Park 0.6 miles from Hwy. 203 in a sagebrush filled wash.

From the parking area walk northwest up the wash. You will walk right into the Ravine.

History: Developed by Rob Stockstill in the late '90s.

The Ravine Details

Environment: Sagebrush and pinyon trees, in a sheltered gulch.
Elevation: 7,300 ft.
Season: April to November.
Exposure: Varied.
Rock Type: Polished volcanic tuff.
Bouldering: ★.
Drive From Mammoth: 5 minutes.
Approach: 2 minute walk.

©2004 Maximus Press. *Marty Lewis Photo.*

The Ravine
· Point of View

The Ravine

Park

Approach Map pg 92

Becky Hutto bouldering at **The Ravine**. ©*Kevin Calder Photo.*

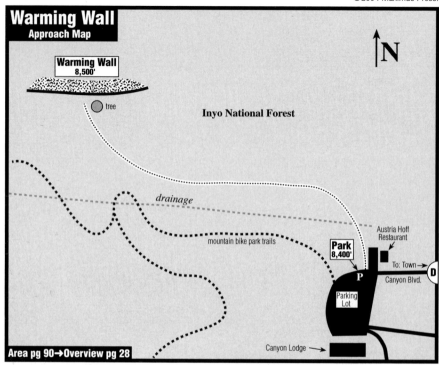

Warming Wall
Approach Map

Warming Wall
8,500'

tree

N

Inyo National Forest

drainage

mountain bike park trails

Austria Hoff
Restaurant

Park
8,400'

To: Town → D

Canyon Blvd.

P

Parking
Lot

Canyon Lodge →

Area pg 90→Overview pg 28

Warming Wall

This convenient wall provides moderate sport climbing within the Town of Mammoth Lakes. The rock is sharp, grainy and of a volcanic origin.

The Approach: From the Town of Mammoth Lakes head west on Hwy. 203. Go straight through the intersection of Minaret Rd. and make the next right on Canyon Blvd. Follow Canyon Blvd. to its end in the tremendous Canyon Lodge parking lot. The Austria Hof Restaurant is the last building on the right, park just beyond it, below a sign that says "Point of Winter Closure".

From here follow a faint trail that heads north into the woods. It then turns left (west) and climbs a shallow drainage.

Warming Wall Details

Environment: Jeffrey pine forest.
Elevation: 8,500 ft.
Season: June to October.
Exposure: South facing, shady forest.
Rock Type: Grainy volcanic tuff.
Sport Climbs: 10 routes, 10a to 11b.
Gear Climbs: 1 route, 5.8.
Drive From Mammoth: 5 minutes.
Approach: 5 minute walk, with a 100 ft. gain.
Special Concerns: The cliff has some graffiti that appeared long before the climbing routes. Although this graffiti lends an urban touch to the cliff, this is a popular area used by mountain bikers. Please keep it clean!

History: This area had been occasionally used for top-roping. It was then developed as a sport climbing area in the late 1980s.

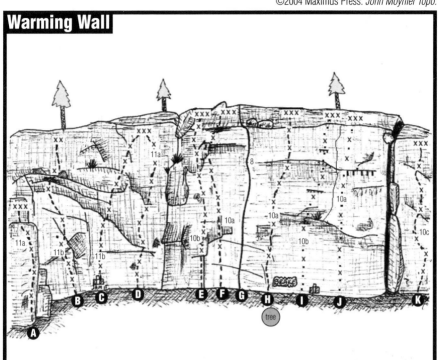

Warming Wall

All pitches are shorter than 25m/80 ft. long.

A. El Nino 11a*
4 bolts. Short steep face. Lower off.
FA: Malcolm Jolley, Meri Jolley, Vivian Farnsworth, 1989.

B. Nuclear Winter 11b***
6 bolts. Technical face, then climb jugs through a roof. Lower off.
FA: Brian Postlethwait, Barry Oswick, 10/1999.

C. Jam It 11b**
7 bolts. Technical face. Lower off.
FA: Malcolm Jolley, Meri Jolley, 1989.

D. Heat Vampire 11a***
8 bolts. Face. Lower off.
FA: Mark Ledel, Malcolm Jolley, 1989.

E. Oh Zone 10b**
9 bolts. Short bulge to a face. Lower off.
FA: Malcolm Jolley, Meri Jolley, 1989.

F. Warming Trend 10a**
5 bolts. Face. Lower off.
FA: Malcolm Jolley, Mark Ledel, 1989.

G. Warming Wall Crack 8*
Gear to 5". Wide crack. Lower off.

H. Faulty Brake 10a***
7 bolts. Nice face behind tree. Lower off.
FA: Malcolm Jolley, Meri Jolley, Gregg Davis, Cynthia Dayhoff, 1989.

I. Ghetto Blaster 10b·
5 bolts. A bouldery start leads to dirty ledgy climbing. Lower off.

J. Hot Flash 10a**
6 bolts. Fun face. Lower off.

K. Greenhouse Effect 10c***
6 bolts. Starts with a strenuous bulge. Lower off.
FA: Malcolm Jolley, Mark Ledel, 1989.

Adapted from the U.S.G.S. 1:24,000 Crystal Crag, Bloody Mtn., Mammoth Mtn. and Old Mammoth Quadrangles.

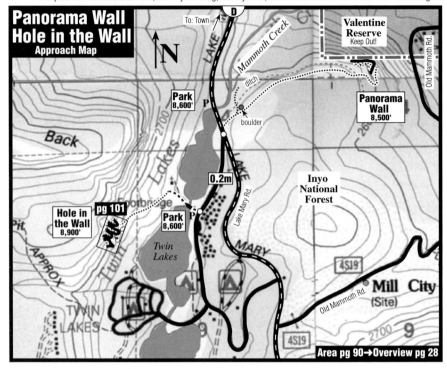

Panorama Wall

Some really hard routes on a gently overhanging wall in a convenient location make this somewhat of a training crag.

The Approach: From the Town of Mammoth Lakes head west on Hwy. 203. At Minaret Rd., Hwy. 203 turns right, but go straight onto Lake Mary Rd. This road passes through a tunnel, then heads up a short grade. Eventually the outlet of Twin Lakes will be reached, park on the right in a paved lot before the lake.

Walk up Lake Mary Rd., go 100 ft. past the bridge and stop 30 ft. before a sign that says "TAMARACK LODGE 1/4→", look for a path on the left side

Panorama Wall Details

Environment: Jeffrey pine forest.
Elevation: 8,500 ft.
Season: June to October.
Exposure: East facing.
Rock Type: Polished volcanic tuff.
Sport Climbs: 4 routes, 11b to 13a.
Drive From Mammoth: 5 minutes.
Approach: 10 minute hike, with a 100 ft. descent.
Special Concerns: The wall is right on the edge of a private ecological study area. Keep it quiet and low key. If the Valentine Reserve posts any climbing restrictions obey them!

of the road. Follow this, after 300 ft. fork right at a boulder and continue on the path that parallels an abandoned ditch (a historical resource—it once fed water to early mining camps). Eventually the path crosses the ditch and drops down to the right, then back left to the base of the crag.

Panorama Wall

Panorama Wall

This is a "quiet crag". Please don't bring your stereo and please don't be loud when climbing here. The slope below is a nature reserve.

A. Project ?
6 bolts. Seam.
P: Todd Graham.

B. Flowstone 12d★★★
6 bolts (gold hangers). Technical and sustained face. Lower off.
FA: Brian Postlethwait, 7/1999.

C. Momentum 12c★★★★
8 bolts. Thin face to right arching seam. Lower off.
FA: Todd Graham, 8/2000.

D. Barbed Wire Utopia
11b★★ or 13a★★★
1st Anchor: 11b★★. 4 bolts. Crack. Lower off.
2nd Anchor: 13a★★★. 9 bolts. Continue past the first anchor, climb a bouldery sustained crux to a thin crack. Lower off.
FA: Todd Graham, 8/2001.

Hole in the Wall

Directly above the popular destination of Twin Lakes lies an expansive cliff band of volcanic rock. Most of it seems pretty chossy. Towards the far left there is an interesting geologic feature known as "Hole in the Wall". For years skiers and snowboarders have made the circuitous descent so that they could make turns through this natural arch. A lot of very steep rock will be found in this cave, so far two routes have been completed. Left of the cave two more climbs will be found on a nice tower of clean rock.

Hole in the Wall Details

Environment: Brushy scree slopes.
Elevation: 8,900 ft.
Season: June to October.
Exposure: Varied.
Rock Type: Volcanic tuff.
Sport Climbs: 4 routes, 11c to 12c.
Drive From Mammoth: 5 minutes.
Approach: 15 minute scramble, with a 300 ft. gain.

In general be careful here, there is a lot of loose rock, and be aware of hikers tossing rocks off the cliffs from above.

The Approach: Map page 98. From the Town of Mammoth Lakes head west on Hwy. 203. At Minaret Rd., Hwy. 203 turns right, but go straight onto Lake Mary Rd. This road passes under a ski lift, then heads up a short grade. The first paved right is for Twin Lakes, turn here, drive 0.2 miles and park on the right.

From here head west across a bridge and past a chapel. Begin to angle up and left on stable talus, keep heading left as the approach degenerates into a loose slidey scree slope. Cross a line of brush, then go up heinous scree to Hole in the Wall. The Z Chute Cliff is 5 minutes left (south) of here around a buttress and through more brush.

History: People have tried climbing here at various times over the years but found the rock too loose to allow reasonably safe routes. In the mid 1990s Bruce Lella realized that with extensive cleaning and good bolts some fun cave climbing could be possible.

Hole in the Wall

The rock in here is a little chossy. With a some traffic these super-steep lines should clean up.

A. Open Project
1 bolt. Right under the arch.
P: Bruce Lella.

B. Broken Earth aka Gravity's Riddle 12c**
7 bolts. Steep cave. Lower off.
FA: Bruce Lella.

C. Mixture of Frailties 12b**
6 bolts. Steep face. Lower off.
FA: Bruce Lella.

D. Open Project
1 bolt. Right under the arch.
P: Bruce Lella.

E. Open Project
1 bolt. Right under the arch.
P: Bruce Lella.

Z Chute Cliff

The rock on this tower is pretty clean.

F. Yard Sale 11c**
7 bolts. Up steep pocketed face. Lower off.
FA: Dave Melkonian, Mike Melkonian, 10/2001.

G. Huck'n Meat 12a***
9 bolts. Overhang to steep pocketed face. Lower off.
FA: Mike Melkonian, Dave Melkonian, 10/2001.

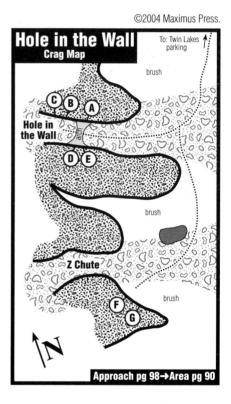

Hole in the Wall
Crag Map

To: Twin Lakes parking

brush

Hole in the Wall

brush

Z Chute

brush

N

Approach pg 98→Area pg 90

Adapted from the U.S.G.S. 1:24,000 Crystal Crag Quadrangle.

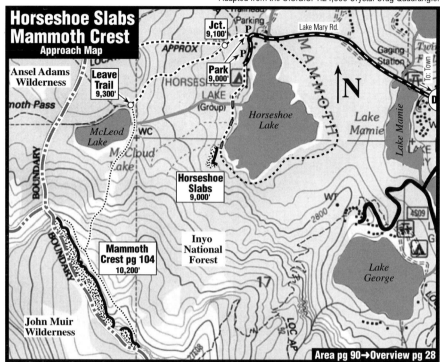

Horseshoe Slabs

The Horseshoe Slabs traditionally have been a top-rope area, but recently a few of these routes have been bolted and provide fun leads. The route anchors are large trees, so bring some long runners.

The Approach: From the Town of Mammoth Lakes head west on Hwy. 203. At a traffic light Hwy. 203 turns right, instead go straight ahead on Lake Mary Rd. Follow this 5 miles to its end at Horseshoe Lake and park. A deforested area is reached (volcanic gasses killed of the trees).

From the parking lot hike south along the west side of the lake on a mountain bike trail. Follow this across a few bridges. The trail then crosses a gully, and passes alongside a little granite buttress, the crag is just beyond towards the right in the forest.

History: This has long been a popular area with local guides as a beginning teaching area.

Horseshoe Slabs Details

Environment: Alpine forest.
Elevation: 9,000 ft.
Season: July to October.
Exposure: East facing, shady forest.
Rock Type: Granite.
Gear Climbs: 10 routes, 5.4 to 10a.
Top-roping: Tree anchors.
Drive From Mammoth: 10 minutes.
Approach: 10 minute walk.
Special Concerns: Horseshoe Lake is a very popular spot, expect to see hikers, mountain bikers and other users.

©2004 Maximus Press. *John Moynier Topo.*

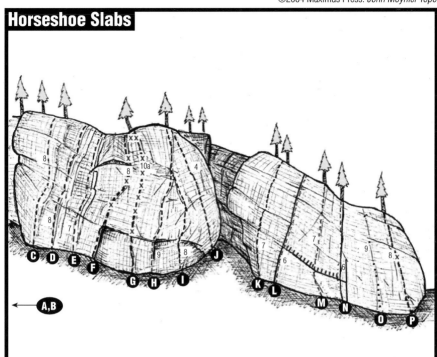

Horseshoe Slabs

Horseshoe Slabs

Most of the route's anchors are trees at the top of the slab. The cliff is well under 25m/80' long.

The first two routes are off to the left on a small tower.

A. Unknown ?
Gear. A crack that goes up the left side of the tower.

B. Unknown ?
2 bolts, gear. Climb the seam past two bolts to a crack that splits the middle of the tower.

C. Top-rope 8*(tr)
Face to a slabby dike.

D. Top-rope 8*(tr)
Climb many parallel dikes.

E. Top-rope 7*(tr)
The left black streak.

F. Wrangler 8**
3 bolts, gear: 2.5" piece. Climb the right black streak. Lower off.
FA: Malcolm Jolley, 1992.

G. Horseman 10a**
6 bolts. Slab. Lower off.
FA: Malcolm Jolley, 1992.

H. Top-rope 9*(tr)
Slabby dikes.

I. Top-rope 8*(tr)
Slabby dikes.

J. Top-rope 4*(tr)
Slab.

K. Top-rope 7*(tr)
Slabby dike.

L. Cowpuncher 6**
Gear to 2". Right leaning crack. Tree anchor.

M. Top-rope 7*(tr)
Follow a dike through a short bulge, then up a slab.

N. Rodeo Rider 6**
Gear to 2". Twin cracks. Tree anchor.

O. Top-rope 9*(tr)
Slab.

P. Blacksmith 8*
1 bolt, gear to 1". Seam. Tree anchor.

Mammoth Crest
Point of View

McLeod Lake

Approach Map pg 102

Mammoth Crest

This expansive band of alpine granite is quite prominent from the Town of Mammoth Lakes. Most of the routes involve two to three pitches of climbing.

The Approach: Map page 102. From the Town of Mammoth Lakes head west on Hwy. 203. At a traffic light Hwy. 203 turns right, instead go straight ahead on Lake Mary Rd. Follow this 5 miles to its end at Horseshoe Lake and park at a deforested area (volcanic gasses killed the trees).

From the parking lot take the Mammoth Pass Trail. Within a couple of minutes go left at a trail junction to McLeod (McCloud) Lake. Upon reaching McLeod (McCloud) Lake skirt clockwise towards the south end of the lake then scramble up a pumice slope right of a huge talus field. Upon reaching a small cliff band head up and right.

History: As with many of the other areas around Mammoth, this crag was first developed by local guides—Yosemite climbers wintering at the ski area. Recently there has been renewed interest, with some new climbs going in.

Mammoth Crest Details

Environment: Alpine talus slope.
Elevation: 10,200 ft.
Season: July to September.
Exposure: Northeast facing, morning sun.
Rock Type: Alpine granite.
Gear Climbs: 13 routes, 8 to 10c.
Sport Climbs: 1 route, 10c.
Drive From Mammoth: 10 minutes.
Approach: 45 minute scramble with a 1,200 ft. gain. Kind of a grunt.

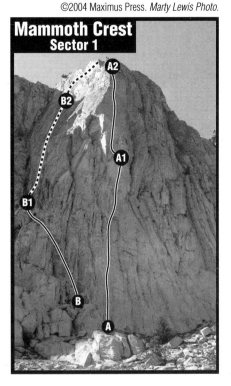

Mammoth Crest - Sector 1

A. Pump Up the Jams 10b***

Pitch 1: Gear to 4". Climb lightning bolt cracks to an obvious shallow chimney in an overhang, belay from a sloping ledge above the chimney.

Pitch 2: 10b***. Gear to 4". Face climb left to a prominent fist and hand crack that splits the headwall near the arete.

Pitch 3: 4th class. Climb jumbled blocks to summit.

Descent: Walk left (south) 50 ft. to a double rope rappel off a tree.

FA: Dean Rosnau, Bryant Phillips, 1994, GU.

B. Black Track 10a**

Pitch 1: Easy 5th. Gear. Scramble up a low angle dihedral for 50m/165', belay from a large boulder.

Pitch 2: Bolts. Climb the steep black streak on perfect holds to a hanging belay.

Pitch 3: 10a**. Bolts. Climb thin face up, then go right to the summit.

Descent: Walk left (south) 50 ft. to a double rope rappel off a tree.

FA: Dean Rosnau, Roy Suggett, 1994, GU.

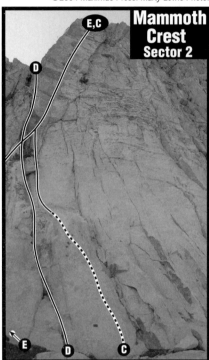

Mammoth Crest Sector 2

Mammoth Crest Sector 3

Crag Photo pg 105

Bob Finn on **Buffalo Chips** 10c***. ©*Errett Allen Photo.*

Mammoth Crest - Sector 2

Intro: Page 104.

C. Requiem 10c**
2 pitches, bolts, gear. Start just right of a small plaque bolted to the cliff. Face to crack. Walk off.
FA: Bruce Lella, Doug Howell, 1992.

D. Reaganomics 9**
2 pitches, gear. Big dihedral. Walk off.
FA: Scott Cole, Bob, 1980s.

E. Gunboat Diplomacy 10a*
2 pitches, gear. Crack, crosses *Reaganomics.* Walk off.
FA: Scott Cole, Chuck Satterfield, 1980s.

Mammoth Crest - Sector 3

F. Summer Daze 9**
2 pitches, gear. Crack. Walk off.
FA: Pete Lowery, Chris Keith, 1990.

See Page 108

Mammoth Crest
Sector 4

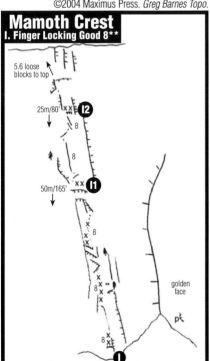

Mamoth Crest
I. Finger Locking Good 8**

5.6 loose
blocks to top

25m/80'

8

8

50m/165'

8

8

golden
face

pt

Mammoth Crest - Sector 4
Intro: Page 104.

G. Pigs in Space 10a*
2 pitches, gear. Start *Ski Tracks*, then go right at the second pitch. Walk off left.

H. Ski Tracks 10a**
2 pitches, gear. Steep cracks. Walk off left.
FA: Ken Yager, Bob Finn, 1980s.

I. Finger Locking Good 8***
Pitch 1: 8***. 9 bolts, gear: thin to 1.5". Corners and face. Bolt anchor, 50m/165' rappel.
Pitch 2: 8***. Gear: thin to 1.5". Awesome finger crack. Bolt anchor, 25m/80' rappel.
FA: Barry Hutten, Greg Barnes, 9/2001.

Mammoth Crest
Sector 5

Crag Photo pg 105

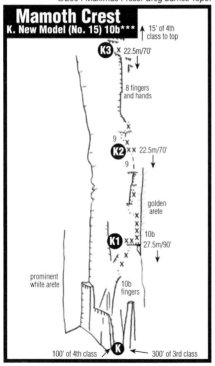

Mamoth Crest
K. New Model (No. 15) 10b***

15' of 4th class to top

K3   X 22.5m/70'

8 fingers and hands

9

K2 xx 22.5m/70'

9

golden arete

10b
27.5m/90'

K1 xx

prominent white arete

10b fingers

100' of 4th class   K   300' of 3rd class

Mammoth Crest - Sector 5
Intro: Page 104.

J. Crestfallen 10c***
10 bolts. Face. Lower off.
FA: Urmas Franosch, Dustin Clark, 10/2002.

K. New Model (No. 15) 10b***
Pitch 1: 10b***. 2 bolts, gear to 2". Climb an arch to a steep face.
Pitch 2: 10b***. 5 bolts, gear to 2". Climb an arete then go left towards cracks, up these to face climbing.
Pitch 3: 9**. 1 bolt, gear to 2". Face climb past a bolt then climb a dihedral.
Descent: Three 30m/100' rappels.
FA: Greg Barnes, Barry Hutten, 9/2001.

L. Buffalo Chips 10c***
Gear. Straight in wide crack. Walk off left.
➤ Photo page 106.
FA: Chuck Cochrane, Bob Finn, 1980s.

Mammoth Crest
Left Side

Sector 6

Hollywood Bowl
2nd class gully

Right Side
pg 105

M

Mammoth Crest
Sector 6

M

Mammoth Crest - Sector 6
Intro: Page 104.

M . Wonder 10c**
Gear to 1". Finger crack. Scramble off right.
FA: Joel St. Marie, Barb Howe, 9/1999.

Mammoth Crest - Left Side

There seems to have been very little activity on this section of cliff.

The exact location of this mysterious climb is unknown.

Finn-Yager 9*
Gear. Crack. Walk off.
FA: Bob Finn, Ken Yager, 1980s.

Adapted from the U.S.G.S. 1:24,000 Crystal Crag and Bloody Mtn. Quadrangles.

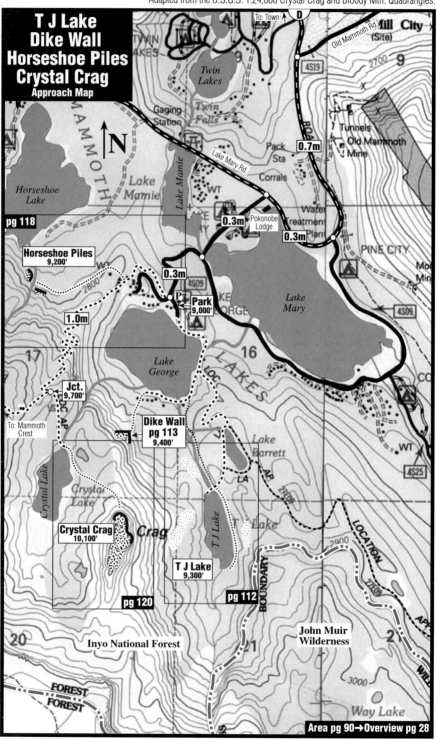

T J Lake

T J Lake has an expansive, but spread out, selection of excellent bouldering, on featured granite, with a handful of roped climbs thrown in.

The Approach: From the Town of Mammoth Lakes head west on Hwy. 203. At a traffic light Hwy. 203 turns right, instead go straight ahead on Lake Mary Rd. Follow this 3.8 miles and turn left at the Pokonobe Lodge. Follow this narrow road 0.3 miles until a "T" intersection is reached. Turn right here and follow the steep winding road 0.3 miles up to the Lake George parking lot.

T J Lake Details

Environment: Alpine lake.
Elevation: 9,300 ft.
Season: July to October.
Exposure: Varied.
Rock Type: Quality granite.
Bouldering: ★★.
Gear Climbs: 2 routes, 5.7.
Sport Climbs: 1 route, 12a.
Drive From Mammoth: 10 minutes.
Approach: 25 minute hike with a 300 ft. gain.

From here hike clockwise around the east shore of the lake. After crossing the outlet stream follow a good trail past some cabins. The T J Lake trail then branches left up a steep grade. After a half mile the trail drops down to the lake. Upon approaching T J Lake one can head clockwise around the lake to the T J Swan Cliff. Around the west side of the lake just beyond the outlet is a small granite formation known as Anaerobia.

Excellent bouldering will be found scattered about on the hillsides around and below the lake. At the south end of T J Lake is a classic square erratic boulder that features a steep cave.

History: The stunning prow of *Anaerobia* (12a) was an early Eastside testpiece first top-roped by Kevin Leary. The square hand traverse boulder was developed in the 1980s. Only recently Rob Stockstill has developed the bouldering on the slopes around the lake.

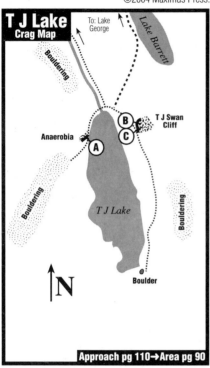

T J Swan Cliff

T J Lake Intro: Page 111. This west facing crag seems to be of volcanic origin. There are a few 1/4" bolts on top of the formation, but these should be supplemented with natural gear for belaying. There are many options for top-roping on either side of the cracks.

B. T J Swan 7★★
Gear to 2". The left crack. 20m/65', gear anchor, walk off right.

C. Myers Crack 7★★
Gear to 2". The right crack. 20m/65', gear anchor, walk off right.

Steve Schneider on **Anaerobia** 12a★★★.

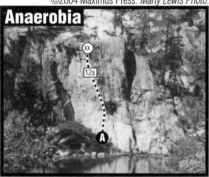

Anaerobia

T J Lake Intro: Page 111. This is a southeast facing buttress. There is an old aid line on the left side.

A. Anaerobia 12a★★★
5 bolts. Steep lieback. Lower off.
➤ Photo this page.
FA: Roland Arsons, 1990. FTR: Kevin Leary.

Dike Wall

The Dike Wall offers fantastic vertical to gently overhanging climbing on granite superbly featured with dikes, plates and seams. Located in a pristine alpine setting, the Dike Wall is one of the most beautiful of the Mammoth areas. This wall features incredible sport climbing, and a few awesome trad leads. All routes have excellent anchors. Top-ropes can be easily jumped from one route to the route on either side.

The East Face gets morning sun. The North Face is a cool shady summer area that is great on hot days. Note that a significant snowbank often lingers at the base of the North Face well into summer. This usually doesn't affect the climbing too much, just start in the moat.

The Approach: Map page 110. From the Town of Mammoth Lakes head west on Hwy. 203. At a traffic light Hwy. 203 turns right, instead go straight ahead on Lake Mary Rd. Follow this 3.8 miles and turn left at the Pokonobe Lodge. Follow this narrow road 0.3 miles until a "T" intersection is reached. Turn right here and follow the steep winding road 0.3 miles up to the Lake George parking lot.

From here hike clockwise around the east shore of the lake. After crossing the outlet stream follow a good trail about a 1/4 mile past many cabins. Just before the last cabin a climbers' path heads south up a steep slope. After a short distance talus will be reached, the Dike Wall is just above.

History: The Dike Wall was a popular top-roping crag during the '80s, that had a handful of traditional leads. During the early '90s bolts were added to many of the top-ropes yielding leadable climbs, but natural placements were still used whenever possible. Recently, due to popular demand, most of the remaining mixed routes have been bolted into sport climbs.

Dike Wall Details

Environment: Alpine talus field.
Elevation: 9,400 ft.
Season: July to October.
Exposure: East and north facing.
Rock Type: Quality granite.
Sport Climbs: 20 routes, 10a to 13b.
Gear Climbs: 5 routes, 5.6 to 11a.
Top-roping: Bolt anchors.
Drive From Mammoth: 10 minutes.
Approach: 20 minute hike, with a 400 ft. gain.

Marty Lewis on **Black Lassie** 10d****. ©*Kevin Calder Photo.*

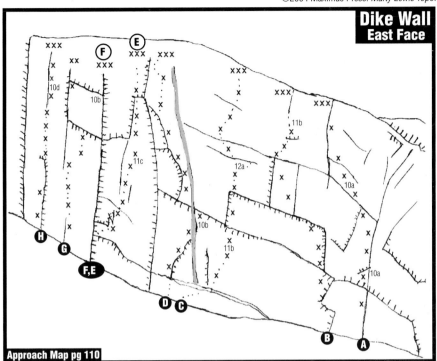

Dike Wall - East Face

Intro: Page 113. This gently overhanging wall receives morning sun.

A. Cromagnon 10a*****
9 bolts. Pass a roof, then follow discontinuous cracks. Lower off. ☞ A loose chossy death route had been climbed on this face by a few individuals (including Kevin Calder) on dicey gear. That route has since exfoliated off of the cliff (notice the debris at the base), yielding a new line that was bolted and has become an instant classic.
FA: Kevin Calder, Marty Lewis, 9/1997, GU.

B. Antibro 11b***
9 bolts. Dihedrals to a bulge. Lower off.
FA: Marty Lewis, Kevin Calder, 9/1997, TD.

C. Secret Agent Man 12a****
10 bolts. Sustained with a crimpy crux. Lower off.
FA: Marty Lewis, Kevin Calder, 8/1998, TD.

D. Grim Reality 10b**
10 bolts. A bouldery face leads to a ledge, then climb big flakes to an easy dihedral then reach right for the anchors. 27.5m/90' lower off.
FA: Marty Lewis, Kevin Calder, 8/1998, TD.

E. Grinder 11c****
9 bolts. Face to a dihedral. Lower off.
FA: Kevin Calder, Marty Lewis, 8/1998, TD.

F. Black Dihedral 10b****
Gear to 3". Stem, jam and lieback up this beautiful corner. Lower off. ☞ A traditional classic. ➤ Front cover photo.

G. Proud Rock Climb 11d***
7 bolts, opt. gear to 0.5". Wander up a face, a little sporty. Lower off.
FA: John Hartman, 1990, GU.

H. Black Lassie 10d****
9 bolts. Climb a dihedral to a black streak. Lower off.
➤ Photo page 88, facing page.
FA: Kevin Calder, Marty Lewis, 9/1997, TD.

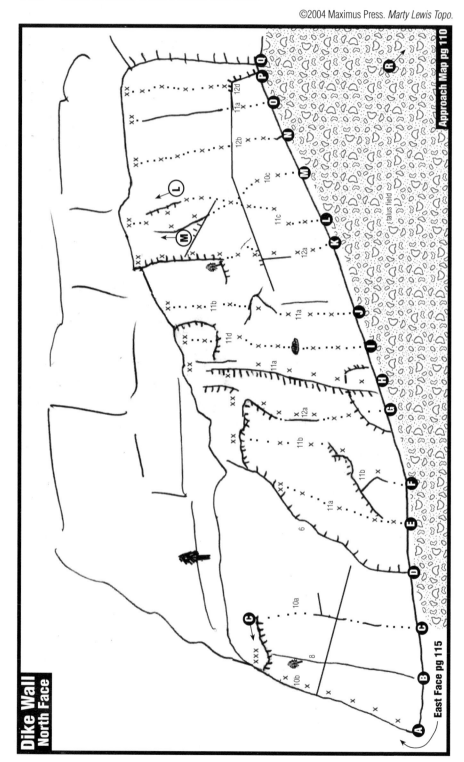

Dike Wall
North Face

Approach Map pg 110

East Face pg 115

Chris McNamara on **Strap-on Tools** 12a****. ©*Kevin Calder Photo.*

Dike Wall - North Face

Intro: Page 113. Many of the routes on this wall were first top-ropes, the route names listed are from the original top-rope ascents.

A. Mongoloid 10b★★
6 bolts. Slabby arete. Lower off.
FA: Kevin Calder, Marty Lewis, 8/1998.

B. Mr. D.N.A. 8★★
Gear to 2". A thin crack leads past a small tree. Lower off.

C. Mr. Kamikaze 10a★(r)
Gear to 2". Dike to face, sporty and nebulous. Gear anchor.

D. Satterfield Corner 6 •
Gear to 2". One move dihedral. Mainly used to access top-rope anchors. Lower off.

E. Quick Lick 11a★★
4 bolts. Face. Lower off.
FA: Urmas Franosch, John Hoffman, 8/2001.

F. Dichotomy 11b★★
4 bolts. Climb past a flake. Lower off.
FA: John Hoffman, Urmas Franosch, 8/2001.

G. Strap-on Tools 12a★★★★
6 bolts. Sustained face to undercling flake. Lower off.
► Photo this page.
FA: Marty Lewis, Kevin Leary, Malcolm Jolley, 8/1992. FTR: Urmas Franosch.

H. Black Leather 11a★★★★
6 bolts. Tricky physical dihedral. Lower off. ☞ Originally a very bold boltless lead. Later 2 bolts were added; one to protect a potential ground fall and the other to protect a 7" section of crack. Ten years later, due to popular demand it has been bolted into a sport climb.
FA: Urmas Franosch, Errett Allen, 1985.

I. Box Lunch 11d★★★
6 bolts. Stem and pinch the twin dikes. Lower off. ☞ The first sport climb at the crag.
FA: Roland Arsons, Dimitri Barton, 1990.

J. Lesbie Friends 11b★★★★
6 bolts. Sustained face. Lower off.
FA: Marty Lewis, Mark Blanchard, 8/1992. FTR: Urmas Franosch.

K. Feather Ruffler 12a★★★
8 bolts. Face to dihedral. Lower off.
FA: Scott Ayers, Urmas Franosch, 8/2001. FTR: Dimitri Barton.

L. Going Both Ways 11c★★★★
9 bolts. Long sustained face. Lower off.
FA: Urmas Franosch, Al Swanson, 8/1997.

M. Double Ender 10c★★★
6 bolts. Pass the initial bulge then go up and left across *Going Both Ways* to a seam. Lower off.
FA: Urmas Franosch, Errett Allen, 1992.

N. Instigator 12b★★
6 bolts. Technical face. Lower off.

O. Dominatrix 11a★★★
1 bolt, gear to 1.5". Face to thin crack. Lower off.
FA: Urmas Franosch, Scott Cole, 1985.

P. Blue Velvet 12d★★★
5 bolts, stick clip. Sporty face. Lower off.
FA: Steve Schneider, Roland Arsons, 1990.

Q. Solo Route 7 •
Gear. Crack. Mainly used to access top-rope anchors. Gear anchor.

This route is located below and to the right of the Dike Wall.

R. Special Fun 13b★★★
4 bolts. Face. Lower off.
FA: Tom Herbert, Roland Arsons, Dimitri Barton, 1990.

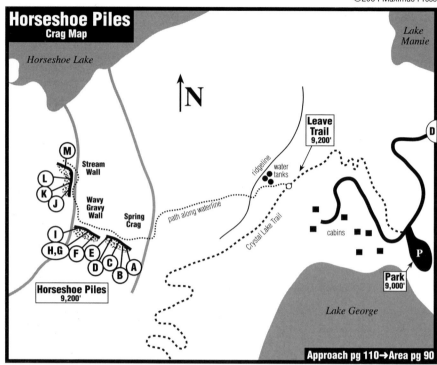

Horseshoe Piles

A small secluded area hidden in the forest above Horseshoe Lake.

The Approach: Map page 110. From the Town of Mammoth Lakes head west on Hwy. 203. At a traffic light Hwy. 203 turns right, instead go straight ahead on Lake Mary Rd. Follow this 3.8 miles and turn left at the Pokonobe Lodge. Follow this narrow road 0.3 miles until a "T" intersection is reached. Turn right here and follow the steep winding road 0.3 miles up to the Lake George parking lot.

Horseshoe Piles Details

Environment: Alpine forest.
Elevation: 9,200 ft.
Season: July to October.
Exposure: North facing, shady.
Rock Type: Granite.
Sport Climbs: 12 routes, 5.8 to 11c.
Gear Climbs: 1 route, 5.9.
Drive From Mammoth: 10 minutes.
Approach: 15 minute walk with a 200 ft. gain.

From here take the Crystal Lake Trail. Hike about 5 minutes until reaching a few water tanks. Leave the trail, walk 150 ft. west past the water tanks and cross the ridgeline. Follow a gentle path along a waterline to the west. Upon reaching a small creek head upstream, the Spring Crag is just across the creek. Contour past the Spring Crag to reach the Wavy Gravy Wall. The Stream Wall is a little further down a steep streambed.

History: It wasn't until the turn of the century that this hidden crag was developed.

Wavy Gravy Wall

Spring Crag
A. Reallyfivenineplus 10c**
8 bolts. Slab to overhang to a slabby crack. Lower off.
FA: Dave Tidwell, 7/2000.

B. D.D.D. 11a****
9 bolts. Sustained left facing dihedral. Harder than it looks. Lower off.
FA: Dan Mulnar, Dave Tidwell, 8/2000.

C. Fall Harvest 10b*
Bolts. Boulder up a vertical section, than climb a slab. Lower off.
FA: Dave Tidwell, Dan Mulnar, 10/2000.

D. Cleaning Lady 9**
6 bolts. Slab. Lower off.
FA: Alan Bartlett, Steve Gerberding, 7/2003.

E. Horseshoe Pits 9*
Gear. Broken dihedral. Lower off.
FA: Al Swanson, 2000.

Wavy Gravy Wall
F. Giving Tree 10d**
7 bolts. Left facing flake start to roof to face. Lower off.
FA: Dave Tidwell, 7/2000.

G. Ambient Groove 11a*
Bolts. Start on a slabby depression, pass a small roof then up a groove. Lower off.
FA: Scott Sederstrom, Dan Mulnar, 6/2000.

H. Wavy Gravy 11c*
Bolts. Clip the 1st bolt on *Ambient Groove* then move right to a vertical face. Lower off.
FA: Scott Sederstrom, Dan Mulnar, 6/2000.

I. Autumn Storm 8**
Bolts. Slab. Lower off.
FA: Todd Graham, 2000.

Stream Wall
Just left of a tree with four trunks.
J. War-Wound 11b**
6 bolts. Long reaches up an overhanging face. Lower off.
FA: Dave Tidwell, 9/2001.

K. Slotster 10c*
5 bolts. Start in big slot then climb face. Lower off.
FA: Dave Tidwell, Dan Mulnar, 6/2001.

L. Crimpoid 11c*
6 bolts. Crimpy lieback start then join *Slotster.* Lower off.
FA: Dave Tidwell, Dan Mulnar, 6/2001.

This route is down the hillside and around the toe of the buttress.
M. This is the Meaning of Life 11a****
11 bolts. Start at a rust patch then climb the long face to a roof finish.
FA: Dave Tidwell, Dan Mulnar, 9/2001.

Crystal Crag
A. North Face 8**
B. Northeast Buttress 8*

Schoolboy
Buttress pg 124

Kilt Wall
pg 123

Highlands
Wall pg 123

Approach

Crystal Crag

This 10,364 ft. peaklet is visible from most points in the Lakes Basin. The west face offers a 3ʳᵈ class route to the summit, this is also the descent for the climbs that top-out. Recently a number of fine sport climbs have been added to the base of this alpine crag. The hangers are so well camouflaged that they are almost invisible. This can cause a bit of confusion as to which route is which.

The Approach: Map page 110. From the Town of Mammoth Lakes head west on Hwy. 203. At a traffic light Hwy. 203 turns right, instead go straight ahead on Lake Mary Rd. Follow this 3.8 miles and turn left at the Pokonobe Lodge. Follow this narrow road 0.3 miles until a "T" intersection is reached. Turn right here and follow the steep winding road 0.3 miles up to the Lake George parking lot.

From here take the Crystal Lake Trail. After 1 mile a trail junction will be reached, go left towards Crystal Lake, upon reaching the lake cross the outlet and skirt the lake clockwise. Soon a sign will be encountered warning of the

Crystal Crag Details

Environment: Alpine talus field.
Elevation: 10,100 ft.
Season: July to September.
Exposure: Northeast facing, morning sun.
Rock Type: Alpine granite.
Sport Climbs: 19 routes, 5.9 to 12a.
Gear Climbs: 7 routes, 5.7 to 5.9.
Drive From Mammoth: 10 minutes.
Approach: 45 minute hike, with a 1,100 ft. gain.

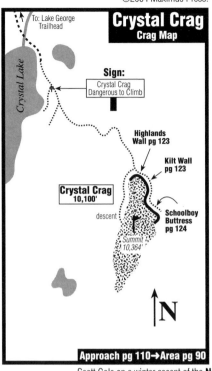

Crystal Crag
Crag Map

To: Lake George Trailhead

Crystal Lake

Sign:
Crystal Crag
Dangerous to Climb

Highlands Wall pg 123

Kilt Wall pg 123

Crystal Crag
10,100'

descent

Schoolboy Buttress pg 124

Summit
10,364'

N

Approach pg 110→Area pg 90

peril of attempting to climb Crystal Crag. From here a path wanders southeast through many granite outcrops to the base of the cliff.

History: The obvious alpine corner systems on the north side were first climbed many years ago. However the area's sport climbing potential was only recently tapped, in a burst of energy, during the summer of 2001, primarily by Scott Ayers.

Scott Cole on a winter ascent of the **North Arete** 7*** of Crystal Crag (1983). ©*Marty Lewis Photo.*

See Page 123

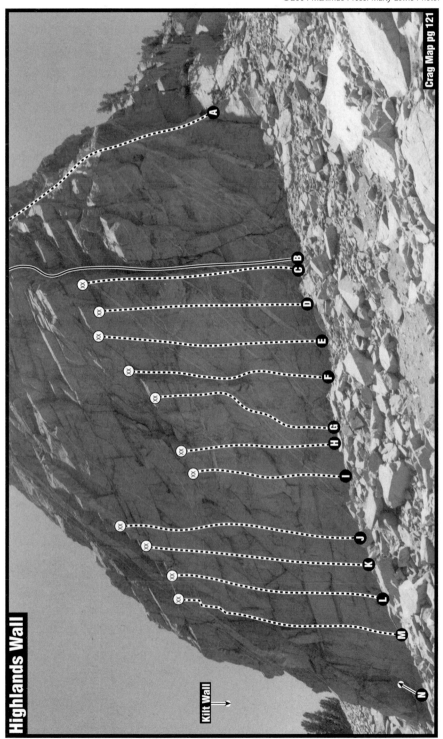

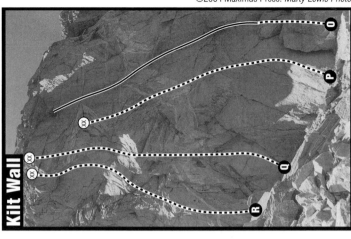

Highlands Wall
Crystal Crag Intro: Page 120.

A. North Arete 7***
Gear to 3". Starts in an obvious right facing corner. Up this (the crux) until the corner starts to fade out a bit and it's easy to break up and left. Take the easiest line up the crest to an amazing crystal band. Then head south along the ridge. ➤ Photo page 121.
Descent: Work you way down the west face (Class 3).

B. North Face 8**
Gear to 3". This climb starts in a dihedral on the prow of the arete. After the first 5.8 pitch, a few easier pitches lead to the summit ridge. Then head south along the ridge.
Descent: Work you way down the west face (Class 3).

C. Macallan 9**
7 bolts. Arete. Lower off.
FA: Scott Ayers, Matt Ciancio, 8/2001.

D. Lagavulin 10c***
10 bolts. Dike and knob climbing to hard finish. Lower off.
FA: Scott Ayers, Matt Ciancio, 8/2001.

E. Springbank 10a***
8 bolts. Dikes to classic thin flake finish. Lower off.
FA: Scott Ayers, Matt Ciancio, 8/2001.

F. Balvenie 9**
2 bolts, gear to 2.5". Face climb to a green right facing corner. Lower off.
FA: Scott Ayers, Matt Ciancio, 8/2001.

G. Cragganmore 9**
7 bolts. Slab start to right angling traverse on big dikes, then up. Lower off.
FA: Scott Ayers, 8/2001.

H. Knockando 10d**
7 bolts. Slab start to a dike, to a steep headwall. Lower off.
FA: Scott Ayers, Matt Ciancio, 8/2001.

I. If It's Not Scottish, It's Crap 11a*
6 bolts. Slab start to face, pass roof crux, then steep finish. Lower off.
FA: Henry Means, Scott Ayers, 8/2001.

J. On the Rocks 10b**
9 bolts. Straight up crossing diagonal ramp to double roofs. Lower off.
FA: Scott Ayers, Lara Wilkinson, 8/2001.

K. Double Barrel 10b**
9 bolts. Straight up crossing diagonal ramps to roof, then steep left facing corner finish. Lower off.
FA: Scott Ayers, Lara Wilkinson, 8/2001.

L. Tumbler 11a***
10 bolts. Small left facing corner start. Straight up to and through obvious break in roof. Traverse right across lip of roof, then back left at the top. Lower off.
FA: Scott Ayers, Lara Wilkinson, 8/2001.

M. But I Don't Drink Scotch 10a**
10 bolts. Left facing corner to dike. Then right facing corner to stance. Then climb the stair stepped arete finish. Lower off.
FA: Scott Ayers, Lara Wilkinson, 8/2001.

N. Northeast Buttress 8*
Gear to 3". This climbs the most obvious corners and ramps to the right of the broken northeast face.
Descent: Work you way down the west face (Class 3).
FA: Vern Clevenger, Bill Dougherty, 1970s.

Kilt Wall

O. Ben Nevis 9**
Gear. Quality clean left facing corner. Fixed gear anchor.

P. Off Kilter 9***
9 bolts. Slab to roof to flakes. Then climb a left facing corner to finish under a roof. Lower off.
FA: Scott Ayers, Urmas Franosch, 8/2001.

Q. View to a Kilt 11a***
10 bolts. Steep corner to slab, to big roof finish. Lower off.
FA: Scott Ayers, Lara Wilkinson, 8/2001.

R. Plaid to the Bone 10d***
12 bolts. Steep face, then step right to a big roof. Lower off.
FA: Scott Ayers, Urmas Franosch, 10/2001.

Schoolboy Buttress
Crystal Crag Intro: Page 120.

A. East Face Right 9*
Gear to 3". Climb three pitches up a left leaning ramp system.
Descent: Work you way down the west face (Class 3).
FA: Vern Clevenger, Galen Rowell, 1970s.

B. Unknown ?
5 bolts. Slab. Lower off.

C. Unknown 9*
Gear to 3.5". Dihedral. Lower off.

D. Little Schoolboy 10c**
8 bolts. Start at a corner on a rounded arete, climb to a roof, then left facing flakes. Lower off.
FA: Lara Wilkinson, Scott Ayers, 8/2001.

E. Le Petit Ecolier 11c**
9 bolts. Start at a dihedral on the arete, then go out left to an overhanging crack to a stance, then finish up the arete. Lower off.
FA: Scott Ayers, Lara Wilkinson, 8/2001.

F. Crystal Whipped 11d***
9 bolts. Stem a box to a slab then climb a hanging right facing corner, next overhanging face and seams. Lower off.
FA: Scott Ayers, Urmas Franosch, 10/2001.

G. East Face Left 8*
Gear to 3". Follow an obvious dihedral all the way to the summit.
Descent: Work you way down the west face (Class 3).
FA: Greg Donaldson, Chuck Calef.

H. School of Rock 12a***
9 bolts. Central left facing corner which curves left. Head straight up to roofs, then step right into an easy corner. Lower off.
FA: Scott Ayers, Lara Wilkinson, 10/2001.

I. 9/11 10c***
9 bolts. Climb the left facing rounded ramp/dihedral to the left of a roof system, then a steep finish then step right to anchors. Lower off.
FA: Urmas Franosch, John Hoffman, 9/2001.

J. Bagpipe 11a**
8 bolts. Prominent blunt arete left of overhanging face. Lower off.
FA: Urmas Franosch, Becky Franosch, 9/2001.

Way Lake

Way Lake is one of the latest bouldering finds in the Mammoth Area. The rock is nicely featured with angular positive holds that can be quite polished. The rock is of a very high quality, some have suggested that it is a form of gneiss.

The Approach: From the Town of Mammoth Lakes head west on Hwy. 203. At a traffic light Hwy. 203 turns right, instead go straight ahead on Lake Mary Rd. Follow this 3.5 miles, then turn left on a paved road that goes around the east side of Lake Mary. After 0.6 miles turn left on a road that leads through Coldwater Campground. Follow this 0.7 miles to the Emerald Lake Trailhead Parking.

From here take the Emerald Lake Trail until reaching a junction, turn right on a trail that leads towards T J Lake. Follow this for 5 minutes than scramble left (southwest) up a short rise to a plateau.

History: Probably the first climbers to boulder here extensively where Brian Carkeet and Chris Passie in the summer of 2001.

Way Lake Details

Environment: Alpine boulderfield.
Elevation: 9,800 ft.
Season: July to October.
Exposure: Varied.
Rock Type: Quality granite.
Bouldering: ★★, 100 problems.
Drive From Mammoth: 10 minutes.
Approach: 30 minute hike with a 700 ft. gain.
Special Concerns: Way Lake is in the John Muir Wilderness.

©2004 Maximus Press.

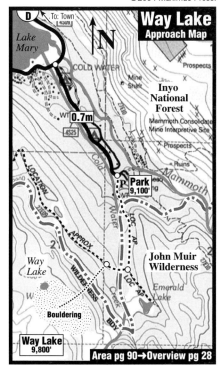

Way Lake Approach Map

Area pg 90→Overview pg 28

See Page 141 Peter Croft on **Cable Guy** 11d***** at the Bear Crag. ©*Kevin Calder Photo.*

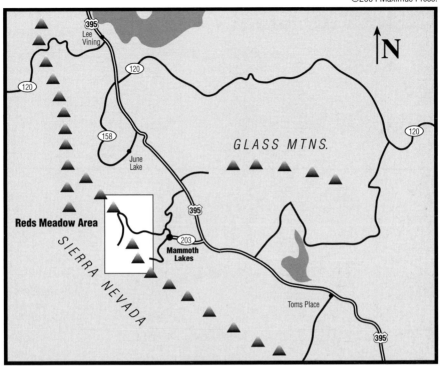

CHAPTER 6

REDS MEADOW AREA

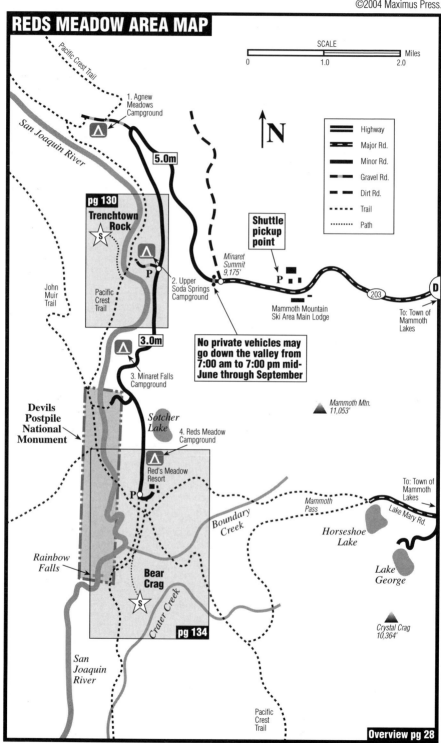

REDS MEADOW AREA MAP

SCALE
0   1.0   2.0   Miles

N

Highway
Major Rd.
Minor Rd.
Gravel Rd.
Dirt Rd.
Trail
Path

Pacific Crest Trail

1. Agnew Meadows Campground

5.0m

San Joaquin River

pg 130
Trenchtown Rock
S

John Muir Trail

Pacific Crest Trail

P

2. Upper Soda Springs Campground

Minaret Summit 9,175'

Shuttle pickup point

P

203

D

To: Town of Mammoth Lakes

Mammoth Mountain Ski Area Main Lodge

3.0m

3. Minaret Falls Campground

No private vehicles may go down the valley from 7:00 am to 7:00 pm mid-June through September

Mammoth Mtn. 11,053'

Devils Postpile National Monument

Sotcher Lake

4. Reds Meadow Campground

Red's Meadow Resort

P

To: Town of Mammoth Lakes

Mammoth Pass

Lake Mary Rd.

Boundary Creek

Horseshoe Lake

Rainbow Falls

Bear Crag
S

Crater Creek

Lake George

Crystal Crag 10,364'

pg 134

San Joaquin River

Pacific Crest Trail

REDS MEADOW AREA BASICS

The Reds Meadow Area is in a beautiful backcountry canyon on the west side of the Sierra Crest. A solitary road goes over Minaret Summit and drops down into the canyon. Two of the more popular tourist attractions in the Mammoth area are located here, Devils Postpile National Monument and Rainbow Falls. This is also the jump off point for hikers, backpackers and mountaineers who want to explore the backcountry around the Minarets. This is a **Fee Area**, currently it costs $7 per person to enter. The fee is waived if you present a valid Golden Eagle Pass.

Getting There

Due to winter snowfall the road to Reds Meadow is only open from mid June until late October. In an effort to limit motor vehicle use, on the narrow curvy road, there is a mandatory shuttle bus that must be used from mid June until just after Labor Day weekend. The shuttle operates from 7:00 A.M. until 7:00 P.M. You may use your own vehicle if you enter outside of these hours.

To get to the Reds Meadow Area (leave Mammoth by 6:40 A.M. to avoid the shuttle bus restriction) drive west on Hwy 203 (Main St.) until Minaret Road, turn right here (still on Hwy 203). Follow this curvy road through the forest past Mammoth Mountain Ski Area (the pickup point for the shuttle) go over Minaret Summit (must be here by 7:00 A.M. to avoid the shuttle) and down the other side.

Amenities

The Red's Meadow Resort

Groceries, a restaurant, lodging and a natural hot spring. ☎ 760-934-2345.

Camping

1. Agnew Meadows Campground

Open mid June to mid September, the fee is $17. Picnic tables, piped water, chemical toilets, elev. 8,400 ft.
☎ 760-924-5500.

2. Upper Soda Springs Campground

Open mid June to mid September, the fee is $15. Picnic tables, piped water, flush toilets, elev. 7,700 ft.
☎ 760-924-5500.

3. Minaret Falls Campground

Open mid June to mid September, the fee is $15. Picnic tables, piped water, chemical toilets, elev. 7,700 ft.
☎ 760-924-5500.

4. Reds Meadow Campground

Open mid June to mid September, the fee is $15. Picnic tables, piped water, flush toilets, showers, elev. 7,700ft.
☎ 760-924-5500.

©2004 Maximus Press.

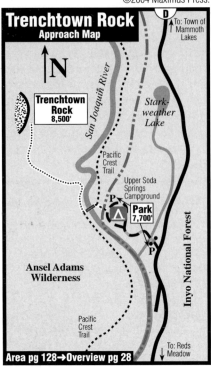

Trenchtown Rock Approach Map

Trenchtown Rock Details

Environment: Forested hillside.
Elevation: 8,500 ft.
Season: July to October.
Exposure: East facing, morning sun.
Rock Type: Quality granite.
Sport Climbs: 7 routes, 5.8 to 11b.
Gear Climbs: 4 routes, 10a to 10c.
Drive From Mammoth: 25 minutes.
Approach: 35 minute scramble with a 800 ft. gain.
Special Concerns: A $7 per person fee is required to cross Minaret Summit. Trenchtown Rock is in the Ansel Adams Wilderness. Motorized drills are prohibited.

Trenchtown Rock

Trenchtown Rock is the massive, Tuolumne-like dome on the west side of the San Joaquin River in the vicinity of the Soda Springs Campground. It is easily seen from the Minaret Vista overlook. This crag offers excellent granite slab climbing reminiscent of Tuolumne Meadows.

The Approach: From the U.S. 395/203 junction (leave Mammoth by 6:40 A.M. to avoid the shuttle bus restriction) drive west on Hwy. 203 until Minaret Road, turn right here (still on Hwy. 203). Follow this curvy road through the forest past Mammoth Mountain Ski Area (the pickup point for the shuttle) go over Minaret Summit (must be here by 7:00 A.M. to avoid the shuttle) and down the other side. Continue down this winding road 5 miles and turn right at the Upper Soda Springs Campground turnoff. Drive into the campground and park right of Site #17 in the Day Use Area. In the fall when the campground is closed, park at the gate and walk 10 minutes through the campground.

From the Soda Springs Trailhead head south and cross the San Joaquin river on a bridge. Then turn right (north) and follow a fisherman's trail to a slabby granite watercourse marked with cairns. Follow this west until almost level with the crag, then traverse right (north) to Trenchtown Rock.

History: Developed in the early 1990s.

Trenchtown Rock- Right Side

The right side is quite monolithic and features a series of thin cracks splitting a polished gold wall. The routes are about 2 pitches long and are best descended by rappeling *Acapulco Gold*.

A. Unknown
Gear. Crack.

B. Acapulco Gold 12?
2 pitches. Thin seam waiting for a redpoint.

C. Catch a Fire 10c***
Pitch 1: 10c***. 1 bolt, gear: R.P.'s to a 3" piece.
Pitch 2: 10a***. Crack to face traverse right.
Descent: Rappel *Acapulco Gold*, two 50m/165' rappels.
FA: Urmas Franosch, Kevin Calder, 9/1994.

D. Unknown 10a**
Gear to 3.5". Crack.

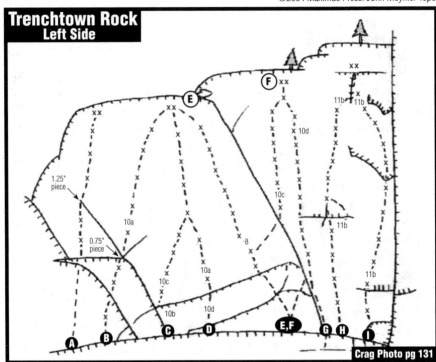

Trenchtown Rock
Left Side

Crag Photo pg 131

Trenchtown Rock - Left Side

Intro: Page 130. The left side of the east face of the dome features a number of excellent slab climbs.

A. Planet Dread 10a★★
5 bolts, gear: 1.25" piece. Slab. 50m/165' rappel.
FA: Bruce Sato, Malcolm Jolley, 8/1993.

B. Bosch Gnarley 10a★★★
7 bolts, gear: 0.75" piece. Slab. 50m/165' rappel.
FA: Malcolm Jolley, Bruce Sato, 8/1993.

C. Prodigal Son 10c★★
7 bolts. Slab. 50m/165' rappel.
FA: Malcolm Jolley, Bruce Sato, 8/1993.

D. Burnin' & Lootin' 10a★★★
10 bolts. Slab. 50m/165' rappel.
FA: Bruce Sato, Malcolm Jolley, 8/1993.

E. Rat in the Kitchen 8★★★
7 bolts. Slab. 50m/165' rappel.
FA: Malcom Jolley, Bruce Sato, 8/1993.

F. That D.A.M.M. Route 10c★★★
8 bolts. Slab. 50m/165' rappel.
FA: Bruce Sato, Malcolm Jolley, 8/1993.

G. Get Up-Stand Up 10d★★★★
10 bolts. Slab. 50m/165' rappel.
FA: Malcolm Jolley, Bruce Sato, 8/1993.

H. Steel Pulse 11b★★★★
9 bolts. Slab. 50m/165' rappel.
FA: Urmas Franosch, Bruce Sato, 10/1994.

I. White Men Can't Rap 11b★★★★
10 bolts. Slab. 50m/165' rappel.
FA: Urmas Franosch, Bruce Sato, 10/1995.

See Page 142

Francois Marsigny on **Chicks Dig It** 11a**** at the Bear Crag. ©*Kevin Calder Photo.*

©2004 Maximus Press.

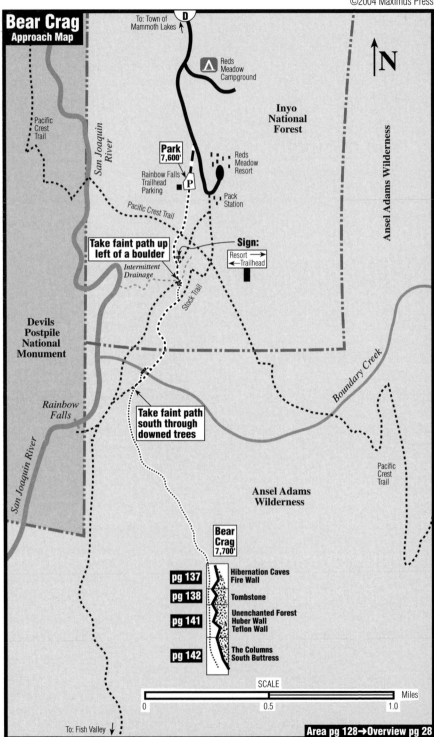

Bear Crag
Approach Map

To: Town of Mammoth Lakes

D

Reds Meadow Campground

Inyo National Forest

Pacific Crest Trail

San Joaquin River

Park 7,600'

Reds Meadow Resort

Rainbow Falls Trailhead Parking

P

Pack Station

Pacific Crest Trail

Take faint path up left of a boulder

Sign:
Resort →
← Trailhead

Intermittent Drainage

Stock Trail

Ansel Adams Wilderness

Devils Postpile National Monument

Boundary Creek

Rainbow Falls

Take faint path south through downed trees

San Joaquin River

Ansel Adams Wilderness

Pacific Crest Trail

Bear Crag 7,700'

pg 137 — Hibernation Caves / Fire Wall

pg 138 — Tombstone

pg 141 — Unenchanted Forest / Huber Wall / Teflon Wall

pg 142 — The Columns / South Buttress

N

SCALE
Miles
0   0.5   1.0

To: Fish Valley

Area pg 128→Overview pg 28

Bear Crag

The 5.11 (or better) climber will find the Bear Crag to be some of the finest sport climbing in the Eastern Sierra. The volcanic rock offers incredible climbing from vertical to radically overhanging, with many columns and roofs. Teflon edges are the name of the game. Finesse, technique, power and endurance are all required to succeed at this crag.

It would have seemed that this crag was destined for popularity, but it is has its flaws: You have to get out of bed, you have to pay $7 and you have to climb 5.11. The good news is, that if you make the effort—you can climb at one of the most spectacular sport crags in the Eastern Sierra in relative solitude.

The Approach: To get to the Bear Crag (leave Mammoth by 6:40 A.M. to avoid the shuttle bus restriction) drive west on Hwy. 203 until Minaret Road turn right here (still Hwy. 203). Follow this curvy road through the forest past Mammoth Mountain Ski Area (the pickup point for the shuttle) go over Minaret Summit (must be here by 7:00 A.M. to avoid the shuttle) and down the other side. Continue down this winding road 8 miles to near its end, then turn right at a dirt parking lot with a sign that says "Rainbow Falls Trailhead Parking" and park.

Follow the hiking trail south. After a short distance cross the Pacific Crest Trail, soon after is a trail junction, the backwards facing sign says "Resort / Trailhead", continue down a short hill to an intermittent drainage. Take a faint path up left of a boulder to a stock trail. Head south down the stock trail until Boundary Creek is reached. To the right is a log crossing. After crossing the creek rejoin the stock trail for 30 ft. Then turn left and follow a faint path south through many burned and downed trees.

History: In the early 1990s the Bear Crag was a hidden, top-secret cliff, only known about by the staunch ground-up brethren. During that time, this hard-to-find crag had only one completed line, the *Garden Route*. Soon after, there was a giant forest fire in the area. After the smoke cleared the Bear Crag could easily be seen from the Fish Valley trail. It was just a matter of time before the rap-bolt thugs showed up and developed this awesome crag.

Bear Crag Details

Environment: Severely burned forest.
Elevation: 7,700 ft.
Season: July to October.
Exposure: West facing, broiling afternoon sun.
Rock Type: The rock is a form of Volcanic Tuff reminiscent of basalt and limestone.
Sport Climbs: 40 routes, 10a to 13c.
Gear Climbs: 1 route, 11d.
Drive From Mammoth: 30 minutes.
Approach: 30 minute hike, with a 100 ft. gain.
Special Concerns: A $7 per person fee is required to cross Minaret Summit. The Bear Crag is in the Ansel Adams Wilderness. Motorized drills are prohibited. Do not leave webbing anywhere on the crag, if you have to bail out before the top of a route sacrifice a carabiner. When at the Bear Crag please go 100 ft. past either end of the crag when you have to relieve yourself.

Hibernation Caves
Bear Crag Intro: Page 135.

A. Arete Already 10c***
7 bolts. Climb the arete. Lower off.
FA: Urmas Franosch, Kelly Cordner, 8/1996, TD.

B. Exappeal 10b**
7 bolts. Vertical face on the right of a dihedral. Lower off.

C. Little Walt 11a*
8 bolts. Climb a mini-dihedral then go left through bulge. Lower off.
FA: Janie Chodosh, Fred Berman, 7/1997, TD.

See Page 142

Karine Croft on **Chicks Dig It** 11a****. ©*Kevin Calder Photo.*

©2004 Maximus Press.

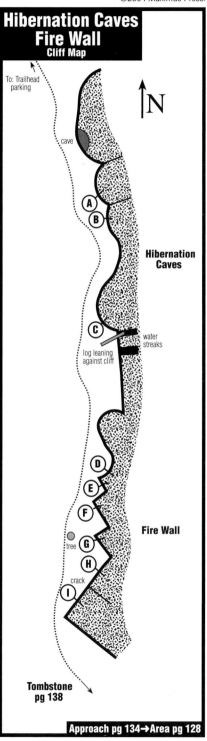

Hibernation Caves
Fire Wall
Cliff Map

To: Trailhead parking

N

cave

Ⓐ
Ⓑ

Hibernation Caves

Ⓒ
water streaks
log leaning against cliff

Ⓓ
Ⓔ
Ⓕ
tree Ⓖ
Ⓗ
crack
Ⓘ

Fire Wall

Tombstone pg 138

Approach pg 134➜Area pg 128

Fire Wall
Bear Crag Intro: Page 135.

D. White Lightning 12a**
8 bolts. Pass a bulge then climb the white streak on the face between cracks, a little contrived. Lower off.
FA: Mike Cann, 10/1995, TD.

E. White African 11c**
7 bolts, stick clip. A bouldery start leads to a roof, then climb the dihedral. Lower off.
FA: Marty Lewis, Fred Berman, 8/1996, TD.

F. Project
2 bolts. Face.
P: John Bachar.

G. Smoked Cake 11a**
8 bolts. Strenuous face climbing leads to a gold arete. Lower off.
FA: Fred Berman, Janie Chodosh, 8/1996, TD.

H. Serpico 12a***
9 bolts. Steep blocky gray roofs lead to a crimpy white headwall. Lower off.
FA: Fred Berman, Mike Cann, 10/1995, TD.

I. Texas Chainsaw Massacre 12b**
9 bolts. A very steep face leads to a technical black headwall. A little loose. Lower off.
FA: Marty Lewis, Fred Berman, Doug McDonald, 9/1996, TD.

©2004 Maximus Press. *John Moynier Photo.*

Fire Wall

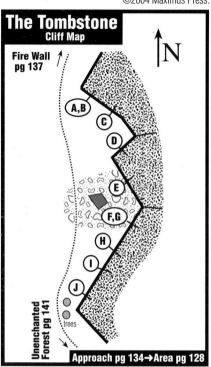

The Tombstone
Cliff Map

Fire Wall
pg 137

↑N

A,B
C
D
E
F,G
H
I
J

trees

Unenchanted
Forest pg 141

Approach pg 134→Area pg 128

Marty Lewis on the **Reanimator** 11d****.

The Tombstone

Bear Crag Intro: Page 135. This imposing cliff is quite overhanging.

A. Dilate 11d***
9 bolts. Climb the left leaning dihedral to double roofs. Lower off.
FA: Fred Berman, Steve Bacon, Janie Chodosh, Marty Lewis, 8/1996, TD.

B. Regurgitator 11b****
8 bolts. Steep face, clip first 2 bolts of *Dilate* then go right through bulges and a roof. Lower off.
FA: Kevin Calder, Marty Lewis, 9/1996, TD.

C. Stairway to Heaven 10a**
6 bolts. A technical move leads to a jug haul. Lower off.
FA: Urmas Franosch, Kelly Cordner, 7/1996, GU.

D. Perpetrator 12c***
11 bolts. Climb the white arete to a steep black headwall. Lower off.
FA: Fred Berman, Mark Blanchard, 10/1995, TD.

E. Reanimator 11d****
10 bolts. A quick bulge leads to a moderate face, then climb a steep strenuous seam. Lower off. ☞ A great climb and a disturbing horror film (it's so bad it's good).
➤ Photo this page.
FA: Marty Lewis, Mike Cann, Rob Stockstill, 10/1995, TD.

F. Sidearm 11d**
3 bolts, gear to 2". Climb face for 3 bolts then move left into a massive dihedral that arcs right. Lower off.
FA: Doug McDonald, 9/1997, TD.

G. Tombstone (Open project) 14a?
10 bolts. Ascends a steep rust colored face. Lower off.
P: Doug McDonald.

H. To the Grave 12d*****
11 bolts (1 chain draw). Steep seam through a difficult roof to a steep dihedral. Lower off. ☞ This beautiful line was the 2nd route completed at the Bear Crag.
FA: Doug McDonald, Marty Lewis, Fred Berman, Brian Ketron, 7/1995, TD.

I. Brain Dead 13b****
11 bolts. Roofs to a steep seam. Lower off. ☞ This difficult line was bolted in 1996 and proved to be too much for the route preparers. Six years later a visiting hardman was able to send it.
FA: Juergen Gottfried, 9/2002. Bolts: Fred Berman, Marty Lewis, TD.

J. Tales From the Crypt 12c****
8 bolts (1 chain draw). A steep seam through a roof, then up the technical headwall. Lower off.
FA: Fred Berman, Marty Lewis, 8/1995, TD.

The Tombstone

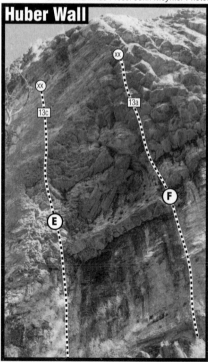

Unenchanted Forest
Bear Crag Intro: Page 135.

A. Project
3 bolts. Face.
P: Steve Calder.

B. Barely Canadian 11c★★★
12 bolts. Steep arete leads to a left leaning dihedral.
27.5m/90' lower off.
FA: Kevin Calder, Marty Lewis, 10/1999, GU.

C. Penetrator 12b★★★★★
13 bolts. Climb a quick face, then move right to a gently overhanging face through small roofs, then pass a big roof on the left, sustained and strenuous. 27.5m/90' lower off.
FA: Marty Lewis, Kevin Calder, Fred Berman, 9/1996, TD.

D. Idiot Savant 12c★★
11 bolts, stick clip. Steep face through roofs, a little loose. Lower off.
FA: Fred Berman, Marty Lewis, Kevin Calder, Janie Chodosh, 7/1997, TD.

Huber Wall
The section of cliff left of *I Fly* looked so difficult that the Huber brothers seemed like the perfect candidates to develop it. We're still waiting.

E. I Fly 13c★★
8 bolts. Start in a dihedral then climb a very steep face, a little loose. Lower off.
FA: Doug McDonald, 8/1996, TD.

F. Tension Tamer 13a★★★★
10 bolts. Face climb to steep blocky roofs. Lower off.
FA: Doug McDonald, 10/1995, TD.

G. Grain Tamer 12c★★
9 bolts. Work up and right on a steep blocky face. Lower off.
FA: Doug McDonald, 9/1995, TD.

H. Project
1 bolt. Column.
P: Mike Cann.

I. Project
1 bolt. Column.
P: Marty Lewis.

Teflon Wall
This section of cliff has a concentration of awesome vertical face climbs on near perfect rock.

J. Cone of Silence 12a★★★★
12 bolts. Dihedrals lead to a roof. 30m/100' lower off.
FA: Marty Lewis, Kevin Calder, 10/1997, TD.

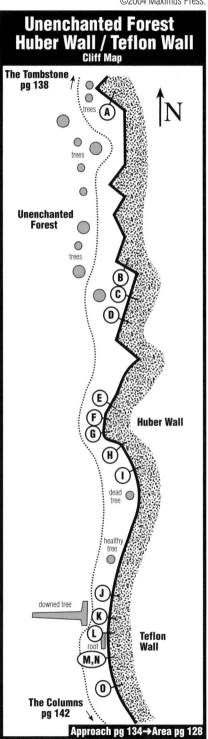

Unenchanted Forest
Huber Wall / Teflon Wall
Cliff Map

The Tombstone
pg 138

trees
A

trees

Unenchanted
Forest

trees

B
C
D

E
F
G
H
I

Huber Wall

dead
tree

healthy
tree

J
K
L
M,N
O

downed tree

root

**Teflon
Wall**

The Columns
pg 142

Approach pg 134→Area pg 128

Teflon Wall

K. Cable Guy 11d*****
13 bolts. Gently overhanging dihedrals lead to a thin face, then pass a roof. 30m/100' lower off. ➤ Photo page 126.
FA: Kevin Calder, Marty Lewis, 6/1999, TD.

L. Cupcake 11c**
12 bolts. Vertical column to a left leaning corner, a bit of a squeeze on the *Garden Route*. 27.5m/90' lower off.
FA: Unknown, 11/1995. Bolts: Joe Rousek, John McDonald, TD.

M. Garden Route 11c*****
10 bolts. Sustained vertical columns, a little sporty. 30m/100' lower off. ☞ Originally this route continued above the first anchor (it was added later) and past 2 more bolts to an anchor on the top. From here you went up a heinous 45° pumice slope and then traversed off right. This visionary line was the first route done at the Bear Crag.
FA: John Hartman, 1992, GU.

N. Right Again 10d****
11 bolts. Clip first 5 bolts of the *Garden Route*, then go right past a bolt, then go right again across *Hamster Style*, then up a dihedral. 30m/100' lower off.
FA: Karine Croft, Peter Croft, Marty Lewis, Kevin Calder, Jay Zimmerman, 6/1999, TD.

O. Hamster Style 11b****
13 bolts. One crumbly move gets you to varied climbing straight up dihedrals. 30m/100' lower off.
Variation: 11b****. 12 bolts. Start on *Right Again*, then finish on *Hamster Style*. 30m/100' lower off.
FA: Marty Lewis, Kevin Calder, 6/1999, TD.

©2004 Maximus Press.

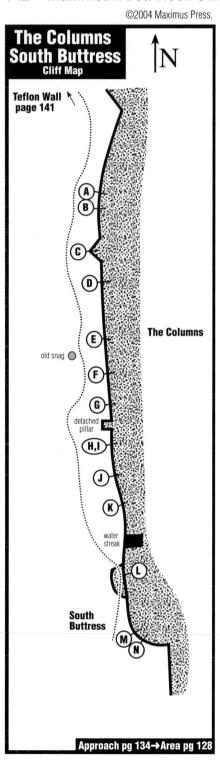

The Columns South Buttress
Cliff Map

↑N

Teflon Wall
page 141

(A)
(B)

(C)

(D)

The Columns

(E)

old snag ○

(F)

(G)

detached
pillar

(H,I)

(J)

(K)

water
streak

(L)

South
Buttress

(M)
(N)

The Columns
Bear Crag Intro: Page 135.

A. Mercy Buckets 12a****
8 bolts. Steep tiered gold roofs, strenuous. Lower off.
FA: Todd Graham, 11/1995, TD.

B. Flamed Thrower 12b****
9 bolts (1 chain draw). Strenuous blocky roofs. Lower off.
FA: Todd Graham, 8/1996, TD.

C. Flying Circus 12c****
8 bolts (1 chain draw). Steep gold arete. Lower off.
➤ Photo facing page.
FA: Todd Graham, 10/1995, TD.

D. Gold Rush 12b***
8 bolts. Steep blocky face, dyno crux. Lower off.
FA: Todd Graham, 11/1995, TD.

E. Chicks Dig It 11a****
8 bolts. Roof to face to roof, steep and fun. Lower off.
➤ Photo pages 133, 136.
FA: Kevin Calder, Marty Lewis, Kelly Boardman, 9/1996, GU.

F. Project
3 bolts. Face.
P: John Hartman.

G. Ashes to Ashes 11d**
13 bolts. Face to roof to black bulge, a little dirty. 27.5m/
90' lower off.
FA: Todd Graham, 9/1996, TD.

H. Holy Smoke 11c**
12 bolts. Clip the first 2 bolts of *Friendly Fire* then go left
up a vertical column to a black bulge. 27.5m/90' lower off.
FA: Todd Graham, 7/1996, TD.

I. Friendly Fire 11b*****
12 bolts. Sustained vertical column, excellent. 27.5m/90'
lower off.
FA: Todd Graham, 6/1996, TD.

J. Easy Rider 11c***
12 bolts. Quick bulge to a vertical column. 27.5m/90'
lower off.
FA: Mike Cann, 11/1995, TD.

K. Stepping Stone 11d*
12 bolts. Pass a bulge then head up and left. 27.5m/90'
lower off.
FA: Mike Cann, 11/1995, TD.

L. Project
7 bolts. A steep bulge leads to face climbing.

South Buttress
Bear Crag Intro: Page 135. The sun
hits this part of the crag first.

M. Jagged Sky 12a*****
7 bolts. Awesome steep blocky arete. Lower off.
FA: Todd Graham, 11/1995, TD.

N. Horizon X 11c*
5 bolts. Steep blocky face. Lower off.
FA: Todd Graham, 11/1995, TD.

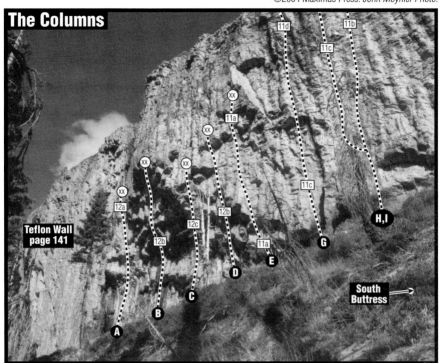

The Columns

11d

11b

11c

xx

11a

xx

11c

xx

xx

xx

12a

Teflon Wall page 141

12c

12b

H,I

12b

11a

G

D

E

C

South Buttress →

B

A

South Buttress

xx

12a

xx

11c

M   **N**

See Page 172

Marty Lewis on **Lack of Honor** 11d*** at Clark Canyon. ©*John Moynier Photo.*

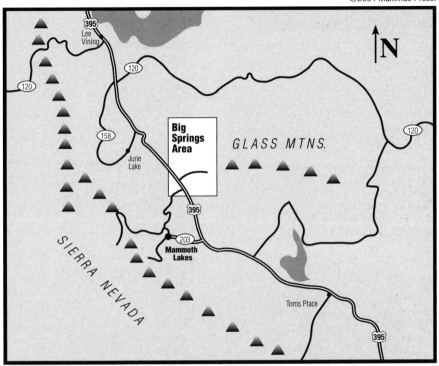

CHAPTER 7

BIG SPRINGS AREA

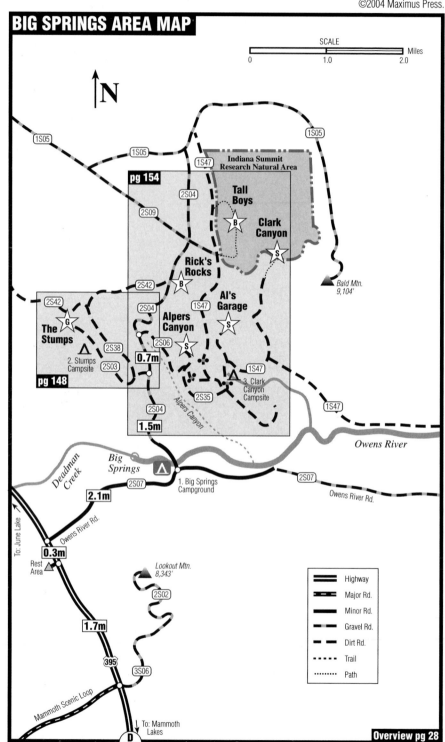

BIG SPRINGS AREA MAP

SCALE

0   1.0   2.0   Miles

N

1S05

1S05

1S05

1S47

Indiana Summit
Research Natural Area

pg 154

2S04

Tall
Boys

2S09

B

Clark
Canyon

S

Rick's
Rocks

Bald Mtn.
9,104'

2S42

B

Al's
Garage

2S42

1S47

G

2S04

Alpers
Canyon

S

The
Stumps

2S38

S

2S06

2. Stumps
Campsite

2S03

0.7m

pg 148

Alpers Canyon

1S47

2S35

3. Clark
Canyon
Campsite

1S47

2S04

1.5m

Owens River

Deadman Creek

Big
Springs

2S07

1. Big Springs
Campground

2S07

2.1m

Owens River Rd.

Owens River Rd.

To: June Lake

0.3m

Rest
Area

Lookout Mtn.
8,343'

2S02

1.7m

Highway

Major Rd.

Minor Rd.

395

3S06

Gravel Rd.

Dirt Rd.

Trail

Mammoth Scenic Loop

Path

To: Mammoth
Lakes

D

BIG SPRINGS AREA BASICS

T he Big Springs Area is located in a dense Jeffrey pine forest on the east side of U.S. 395 just north of Mammoth. The cliffs are eroded outcrops of welded volcanic tuff, including the largest sport crag in the Mammoth Region—Clark Canyon. This area receives a large amount of snowfall in winter, so climbing is often not possible until late spring. The roads in this area, although graded, are often narrow, roughly washboarded and lined with sagebrush. Please drive slow and cautiously and park as far off the roads as possible so others may pass.

Getting There

To get to the Big Springs Area start at the U.S. 395/203 junction and drive north on U.S. 395. After 7 miles a rest area is passed. 0.3 miles further turn right on the paved Owens River Rd. (2S07). Follow this road 2.1 miles to a left turn at Big Springs Campground (2S04). This road heads north past the campground, turns to dirt and begins to wind up a grade.

Amenities

No amenities are available in this area. Back in the town of Mammoth Lakes is where it all goes down.

Camping

1. Big Springs Campground

Open May through October, **there is no fee**. Picnic tables, no potable water, vault toilets, elev. 7,300 ft.
☎ 760-647-3044.

Primitive Camping

In this area it is possible to discretely camp for free, almost anywhere away from paved roads, as long as you are not on private property. Check with the Forest Service in Lee Vining for more information. Do not camp in the parking area for the crags.

2. Stumps Campsite

Primitive camping in a nice valley near The Stumps. No water, elev. 7,700 ft.

3. Clark Canyon Campsite

Primitive camping near Clark Canyon. No potable water, elev. 7,200 ft.

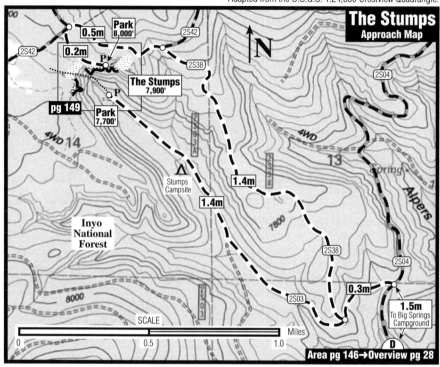

Adapted from the U.S.G.S. 1:24,000 Crestview Quadrangle.

The Stumps

The Stumps are at the head of a long valley that had been extensively logged, leaving behind an ocean of stumps (hence the name). Funny thing is—20 years later, they are nowhere to be found, having been overgrown by a thick forest of juvenile pine trees—making it look more like Christmas tree valley.

The Stumps offer moderate volcanic crack climbing and bouldering in a secluded location. It is kind of a small traditional version of Clark Canyon, with an easier approach and no crowds.

The Stumps Details

Environment: Forested valley.
Elevation: 7,900 ft.
Season: May to mid November.
Exposure: Varied, mostly south facing.
Rock Type: Volcanic Tuff.
Gear Climbs: 21 routes, 5.6 to 11b.
Bouldering: ★★.
Sport Climbs: 1 route, 12b.
Drive From Mammoth: 20 minutes.
Approach: 5 minute pumice slope with a 200 ft. gain.

The Approach: To get to the Stumps start at the U.S. 395/203 junction and drive north on U.S. 395. After 7 miles a rest area is passed. 0.3 miles further turn right on the paved Owens River Rd. (2S07). Follow this road 2.1 miles to a left turn at Big Springs Campground (2S04). This road heads north past the campground, turns to dirt and begins to wind up a grade. After 1.5 miles turn left on road 2S03. Follow this for 1.7 miles (a few roads branch here and there,

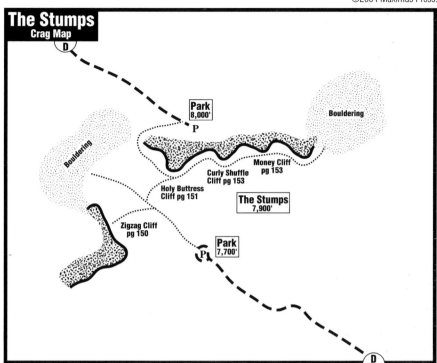

The Stumps
Crag Map

Park
8,000'

Bouldering

Bouldering

Money Cliff
pg 153

Curly Shuffle
Cliff pg 153

Holy Buttress
Cliff pg 151

The Stumps
7,900'

Zigzag Cliff
pg 150

Park
7,700'

Bouldering

Rick Cashner at the **Stumps** (1984). ©*Errett Allen Photo.*

stay on the main road) until it dead ends in an amphitheater. From the parking area hike loose pumice to the crag.

It is also possible to park right at the top of the Holy Buttress Cliff. After getting on road 2S03 drive 0.3 miles and turn right at the junction of road 2S38. Follow this road 1.9 miles and turn left at a 4-way junction. After 0.2 miles the parking area is reached. The crag is right below.

History: Developed in the 1980s by the usual suspects. The awesome bouldering to the east of the main wall was first sampled by Dimitri Barton, John Bachar, Dave Griffith and Neil Newcomb.

Zigzag Cliff

Crag Map pg 149

Kevin Calder on the first ascent of **Calder's Knobs**

Zigzag Cliff

Stumps Intro: Page 148. This little cliff faces east so it is nice and cool in the afternoon. Routes are less than 25m/80 ft. long, walk off right.

A. Orange Zigzag 9***
Gear. Dogleg crack. Gear anchor.
☞ Kind of a Stumps classic.
FA: Grant Hiskes, Errett Allen, Ken Yager, Marylyn Wisner, 5/1984.

B. Knuckle Nutz 10a**
Gear. Crack. Gear anchor.
FA: Ken Yager, Grant Hiskes, Marylyn Wisner, 5/1984.

C. Roll 'em Easy 9*
Gear. Crack. Gear anchor.
FA: Errett Allen, Grant Hiskes, Marylyn Wisner, Ken Yager, 5/1984.

©2004 Maximus Press. *John Moynier Topo.*

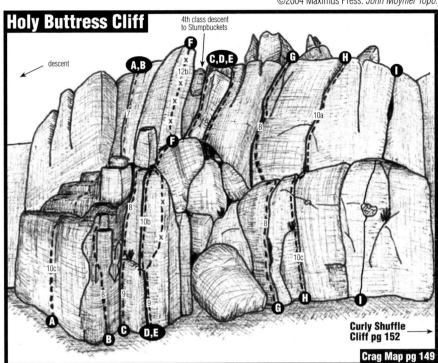

Holy Buttress Cliff

4th class descent
to Stumpbuckets

descent

Curly Shuffle
Cliff pg 152

Crag Map pg 149

Holy Buttress Cliff
Stumps Intro: Page 148. Walk off left.

A. Calder's Knobs 10c*(r)
Gear. Boulder up some knobs (basically free solo) then finish up a crack. Gear anchor. ➤ Photo facing page.
FA: Kevin Calder, 6/1984.

B. Holy Buttress 8***(r)
Gear to 2.5". Face to crack. Gear anchor.
FA: Grant Hiskes, Ken Yager, 8/1983.

C. Rat Race 9*
Gear to 3". Dihedral. Gear anchor.
FA: Grant Hiskes, Marylyn Wisner, Ken Yager, 8/1983.

D. Vertebrae 10b**
Gear to 2.5". Dihedral. Gear anchor.
FA: Ken Yager, Dave Schultz, 8/1983.

E. Got Ribs ?
2 bolts, gear to 2.5". Start *Vertebrae* then go right past bolts. Gear anchor.

F. Stumpbuckets 12b***
4 bolts. Steep face. Bolt anchor. ➤ Photo pages 22, 152.
FA: Dimitri Barton, John Bachar, 1987.

G. Dr. Strange Glove 8·
Gear. Crack. Gear anchor.
FA: Ken Yager, Grant Hiskes, 6/1984.

H. Slim Pickens 10c**
Gear. A thin seam leads to a ledge, then climb a dihedral. Gear anchor.
FA: Ken Yager, Grant Hiskes, 8/1983.

I. Rude Intrusion 9*
Gear. Climb the crack past a bulging intrusion of rock, finish on a right leaning V-slot. Gear anchor.
FA: Alan Bartlett, Laurel Colella, 5/2000.

John Bachar on **Stumpbuckets** 12b*** (1987). ©*Dimitri Barton Photo.*

©2004 Maximus Press. *John Moynier Topo.*

Curly Shuffle Cliff

Money
Cliff →

← Holy Buttress
Cliff pg 151

← descent

rappel
station
x x

Ⓐ

Ⓑ

10b

Ⓒ

Ⓓ

x

11a

x

Ⓔ

Ⓕ

11b

10a

10a

10a

x

7

Ⓐ

Ⓑ

Ⓒ

Ⓓ,Ⓔ

Ⓕ

Crag Map pg 149

Curly Shuffle Cliff

Stumps Intro: Page 148. Walk left to a bolted rappel station to descend from these climbs.

A. Give a Hoot 7·
Gear. Dihedral. Gear anchor.
FA: Marylyn Wisner, Errett Allen, 8/1983.

B. Whoop Whoop Roof 10b*
Gear. Face to crack to roof. Gear anchor.
FA: Neil Newcomb, Bill Trethewey, Dan Robbins, 8/1983.

C. Smiling Faces 10a*
Gear to 1". Dihedral. Gear anchor.
FA: Grant Hiskes, Errett Allen, Sean Plunkett, 5/1984.

D. Stumpjumper 11a**
3 bolts, gear. Climb *H & R Block*, then go left up a face. Gear anchor.
FA: Neal Newcomb, Tim Noonan, Grant Hiskes, 1985.

E. H & R Block 10a**
Gear to 2.5". Crack. Gear Anchor.
FA: Grant Hiskes, Ken Yager, 5/1984.

F. Curly Shuffle 11b**
Gear. A slabby dihedral leads to a steep crack. Gear anchor.
FA: Ken Yager, Grant Hiskes, 8/1983.

Money Cliff

G. Corner Market 7*
Gear. Dihedral. Bolt anchor.

H. Eastern Winds 9**(r)
2 bolts, gear to 2". Face. Bolt anchor.
FA: Grant Hiskes, 1990.

I. Good 'n Plenty 7*
Gear. Climb past blocks to a crack. Gear anchor.
FA: Grant Hiskes, 8/1983.

J. E.Z. Money 6***
Gear. Crack. Bolt anchor.
FA: Ken Yager, Errett Allen, 8/1983.

Adapted from the U.S.G.S. 1:24,000 Crestview Quadrangle.

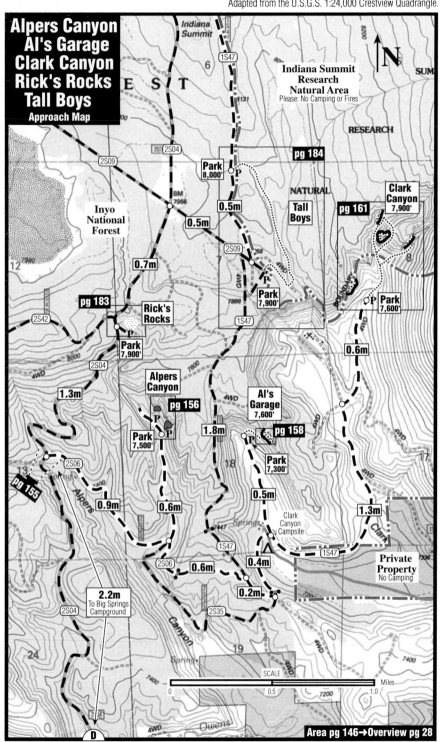

Alpers Canyon
Al's Garage
Clark Canyon
Rick's Rocks
Tall Boys
Approach Map

Indiana Summit Research Natural Area
Please: No Camping or Fires

Inyo National Forest

pg 184

pg 161

Clark Canyon 7,900'

NATURAL

Tall Boys

Park 8,000'

Park 7,600'

0.5m

0.5m

0.7m

pg 183

Rick's Rocks

Park 7,900'

Park 7,900'

0.6m

1.3m

Alpers Canyon

pg 156

Al's Garage 7,600'

pg 158

1.8m

Park 7,500'

Park 7,300'

pg 155

0.9m

0.6m

0.5m

1.3m

Clark Canyon Campsite

Private Property
No Camping

2.2m
To Big Springs Campground

0.6m

0.4m

0.2m

SCALE

Miles

0   0.5   1.0

Big Springs Area
Point of View

To: Rick's Rocks and Tall Boys

Sign

To: Alpers Canyon
Al's Garage
Clark Canyon

(2S04)

(2S06)

This point is 2.2 miles north of Big Springs Campground on road 2S04

Alpers Canyon

Alpers Canyon features a number of obscure towers scattered about on the hillside northeast of the road.

The Approach: To get to Alpers Canyon start at the U.S. 395/203 junction and drive north on U.S. 395. After 7 miles a rest area is passed. 0.3 miles further turn right on the paved Owens River Rd. (2S07). Follow this road 2.1 miles to a left turn at Big Springs Campground (2S04). This road heads north past the campground, turns to dirt and begins to winds up a grade and then drops into Alpers Canyon at 2.2 miles. Turn right here on the easily missed road 2S06. Follow this road 0.9 miles and turn left at the second unmarked road. Follow this road up canyon 0.6 miles to the small parking area at the base of Mind Dart Rock or drive a hair farther to the point where the dirt road crosses the main drainage for Heart Rock.

History: Most of the sport climbs were developed in the early 1990s.

Alpers Canyon Details

Environment: Jeffrey pine forest.
Elevation: 7,500 ft.
Season: May to mid November.
Exposure: Mostly south facing.
Rock Type: Volcanic Tuff.
Sport Climbs: 12 routes, 5.7 to 12d.
Gear Climbs: 2 routes, 10c and 11b.
Drive From Mammoth: 20 minutes.
Approach: 2 minute pumice walk.

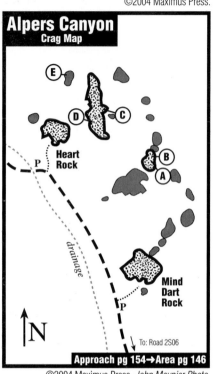

Alpers Canyon
Crag Map

E

D   C

Heart
Rock
P

B

A

N

drainage

Mind
Dart
Rock
P

To: Road 2S06

Approach pg 154→Area pg 146

Alpers Canyon

Intro: Page 155. These routes are scattered about the slidey pumice slopes behind the main formations.

A. Alpo 11b**
5 bolts. Face. Lower off.
FA: Grant Hiskes, Ken Yager, early 1990s.

B. Lurch 11c*
4 bolts. Face. Lower off.
FA: Ken Yager, Grant Hiskes, early 1990s.

C. Rogue's Gallery 11a*
4 bolts. Face. Lower off.
FA: Kevin Fosburg, early 1990s.

D. Plukin' Too Hard 12d**
6 bolts. Pass a bulge to seams. Unknown finish.
FA: Kevin Fosburg, early 1990s.

E. Sporty Shorty 12a*
2 bolts. Face. Lower off.

Mind Dart Rock

F

XX

H   G   F

Mind Dart Rock
Alpers Canyon Intro: Page 155.

F. Mind Dart 11b***
Gear. Dihedral. Gear anchor, scramble off north until reaching a saddle then head down and right.
☞ Kind of an old school Mammoth Area testpiece.
➤ Photo facing page.
FA: Rick Cashner, Grant Hiskes, 6/1984.

G. Body English 10a**
4 bolts, opt. gear to 1". Face between seams. Lower off.
FA: Bruce Hawkins, Alan Bartlett, 7/2000.

H. Sierra Phantom 7*(r)
3 bolts. Start on the left side of an arete, then cross right and climb the black streak. Lower off.
FA: Alan Bartlett, Laurel Colella, 7/2000.

Altoids is found 100 ft. up and left.

I. Altoids 8**
5 bolts. Vertical face on a tower. Lower off.
FA: Mark Bowling, Steve Gerberding, Alan Bartlett, 8/2000.

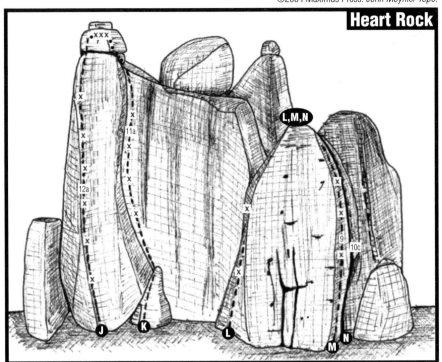

Heart Rock

Rick Cashner on the first ascent of **Mind Dart** 11b***. ©*Errett Allen Photo.*

Heart Rock
Alpers Canyon Intro: Page 155.

J. Heartburn 12a***
6 bolts. Sustained arete, a little crunchy. Lower off.
K. Nasty Habits 11a**
4 bolts. Dihedral. Lower off.
FA: S. Mankenberg, Dave Yerian, Grant Hiskes, 4/1984.
L. Unknown ?
2 bolts. Dark slab. Gear anchor.
M. Mandarin Orange 9*
3 bolts. Face. Gear anchor.
N. Sugar Baby 10c*
Gear. Dihedral to thin crack. Gear anchor.
FA: Grant Hiskes, 4/1984.

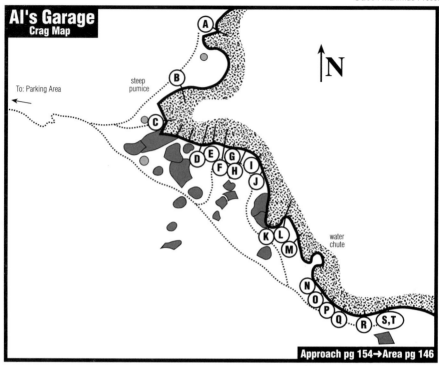

Al's Garage

This cool new discovery seems destined for popularity, it's a lot easier to get to than Clark Canyon and has numerous moderate sport climbs. Expect the routes to be a little crunchy though, but over time they should really clean up.

The Approach: Map page 154. To get to Al's Garage start at the U.S. 395/203 junction and drive north on U.S. 395. After 7 miles a rest area is passed. 0.3 miles further turn right on the paved Owens River Rd. (2S07). Follow this road 2.1 miles to a left turn at Big Springs Campground (2S04). This road heads north past the campground, turns to dirt and begins to winds up a grade and then drops into Alpers Canyon at 2.2 miles. Turn right here on the easily missed road 2S06. Follow this road just over a mile to a cattle gate. A half mile past this gate, road 2S06 joins with 1S47 (coming in on the left), and soon passes through a second cattle gate. From here continue 0.4 miles on this road down past a rough section (low clearance vehicles not recommended), through a meadow (the Clark Canyon Campsite) cross a drainage and turn left. Follow

Al's Garage Details

Environment: Jeffrey pine forest.
Elevation: 7,600 ft.
Season: May to mid November.
Exposure: Southwest facing.
Rock Type: Volcanic Tuff.
Sport Climbs: 16 routes, 5.8 to 11a.
Gear Climbs: 3 routes, 5.9 to 10a.
Drive From Mammoth: 25 minutes.
Approach: 10 minute pumice hike with a 300 ft. gain.

this road for 0.5 miles to the parking area.

Hike up the steep pumice slope via a path that goes up and right to the base of the crag.

History: Developed by Alan Hirahara over a couple of summers.

Al's Garage

These routes on the west face of the buttress around and left of the main wall about 100 feet up the hillside.

A. Project ?
3 bolts. Dihedral.

B. On the Fringe 10a**
5 bolts. Crack to arete. Lower off.
FA: Alan Hirahara, early 2000s.

This route is on the toe of the buttress.

C. Kill the Buddha 8*
6 bolts. Face. Lower off.
FA: Alan Hirahara, early 2000s.

Routes D through J are on a big slab above a blocky terrace.

D. Yin and Yang 9*
Gear to 3.5". Starts 3 ft. right of a 4 ft. block. A brushy hand crack leads to a right leaning double crack, mantle a ledge then move left into a brushy gully, from here head right to the anchors of *Karma*. Lower off.
FA: Scott Cole, Kevin Calder, 1980s.

E. Dharma 9*
Gear to 1.5". The middle crack. Start in a brushy depression, pass a wide pod then a finger crack leads to the top. Lower off.
FA: Alan Hirahara, early 2000s.

F. Karma 10a**
Gear to 2.5". Climb a finger crack, at the top step left to *Dharma*, then go back right. Lower off.
FA: Scott Cole, Kevin Calder, 1980s.

G. Sangha 10a**
6 bolts. Seam to a left facing flake. Lower off.
FA: Alan Hirahara, early 2000s.

H. Jhana 9***
5 bolts. Face climb to a left facing scoop, then up a steep lieback flake, a little sporty. Lower off.
FA: Alan Hirahara, early 2000s.

I. Samadhi 10b**
5 bolts. Technical face to a seam. Lower off.
FA: Alan Hirahara, early 2000s.

J. Wake-n-Bake 11a****
9 bolts. Killer thin crack/seam to arete to pocketed face. Lower off.
FA: Dave Tidwell, Alan Hirahara, early 2000s.

On a slabby tower that juts out.

K. Sound of One Hand Slapping 8*
7 bolts. Slabby arete. Lower off.
FA: Alan Hirahara, early 2000s.

L. Aviary 8**
10 bolts. Climb just left of a corner then continue up the pocketed face. Lower off.
FA: Alan Hirahara, early 2000s.

M. Triple Delight 10b****
10 bolts. Start up an arete, then pass multiple roofs and bulges. Use a long runner on the 6th bolt to limit rope drag. 30m/100' lower off.
FA: Alan Hirahara, early 2000s.

Wall right of water chute.

N. Vertigo 10b***
7 bolts. Face. Lower off.
FA: Alan Hirahara, early 2000s.

O. Acrophobia 10c***
10 bolts. Thin start to corner to crack/arete crux then continue up the arete. 30m/100' lower off.
FA: Alan Hirahara, early 2000s.

P. East Side Days 9*
7 bolts. Face to right tending ramp to corner then up a face. A little loose. Lower off.
FA: Alan Hirahara, early 2000s.

Q. East Side Daze 9***
8 bolts. Climb a face, then step right at a bush, pass a bulge, then up a steepening slab. Lower off.
FA: Alan Hirahara, early 2000s.

R. Chronic 10b**
7 bolts. Boulder up a mini-dihedral, then face climb up to a right leaning arete. A little loose. Lower off.
FA: Alan Hirahara, early 2000s.

S. Middle Way 10a**
10 bolts. Start in a stemming corner, then climb up the middle of the face past two big holes, then up a steep corner. Lower off.
FA: John German, Alan Hirahara, early 2000s.

T. Chase the Dragon 10a**
10 bolts. Start the *Middle Way*, after 1 bolt step right and lieback a flake, then move right to a devious airy mantel, then up an exciting face. 30m/100' lower off.
FA: Alan Hirahara, John German, early 2000s.

Labels on photo:
Clark Canyon Point of View
Potato Patch pg 177
Main Island pg 168
Area 13 pg 163
The Wave pg 168
Parking Lot Rock pg 162
Park

Clark Canyon

Clark Canyon is the most popular and highly developed sport crag in the Mammoth Area. The canyon is in a beautiful setting with views of Mt. Morrison and the Sierra Nevada crest. The rock is littered with pockets, jugs and edges. Once a little chossy this crag has really cleaned up.

The Approach: Map page 154. To get to Clark Canyon start at the U.S. 395/203 junction and drive north on U.S. 395. After 7 miles a rest area is passed. 0.3 miles further turn right on the paved Owens River Rd. (2S07). Follow this road 2.1 miles to a left turn at Big Springs Campground (2S04). This road heads north past the campground, turns to dirt and begins to winds up a grade and then drops into Alpers Canyon at 2.2 miles. Turn right here on the easily missed road 2S06.

Clark Canyon Details

Environment: Jeffrey pine forest.
Elevation: 7,900 ft.
Season: May to mid November
Exposure: Varied, shady forest.
Rock Type: Volcanic Tuff.
Sport Climbs: 102 routes, 5.6 to 12d.
Gear Climbs: 8 routes, 5.7 to 10b.
Bouldering: ★★.
Drive From Mammoth: 35 minutes.
Approach: 15 minute brushy walk, with a 300 ft. gain.
Special Concerns: Clark Canyon can have an almost gym type atmosphere; routes can be short and packed in, often sharing holds. Some were originally highball boulder problems that are now bolted. While this ethic has been accepted at Clark Canyon, it is not appropriate at any other crags in the Mammoth area.

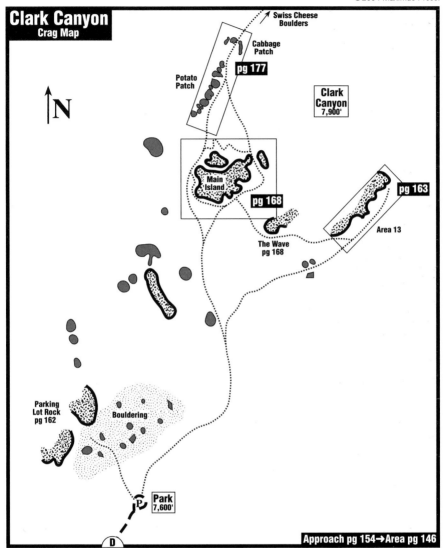

Clark Canyon
Crag Map

Swiss Cheese
Boulders

Cabbage
Patch

pg 177

Potato
Patch

Clark
Canyon
7,900'

N

pg 163

Main
Island

pg 168

Area 13

The Wave
pg 168

Parking
Lot Rock
pg 162

Bouldering

Park
7,600'

D

Approach pg 154→Area pg 146

Follow this road just over a mile to a cattle gate. A half mile past this gate, road 2S06 joins with 1S47 (coming in on the left), and soon passes through a second cattle gate. From here continue 1.7 miles on this road down past a rough section (low clearance vehicles are not recommended), through a meadow (the Clark Canyon Campsite) and around a ridge into the east branch of Clark Canyon. At a 4-way intersection turn right and follow this road 0.6 miles to a loop parking area.

From here walk northeast up a brushy gully. After a few minutes a boulder will be reached. The trail to Area 13 is up the right fork of another gully. Or continue on the main trail a few more minutes to another junction. Going right leads to the Alcove, left leads to the Stoned Wheat Thin Cliff and the Potato Patch.

History: In the late 1970s Jim Stimson and Bill Taylor found and climbed at the Swiss Cheese Boulders. In the 1980s Clark Canyon was known as a highball bouldering area, Roland Arsons, John Bachar, Dimitri Barton, Dave Bengston, Ron Kauk and other climbers from Tuolumne Meadows would go there for a change of pace, onsight soloing many of the best lines. Most of the cracks were done at this time also, either free solo or using natural gear.

During the early 1990s the first wave of bolted climbs went up in Clark Canyon by a group of Yosemite climbers transplanted to Mammoth Lakes, and a group of Yosemite climbers that spent the summers in Tuolumne Meadows. Many of the original free solos were bolted and named at this time.

During the late 1990s, Mammoth Local Alan Hirahara began filling in most of the remaining lines at Clark Canyon. At Area 13, with the exception of the original cluster of lines, Alan almost single-handedly bolted the huge stretches of cliff on either side. He ended up creating the best moderate sport climbing cliff in the Mammoth Area. Alan also invested a huge amount of energy replacing the old sling wad belays with modern metal anchors.

The names and first ascent information given for Clark Canyon are the climbers who spent the time and money bolting the routes and establishing the anchors. The original free soloists seem fine with this ethic—and hey, if you like, you can free solo them too—John Bachar still does!

Parking Lot Rock

Crag Map pg 161

Dave Titus on **Pachuco** 8***. ©*Marty Lewis Photo.*

Parking Lot Rock

Clark Canyon Intro: Page 160. This is the interesting pair of towers to the northwest, right above the parking area. Some good boulder problems will be passed on the way to the base. Their are a few climbs here, however most of the climbing is found farther up the canyon to the northeast.

A. Unknown 10a*
7 bolts. Face. Lower off
B. Stick to Your Ribs 10a*
6 bolts. Climb the black streak. Lower off.
FA: Dan McDevitt, 1990.
C. Project
3 bolts. Prow.
P: John Bachar, Al Swanson.
D. Unknown ?
? bolts. Striking face.

See Page 165

©2004 Maximus Press.

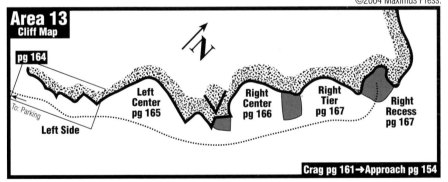

Area 13
Cliff Map

pg 164

To: Parking

Left Side

Left Center pg 165

Right Center pg 166

Right Tier pg 167

Right Recess pg 167

Crag pg 161➔Approach pg 154

Area 13

Not quite as top secret as Area 51, Area 13 was still a mysterious place. The 1996 edition of this book had only a crude map of Clark Canyon, with a system of numbered topos. On the edge of the map was the cryptic inscription "Area 13➔". The unsuspecting climber had to walk off the edge of the map, in the direction of the arrow, until they ran into a cliff. Then on page 60 a vague topo was found that only added to the mystique.

It turns out that Area 13 isn't a UFO crash site. And those strange tracks on the side of Bald Mtn. are just game trails. Area 13 is just simply an expansive cliffband, with the longest, easiest sport climbs at Clark Canyon.

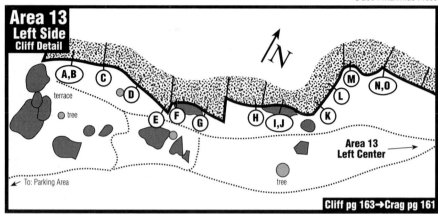

Cliff pg 163→Crag pg 161

Area 13 - Left Side

Clark Canyon Intro: Page 160.

A. Exqueeze Me 7*

7 bolts. Clip the first bolt of *Mobetta Fogetta* then step left and climb the face to a short arete, then continue up and left to a bulge. Kind of a squeeze. Lower off.
FA: Alan Hirahara, late 1990s.

B. Mobetta Fogetta 7***

7 bolts. Climb the face just left of a brushy crack to a mini-dihedral on an arete. Lower off.
FA: Alan Hirahara, late 1990s.

C. Now and Zen 8*

12 bolts. Start up the brushy crack then step right and climb the right wall of a dihedral, up a ramp, then through a blocky bulge. 35m/115' lower off.
FA: Alan Hirahara, 2002.

D. Drop Zone 8****

8 bolts. Climbs the middle of the slab. Lower off.
FA: Alan Hirahara, John German, late 1990s.

E. Bodhisattva 7****

8 bolts. Climbs the left edge of the broken crack, higher up step right and climb the double cracks past the belay for *Too Many Princesses*. Lower off.
FA: Alan Hirahara, John German, 2002.

F. Too Many Princesses 7·

7 bolts. Climbs the right edge of the broken crack, higher it squeezes into the previous route. Lower off.
FA: Alan Hirahara, late 1990s.

G. IEPA! 8**

8 bolts. Climb the face, the end is a little nebulous, either go right up the crack or left up the face. Lower off.
FA: Alan Hirahara, late 1990s.

H. Ugly, Fat and Mean, Come to Mammoth, Be a Queen 7****

9 bolts. Face climb up stacked blocks then step left onto an airy arete. Lower off.
FA: Alan Hirahara, late 1990s.

I. This Ain't No Weenie Roast 10b**

11 bolts. Pass a bulge, then move left across a slab to an easy dihedral, higher up step right and climb the exciting face finish. 30m/100' lower off.
FA: Alan Hirahara, late 1990s.

J. Chapusero 11a**

10 bolts. Climb *This Ain't No Weenie Roast* to its 3rd bolt, then go right up a slabby finger crack to the belay ledge of *Wild Will's Arete*, from here climb the left side of the arete, clipping bolts that seem to far left. Lower off.
FA: Alan Hirahara, late 1990s.

Variation: 10a**. 5 bolts. Climb *Chapusero* to the 5th bolt, then go to the midway belay on *Wild Will's Arete*. Lower off.

K. Wild Will's Arete 8*****

11 bolts. Face climb to the arete, pass the midway anchors, then up a dihedral to an airy arete finish. 35m/115' lower off. ☞ Can be broken into 2 pitches.
FA: Jerry, Sigrid, Lynnea and William Anderson, 8/1994.

L. Digit Delight 9***

8 bolts. Face to seam.
FA: Jerry, Sigrid, Lynnea and William Anderson, 8/1994.

M. Chupacabras 8**

8 bolts. Climb either an arete/dihedral on the left or a seam on the right. The bolts go right up the strength between these weaknesses.
FA: Alan Hirahara, Jim Lynch, late 1990s.

N. More Trad Than Rad 10a***

2 bolts, gear to 3.5". Climb the dihedral past 2 bolts, after that there are plenty of gear placements—will they hold? Lower off.
FA: Jerry, Sigrid, Lynnea and William Anderson, 7/1995.

O. Borrowing From Tradition 10b****

9 bolts. Start *More Trad Than Rad*, at the 2nd bolt reach right and enter a steep crack. Lower off.
FA: Jerry, Sigrid, Lynnea and William Anderson, 7/1995.

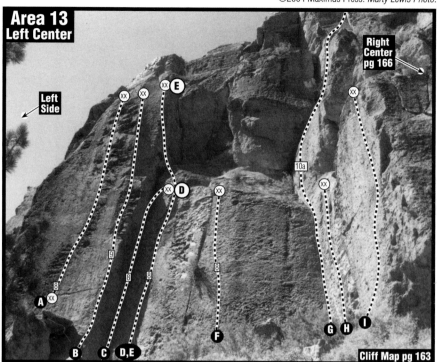

Area 13 - Left Center
Clark Canyon Intro: Page 160.

A. Rock Candy 8****
7 bolts. Scramble up to a ledge with a fixed belay, from here climb the killer off-vertical face. Lower off.
FA: Jim Reed, early 1990s.

B. Bread Line 9***
8 bolts. Start in an awkward dihedral, then up a technical arete, higher up step left to a huecoed blunt arete. 27.5m/ 90' lower off.
FA: Jim Reed, early 1990s.

C. Scorpio 8*
Gear to 3". Dihedral. Lower off.
FA: Grant Hiskes, early 1990s.

D. Chop Chop 8**
4 bolts. Lieback flake. Lower off.
FA: Bill Trethewey, early 1990s. Retrobolts: Alan Hirahara.

E. Pachuco 8***
8 bolts. Climb the *Chop Chop* flake, then step left and climb the right side of a blunt arete. 30m/100' lower off.
➤ Photo page 163.
FA: Alan Hirahara, late 1990s.

F. Chilango 8*
3 bolts. Face climb, higher up use the crack on the left when necessary. Lower off.
FA: Alan Hirahara, late 1990s.

G. Cholito 10a***
17 bolts. Start in a left facing corner, then use a flake to pass a bulge, then moderate climbing up and right past a dihedral to the final airy arete. 50m/165' to a two bolt anchor, walk off left (west).
FA: Alan Hirahara, late 1990s.

H. No Left Turn 10a·
4 bolts. Contrived and squeezed in face, it's much harder (10d) if you don't use the left wall. Lower off.
FA: Alan Hirahara, late 1990s.

I. Get Tuff 11c**
4 bolts. Thin face to a seam. Lower off.
FA: Alan Hirahara, late 1990s.

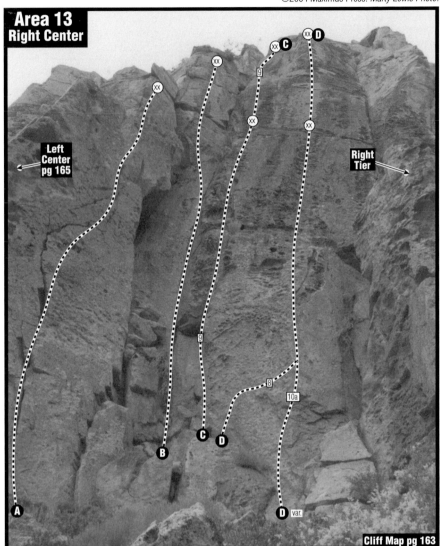

Area 13 - Right Center

Clark Canyon Intro: Page 160.

A. Demasiado 7***

7 bolts. On the left wall of a huge corner, climb a crack to an arete. Lower off.

FA: Alan Hirahara, late 1990s.

B. Backscratcher 7****

8 bolts. Scramble up some blocks then climb a dihedral, move left and chimney past a bulge, then up a gorgeous face. 35m/115' lower off.

FA: Alan Hirahara, late 1990s.

C. Nice Guys Finish Last 9***

13 bolts. Clip the first bolt then move left into a corner, pass a bulge, then climb a long slab. 50m/165', two single rope rappels. ☞ Can be broken into 2 pitches.

FA: Alan Hirahara, late 1990s.

D. No More Mister Nice Guy 8***

12 bolts. A rising traverse (8) or a bouldery direct arete (10a) lead to easy slab climbing, then climb a blunt arete. 50m/165' to a two bolt anchor, walk off right (east). ☞ Can be broken into 2 pitches.

FA: Alan Hirahara, late 1990s.

Area 13 - Right Tier

Clark Canyon Intro: Page 160.

Routes A-C start on a tier and are approached either via a 4th class chimney on the left or straight up easy 5th class face.

A. Inyo Face 9***
11 bolts. Face climb left to reach an arete. Bolt anchor, walk off right (east).
FA: Alan Hirahara, 2002.

B. Lichen It 8**
6 bolts. Goes up the middle slab. 30m/100' lower off.
FA: Alan Hirahara, 2002.

C. Who Dropped the Soap? 8**
5 bolts. Starts next to crack, then go up right hand buttress. Lower off.
FA: Alan Hirahara, 2002.

This route starts on the ground.

D. So it Goes 6***
6 bolts. Face climb straight up, then work right. Lower off.
FA: Alan Hirahara, 2002.

Area 13 - Right Recess

Go to the far right edge of the cliff, then scramble up and left to a ledge below a recess for these next routes.

E. Taboo 8*
6 bolts. Climb past some bushes to an enjoyable double crack. Lower off.
FA: Alan Hirahara, 2002.

F. YRUASOB247? 10b·
11 bolts (missing first 3 hangers). Climb a dihedral then step right and climb a nebulous face; loose, dirty and contrived. Lower off.
FA: Alan Hirahara, 2002.

G. Project ?
2 bolts. Thin crack.
FA: Alan Hirahara.

H. Keough Memorial Buttress 8**
7 bolts (missing first 3 hangers). Start a crack then hand traverse right to an arete. Lower off.
FA: Alan Hirahara, 2002.

©2004 Maximus Press. *John Moynier Photo.*

The Wave

Crag Map pg 161

The Wave

Clark Canyon Intro: Page 160. This is a small tower between Area 13 and the Main Island.

A. Unknown 11d*
4 bolts. Face through a bulge. Lower off
FA: Visiting Japanese climbers, late 1990s.

B. Unknown 10d*
3 bolts. Arete to a bulge. Lower off
FA: Visiting Japanese climbers, late 1990s.

C. Unknown 8**
4 bolts. Face. Lower off
FA: Visiting Japanese climbers, late 1990s.

D. Unknown 8**
3 bolts. Seam to arete. Lower off
FA: Visiting Japanese climbers, late 1990s.

©2004 Maximus Press.

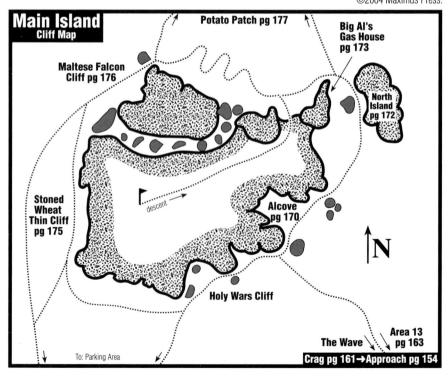

Main Island
Cliff Map

Potato Patch pg 177

Big Al's
Gas House
pg 173

Maltese Falcon
Cliff pg 176

North
Island
pg 172

descent

Stoned
Wheat
Thin Cliff
pg 175

Alcove
pg 170

N

Holy Wars Cliff

To: Parking Area

The Wave

Area 13
pg 163

Crag pg 161→Approach pg 154

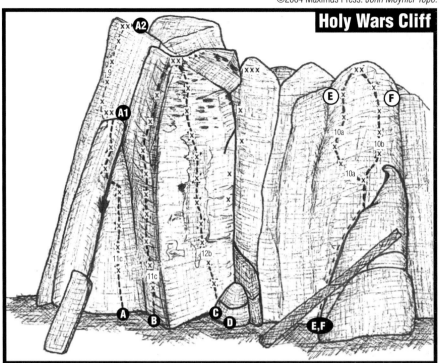

Main Island

Centrally located, the Main Island is home to many fine climbs. The east side features the Alcove. This popular little grotto has a high concentration of short climbs. On the west side, the Stoned Wheat Thin Cliff has some giant 5.10 climbs that are just awesome. Just past there lies a Clark Canyon testpiece; the *Maltese Falcon* (12a).

Holy Wars Cliff

Clark Canyon Intro: Page 160.

A. Crusade 11c*
Pitch 1: 11c*. 6 bolts. Face through cracks. Lower off.
Pitch 2: 9*. 4 bolts. Face. Lower off.
FA: Dave Caunt, 1990.

B. Jihad 11c***
10 bolts. A bouldery bulge leads to a nice face. Lower off.
FA: Grant Hiskes, Ken Yager, 1989.

C. Dirty Dancing 12b****
10 bolts. A technical face leads to a jug haul. Lower off.
FA: Dan McDevitt, Chris Falkenstein, 1990.

D. Unknown ?·
4 bolts. Climb a dihedral then go up and right. Lower off.

E. Welcome to Bohemia 10a**
5 bolts. Face. Lower off.
FA: Errett Allen, Grant Hiskes, 1989.

F. Rocket in My Pocket 10b**
5 bolts. Face. Lower off.
FA: Errett Allen, Ken Yager, 1989.

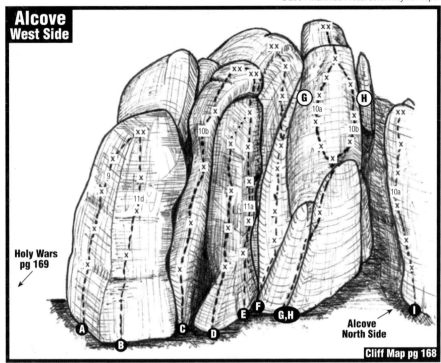

Alcove
West Side

Holy Wars
pg 169

Alcove
North Side

Cliff Map pg 168

Alcove - West Side

Clark Canyon Intro: Page 160.

A. Wholy Cow 9**
4 bolts. Face. Lower off.
FA: Errett Allen, Grant Hiskes, Ken Yager, 1989.

B. El Toro 11d*
3 bolts. A bouldery bulge. Lower off.
FA: Ken Yager, 1989.

C. Freakasaurus 10b**
4 bolts. Blunt arete. Lower off.
FA: Alan Hirahara.

D. Funny Bone 10b**
5 bolts. Face. Lower off.
FA: Dan McDevitt, 1990.

E. Tickled Pink 11a***
5 bolts. Steep face. Lower off.
FA: Dave Bengston, Ken Yager, Grant Hiskes, 1989.

F. Peanut Brittle 9***
6 bolts. Climb the back left corner. Lower off.
FA: Grant Hiskes, 4/1985. Retrobolts: Alan Hirahara

G. Dr. Jeckyl 10a**
6 bolts. Face. Lower off.
FA: Errett Allen, Karen Young, Grant Hiskes, 1989.

H. Mr. Hyde 10b**
6 bolts. Face. Lower off.
FA: Errett Allen, Karen Young, Grant Hiskes, 1989.

Alcove - North Side

I. Craters 10a**
5 bolts. Face. Lower off.
FA: Errett Allen, Grant Hiskes, 1989.

J. What's the Scoop 10c·
5 bolts. Squeeze job out bulge. Lower off.

K. Eightball 10b**
4 bolts. Arete. Lower off.
FA: Karen Young, Errett Allen, Dave Yerian, 1989.

L. Pick Pocket 10c**
4 bolts. Face. Lower off.
FA: Errett Allen, Grant Hiskes, 1989.

M. Stegosaurus 9**
4 bolts. Face. Lower off. ➤ Photo facing page.
FA: Karen Young, Errett Allen, 1989.

N. Double or Nothing 8**
5 bolts. Double crack. Lower off.
FA: Alan Hirahara.

O. Pocket Pool 10b**
4 bolts. Face. Lower off. ➤ Photo rear cover.
FA: Errett Allen, Ken Yager, 1989.

P. Lil' Squirt 7*
2 bolts, gear: 0.75" piece. Face to crack. Lower off.
FA: Ken Yager, Braden Mayfield, 1989.

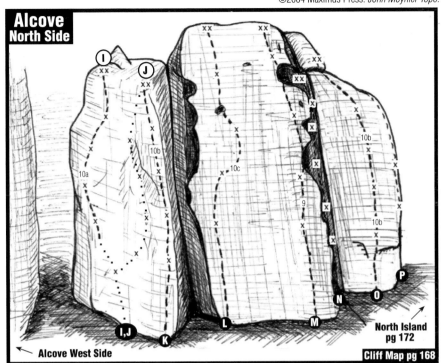

Alcove
North Side

I
J
10b
10a
10c
10b
9
10b
P
N
O
M
L
K
I,J

North Island
pg 172

← Alcove West Side

Cliff Map pg 168

Schatzi Sovich on **Stegosaurus** 9**. ©*Greg Epperson Photo.*

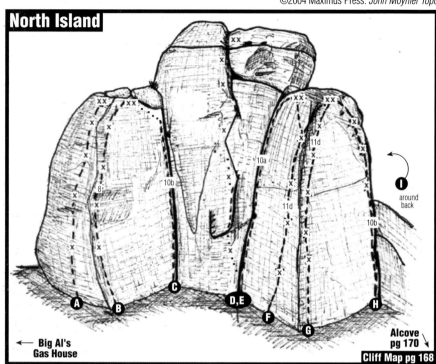

North Island

Clark Canyon Intro: Page 160. This quality piece of rock is covered with sun-baked patina.

A. EZ Duz It 6*
4 bolts. Left side of arete, squeezed in. Lower off.
FA: Alan Hirahara.

B. Something for Everyone 8**
4 bolts. Right side of arete. Lower off.
FA: Malcolm Jolley, Gregg Davis, 1990.

C. Stem Christy 10b**
Gear to 1". Clean dihedral. Lower off.
FA: Grant Hiskes, Ken Yager, 8/1983.

D. Court Martial 10a**
5 bolts. Start *Conduct Unbecoming* then move left into a steep crack. Lower off.
FA: Alan Hirahara.

E. Conduct Unbecoming 10a*
Gear to 1". Dihedral. Lower off.
FA: Malcolm Jolley, Gregg Davis, 1990.

F. Too Close for Comfort 11d*
4 bolts. Face. Lower off.
FA: Alan Swanson, Kelly Rich, early 1990s.

G. Lack of Honor 11d***
5 bolts. Arete. Lower off. ➤ Photo page 144.
FA: Malcolm Jolley, Gregg Davis, Bruce Lella, 1990.

H. Dishonorable Discharge 10b**
3 bolts, gear to 2". Dihedral to face. Lower off.
FA: Malcolm Jolley, Gregg Davis, 1990.

This route is located around to the right on the east face of the tower.

I. Tips n' Toes 10b*
4 bolts. Face climb past a horizontal to a blunt arete. Lower off.
FA: Jerry, Sigrid, Lynnea and William Anderson, 1993.

©2004 Maximus Press. *Marty Lewis Photo.*

Big Al's Gas House

Cliff Map pg 168

Big Al's Gas House

Clark Canyon Intro: Page 160.

This route is located just left of the North Island on an east facing tower.

A. Big Al's Gas House 12a**
4 bolts. Gently overhanging face. Lower off.
FA: Alan Swanson, Bruce Morris, 1990.

The following routes are found by heading north through a gap between *Big Al's Gas House* and the North Island and then heading down and left.

B. One Bolt Wonder 11b·
1 bolt. Silly face. Gear anchor, rappel down *Big Al's Gas House.*
FA: Alan Swanson, Bruce Morris, early 1990s.

C. On the Boardwalk 10d*
5 bolts. Dihedral to arete. Lower off.
FA: Alan Hirahara, Barry Oswick.

D. Stray Cat Strut 10c*
Gear. Dihedral. Gear anchor, rappel down *Big Al's Gas House.*
FA: Grant Hiskes, Neil Newcomb, Tim Noonan, 1983.

Stoned Wheat Thin Cliff

Maltese Falcon pg 176

Cliff Map pg 168

Stoned Wheat Thin Cliff

Clark Canyon Intro: Page 160. As you approach the Main Island keep left to reach this imposing sun baked wall. Some of the biggest and the best routes at Clark Canyon are found here.

A. Woodywhacker 11a***

9 bolts. Bouldery overlaps lead to a ledge, then climb steep flakes and pockets. Lower off.
FA: Alan Hirahara.

B. Get Your Dicken's Cider 10b**

5 bolts. Start behind a tree left of a crack. Climb a face to a bulge. Lower off.
FA: Alan Hirahara.

C. Funky Yet Spunky 10c**

6 bolts. Climb to the 2nd bolt, then either step down and left or go straight up to a ledge, from here steep pockets lead to the anchor. Lower off.
FA: Alan Hirahara.

D. Womb With a View 10d***

Pitch 1: 10b***. 7 bolts. Start in a burly dihedral, after 6 bolts go way right past 1 more bolt to a sling wad on a ledge. ☞ Originally the dihedral was protected with gear. **Pitch 2:** 10d***(r). 5 bolts. Step left and climb the pocketed face.
Descent: 50m/165' rappel or walk off.
FA: Errett Allen, 1990. Retrobolts: Barry Oswick, Marshall Minobe, Alan Hirahara.

E. Driller Instinct 10d*****

17 bolts. Start in the burly *Womb With a View* dihedral, then step right and climb a fantastic steepening arete. 45m/150' rappel. ☞ Possibly the best route in Clark Canyon.
FA: Barry Oswick, Marshall Minobe, Alan Hirahara.

F. Brain Tissue 10b**(r)

8 bolts. Start in a flared offwidth, then face climbing leads to a sporty arete. 30m/100' lower off.
FA: Errett Allen, 1990.

G. Stoned Wheat Thin 10a**

1 bolt, gear to 3.5". Varying crack. 30m/100' lower off.

H. Pull My Finger 10a****

17 bolts. Start in a dihedral, cross right, climb a slab to a belay, from here climb vertical face utilizing the *Stoned Wheat Thin* crack past its belay, then continue past various bulges. 55m/180' pitch, bolt anchor, 3rd class walk off to the east. ☞ Can be broken into 3 pitches.
FA: Alan Hirahara, Barry Oswick.

Stoned Wheat Thin
Right Side

Cliff Map pg 168

Marty Lewis on **Maltese Falcon** 12a****. ©*John Moynier Photo.*

©2004 Maximus Press. *Marty Lewis Photo.*

Maltese Falcon Cliff
Clark Canyon Intro: Page 160.

South facing on a small tower.
A. Little Thang 10c*
4 bolts. Arete. Lower off.
FA: Dan McDevitt, 1990.

B. Maltese Falcon 12a****
6 bolts. A steep face leads to a technical crux. Lower off.
➤ Photo this page.
FA: Dan McDevitt, 1990.
C. Goldielocks 10a**
Gear to 3.5". Dihedral. Gear anchor, walk off.
FA: Grant Hiskes, Ken Yager, 6/1983.
D. Porridge 8**
6 bolts. Climb a slab to a big dihedral. Lower off.
FA: Alan Hirahara.

Around to the left up a pumice hill.
E. Shadow 12d***
6 bolts. Technical face leads to a steepening headwall.
Lower off.
FA: Dave Bengston, 1990.

Potato Patch Cabbage Patch
Cliff Map

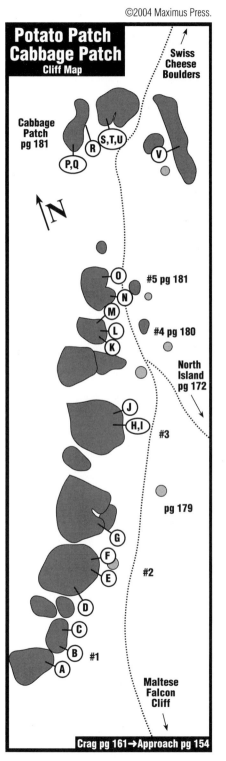

Swiss Cheese Boulders

Cabbage Patch pg 181

S,T,U

R

P,Q

V

N

#5 pg 181

O

N

M

L

K

#4 pg 180

North Island pg 172

J

H,I

#3

pg 179

G

F

E

#2

D

C

B

#1

A

Maltese Falcon Cliff

Crag pg 161➔Approach pg 154

Potato Patch #1

Potato Patch

The Potato Patch is one of the most popular spots at Clark Canyon. As you walk up the gentle pumice filled valley, a series of giant, gently overhanging, potato shaped boulders are passed. The routes tend to be short and pumpy. The "potatoes" all face east, so it's nice and shady in the afternoons.

If you continue up canyon past the Cabbage Patch you will encounter the Swiss Cheese Boulders, a top-roping and highball bouldering area.

Potato Patch #1
Clark Canyon Intro: Page 160.
A. Bucket Brigade 10c***
5 bolts. Face. Lower off.
FA: Grant Hiskes, 1990.
B. Extra Wasabi Please 10b*
4 bolts. A steep bouldery start, then work up and right on easy face. Lower off.
FA: Alan Hirahara.
C. This Spud's For You 10a**
4 bolts. Technical face to a fun juggy finish. Lower off.
FA: Alan Hirahara.

The brothers Ossofsky enjoying **Ruffles** 10a***. ©*Kevin Calder Photo.*

©2004 Maximus Press. *Marty Lewis Photo.*

Diana Jew on **King Spud** 11b***. ©*Perri Nguyen Photo.*

©2004 Maximus Press. *Marty Lewis Photo.*

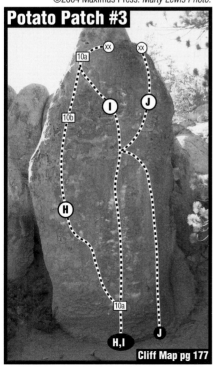

Cliff Map pg 177

Potato Patch #2 and #3

Clark Canyon Intro: Page 160.

D. Spud Launcher 9***

6 bolts. Stem up, then go right on flakes and plates.
Lower off.
FA: Alan Hirahara.

E. Spud Boy 11c****

7 bolts. Steep face. Lower off.
FA: Louie Anderson, Pierre Daigle, 7/1994.

F. King Spud 11b***

5 bolts. Steep face. Kind of sporty until you clip the 2nd
bolt (the 1st bolt is way off right to protect a contrived 12a
start). Lower off. ➤ Photo this page.
FA: Dave Caunt, Dave Bengsten, 1990.

G. Epiglottis 9**

4 bolts. Scramble up to a steep trough, then up slabby
face. Lower off.

H. Funyuns 10b**

4 bolts. A minor variation, same start and finish as
Ruffles; it's like deja vu all over again. Lower off.
FA: Jeff Higashiyama, Alan Hirahara, 1996.

I. Ruffles 10a***

4 bolts. Start on a steep bulge, then continue up gently
overhanging juggy face. Lower off. ➤ Photo facing page.
FA: Grant Hiskes, Urmas Franosch, 1989.

J. Velveeta 10a*

4 bolts. Arete to face, shares 3rd bolt of *Ruffles.* Lower off.
FA: Errett Allen, 1990.

Matt Spurlin on **Thunderball** 11c***. ©*Perri Nguyen Photo.*

©2004 Maximus Press. *John Moynier Topo.*

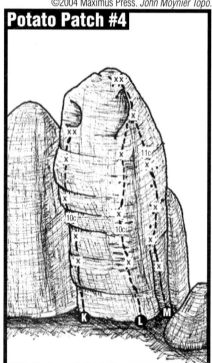

Potato Patch #4

Clark Canyon Intro: Page 160.

K. Well Hung 10c**
4 bolts. Steep face. Lower off.
FA: Errett Allen, early 1990s.

L. Mini Madness 10c**
4 bolts. Steep face. Lower off.
FA: Dan McDevitt, Sue McDevitt, 1990.

M. Thunderball 11c***
5 bolts. Technical face to sequential pockets. Lower off.
➤ Photo this page.
FA: Dan McDevitt, 1990.

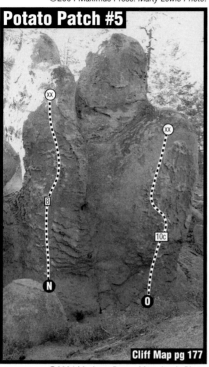

Potato Patch #5

Cliff Map pg 177

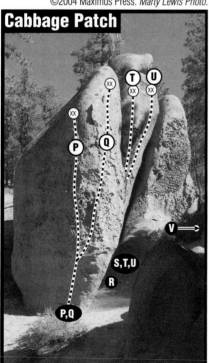

Cabbage Patch

Potato Patch #5
Clark Canyon Intro: Page 160.

N. Hash Brownies 8**
4 bolts. Juggy face. Lower off.
FA: Jeff Higashiyama, Alan Hirahara, 1996.

O. Killer Green Spud 10c*
4 bolts. Climb a short bulge; a boulderer's delight. Lower off.
FA: Jeff Higashiyama, Alan Hirahara, 1996.

Cabbage Patch
Clark Canyon Intro: Page 160.

P. Spudnik 9*
3 bolts. A quick bulge leads to pockets. Lower off.
FA: Jeff Higashiyama, Alan Hirahara.

Q. Pull Your Spud 10a**
3 bolts. Steep arete to pockets. Lower off.
FA: Jeff Higashiyama, Alan Hirahara, 1996.

R. Chalk in My Eye 10d*
3 bolts. Strenuous gently overhanging pockets. Lower off.
FA: Jeff Higashiyama, Alan Hirahara, 1996.

These next three routes are definitive squeeze jobs. The ratings are for following the bolt lines closely. The routes are easier if you go left and harder if you work right.

S. Spudley Do-Right 8*
4 bolts. Steep arete then step left to a slab. Lower off.
FA: Alan Hirahara.

T. Hung Like a Spud 10d*
4 bolts. Overhanging arete to slab. Lower off.
FA: Alan Hirahara, 1996.

U. Twice Baked 11c*
4 bolts. Steep face to lieback to pocketed bulge. Lower off.
FA: Alan Hirahara.

Small west facing tower.

V. James Bong Agent 420 10d**
4 bolts. Jugs to technical face. Lower off.
FA: Alan Hirahara, 1996.

Rick's Rocks

Rick's Rocks

Rick's Rocks is one of the better off the beaten path bouldering spots in the Mammoth Area.

The Approach: Map page 154. From the U.S. 395/203 junction drive north on U.S. 395. After 7 miles a rest area is passed. 0.3 miles further turn right on the paved Owens River Rd. (2S07). Follow this road 2.1 miles to a left turn at Big Springs Campground (2S04). This road heads north past the campground, turns to dirt and begins to winds up a grade, it then drops into Alpers Canyon and climbs back out. At 3.5 miles, near the top of a steep grade, some boulders will be seen on the right. Turn right soon after on a dirt road that dead ends in 100 ft., at a parking spot on a ridge.

Traverse: both ways The chowder has blown

There is some bouldering on the south side of the ridge, but most of the problems are a short stroll to the north in a gully.

History: Mostly developed by Rick Cashner in the early 1980s. Bachar had some Boulders, so it seemed fitting that Rick should get some rocks.

Rick's Rocks Details

Environment: Jeffrey pine forest.
Elevation: 7,900 ft.
Season: May to mid November.
Exposure: Varied, in a southeast facing valley.
Rock Type: Volcanic tuff.
Bouldering: ★★★.
Drive From Mammoth: 20 minutes.
Approach: 5 minute walk.

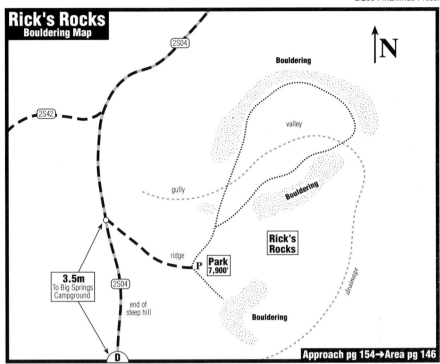

Tall Boys

Nestled in an old growth Jeffrey pine forest, this crag lies within the boundaries of the Indiana Summit Natural Area. The north portion of the Tall Boys consists of a long line of east facing cliffs, the cliffs provide some of the best moderate highball bouldering in the Mammoth Area. There are a few fixed anchors, but it would be wise to bring gear if you want to do a lot of top-roping. The rock often has endless series of letter box slots making even the steepest line go in the 5.8 to 10a range. The south portion of the Tall Boys is home to a more conventional boulderfield that is quite expansive and has tons of potential for those willing to explore.

Tall Boys Details

Environment: Unlogged Jeffrey pine forest.
Elevation: 7,900 ft.
Season: May to mid November
Exposure: Varied.
Rock Type: Volcanic tuff.
Bouldering: ★★.
Top-roping: Limited.
Drive From Mammoth: 25 minutes.
Approach: 5 to 20 minute walk.

The Approach: Map page 154. From the U.S. 395/203 junction drive north on U.S. 395. After 7 miles a rest area is passed. 0.3 miles further turn right on the paved Owens River Rd. (2S07). Follow this road 2.1 miles to a left turn at Big Springs Campground (2S04). This road heads north past the campground, turns to dirt and begins to winds up a grade, it then drops into Alpers Canyon and climbs back out, at 4.2 miles turn right on road 2S09.

For the North Parking Area follow this road 0.5 miles and turn left on road 1S47. Follow this road 0.5 miles and park on the right in front of a sign that says "Indiana Summit Natural Area-Motor Vehicles Prohibited". From here hike northeast towards a gap on a faint abandoned dirt road. Soon a cliff band will be seen on the right, skirt south below this, after 5 minutes the big stuff will be reached. If you continue 10 minutes further south you enter a valley with bouldering on both sides.

For the South Parking Area continue down road 2S09 to its end. The boulders are right below to the right (south).

History: Developed in the early 1980s.

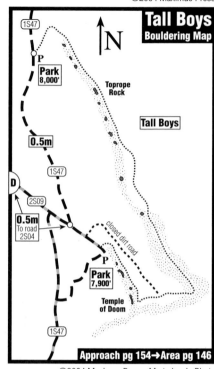

Tall Boys
Bouldering Map

Approach pg 154→Area pg 146

Toprope Rock

Kevin Calder bouldering at the **Tall Boys** (1987). ©*Marty Lewis Photo.*

Marty Lewis on **The Hole** V3 at Deadman I. ©*Kevin Calder Photo.*

See Page 197

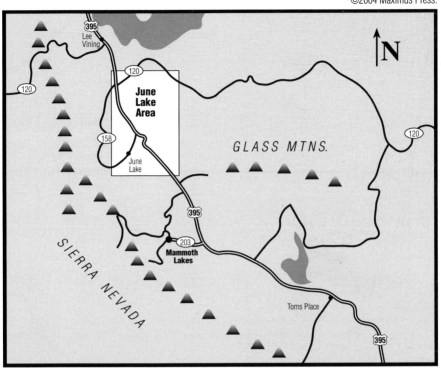

CHAPTER 8

JUNE LAKE AREA

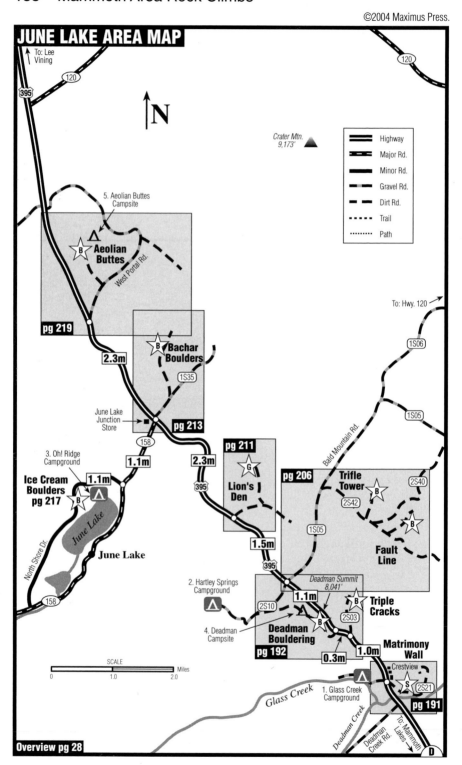

JUNE LAKE AREA MAP

To: Lee Vining

120

395

N

Crater Mtn.
9,173'

| Highway |
| Major Rd. |
| Minor Rd. |
| Gravel Rd. |
| Dirt Rd. |
| Trail |
| Path |

To: Hwy. 120

5. Aeolian Buttes Campsite

Aeolian Buttes

West Portal Rd.

pg 219

2.3m

Bachar Boulders

1S35

1S06

1S05

June Lake Junction Store

pg 213

158

1.1m

2.3m

395

pg 211

Lion's Den

pg 206

Bald Mountain Rd.

Trifle Tower

2S40

2S42

Fault Line

2S05

3. Oh! Ridge Campground

Ice Cream Boulders pg 217

1.1m

North Shore Dr

June Lake

June Lake

158

1.5m

395

1S05

2. Hartley Springs Campground

Deadman Summit
8,041'

1.1m

Triple Cracks

2S03

4. Deadman Campsite

2S10

Deadman Bouldering

pg 192

0.3m

1.0m

Matrimony Wall

Crestview

2S21

pg 191

SCALE
0   1.0   2.0   Miles

1. Glass Creek Campground

Glass Creek

To: Mammoth Lakes

Deadman Creek Rd.

Deadman Creek

D

JUNE LAKE AREA BASICS

The June Lake Area has the highest concentration of quality bouldering in the Mammoth Area. You won't find anything like the Buttermilk Boulders or the Happy Boulders, but what you will find is cool summer temperatures and good old fashioned highball bouldering on vertical to gently overhanging pocketed faces. These problems predate the propensity to name every problem, sit-down starts, and the V-scale.

Most of the bouldering found here is pretty moderate, the emphasis was more on mental control and being solid off the deck. However, there usually are a few V-desperates at each crag, which is pretty impressive, considering most of them were done in EBs and tube socks back in the day.

Getting There
To get to the June Lake Area start at the U.S. 395/203 junction and drive north on U.S. 395 for 9 to 17 miles. The crags are all located a short distance from the highway.

Amenities
June Lake Junction Store
General store and gas station.
☎ 760-648-7509.
June Lake Village
Two miles down Hwy. 158 is the resort town of June Lake. Numerous amenities will be found here.

Camping
1. Glass Creek Campground
Open May through October, **there is no fee**. Picnic tables, no potable water, vault toilets, elev. 7,600 ft.
☎ 760-647-3044.

2. Hartley Springs Campground
Open June through September, **there is no fee**. Picnic tables, no potable water, vault toilets, elev. 8,400 ft.
☎ 760-647-3044.
3. Oh! Ridge Campground
Open May through October, the fee is $13. Picnic tables, piped water, flush toilets, elev. 7,600 ft. ☎ 760-647-3044.

Primitive Camping
In this area it is possible to discretely camp for free, almost anywhere away from paved roads, as long as you are not on private property. Check with the Forest Service in Lee Vining for more information. *Please do not camp in the parking areas of the boulders.*

4. Deadman Campsite
Primitive camping in a valley near the bouldering. No water, elev. 7,900 ft.
5. Aeolian Buttes Campsite
Primitive camping with big views at the top of the Aeolian Buttes. No water, elev. 7,400 ft.

Matrimony Wall

This convenient little crag has excellent rock and offers short, fun sport climbing.

The Approach: From the U.S. 395/203 junction drive north on U.S. 395 8.7 miles to Glass Creek Rd. Turn right here into the Crestview Maintenance Station, then turn right again on a paved service road that leads to a gravel storage area. From here head left down a dirt road (2S21) for 0.4 miles to a pullout on the left, just before the crag.

Walk north up a short pumice hill.

History: Developed primarily by Neil Satterfield in the summer of 2001.

Matrimony Wall Details

Environment: Jeffrey pine forest.
Elevation: 7,600 ft.
Season: April to mid November
Exposure: South facing.
Rock Type: Granite.
Sport Climbs: 7 routes, 10a to 12a.
Gear Climbs: 1 route, 11d.
Drive From Mammoth: 15 minutes.
Approach: 1 minute walk.

Matrimony Wall

A. Mail Order Bride 10b**
6 bolts. Face. Lower off.
FA: Neil Satterfield, Dylan Walford, 2001.

B. Commitaphobe 11b**
6 bolts. Face. Lower off.
FA: Neil Satterfield, Kreighton Bieger, 2001.

C. Traditional Wedding 11d*
3 bolts, gear to 1". Start on *Commitaphobe* after the 3rd bolt go right up a crack. Lower off.
FA: Neil Satterfield, Doug Nidever, 2001.

D. Kreighton's Bastard Child 11a**
5 bolts. Face. Lower off.
FA: Neil Satterfield, Kreighton Bieger, 2001.

E. Drive Through Chapel 10a**
6 bolts. Face. Lower off.
FA: Dylan Walford, Neil Satterfield, 2001.

This route is on a small face just to the right.

F. Astroglide 11c**
5 bolts. Face. Lower off.
FA: Neil Satterfield, Dylan Walford, 2001.

©2004 Maximus Press.

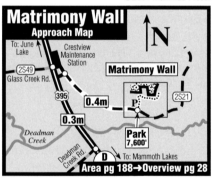

On a tower in front of *Astroglide*.

G. Unknown ?
4 bolts. Face. Lower off.

Around to the right on an east facing overhang.

H. Unknown 12a*
5 bolts. Steep face to slab. Lower off.

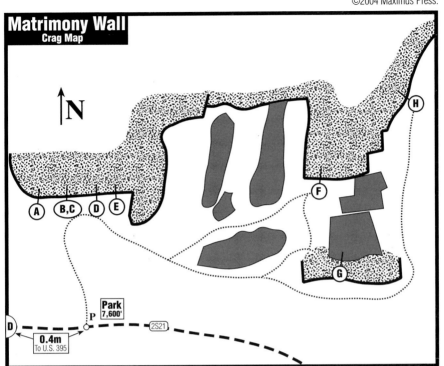

Adapted from the U.S.G.S. 1:24,000 June Lake and Crestview Quadrangles.

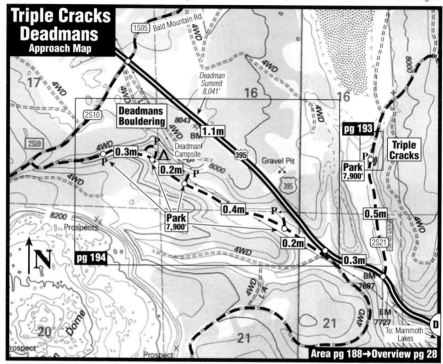

Triple Cracks

The name Triple Cracks is some-what of a misnomer as there are actu-ally about ten cracks here. Most of these are best enjoyed with a top-rope. There is also a bit of bouldering scat-tered about either side of the main for-mation.

This crag has long been a spot for developing crack climbing techniques. This series of steep cracks range from tips to off-hands and include every-thing in between. Although the taller cracks to the left offer short moderate leads or top-ropes; the three cracks in the middle of the cliff are the main attraction that the cliff is named for.

The Approach: From the U.S. 395/203 junction drive north on U.S. 395 for 9.8 miles. In the last mile you will pass a maintenance station on the right and climb a steep grade, turn right at the first turnout on a dirt road (2S21). Follow this up a valley for 0.5 miles and park. The main cliff is on the right.

History: Vern Clevenger, Kevin Leary, Dennis Phillips, Jim Stimson and Bill Taylor all seemed to have climbed here in the late 1970s.

Triple Cracks Details

Environment: Jeffrey pine forest.
Elevation: 7,900 ft.
Season: May to mid November
Exposure: Mostly west facing.
Rock Type: Volcanic tuff.
Top-roping: Gear anchors.
Bouldering: ★.
Drive From Mammoth: 15 minutes.
Approach: 1 minute walk.

"Big Wall" Marty at the **Triple Cracks** (1980). *Kevin Calder Photo.*

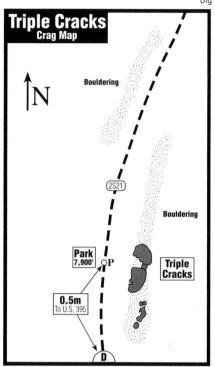

Triple Cracks
Crag Map

N

Bouldering

2S21

Bouldering

Park
7,900' P

Triple
Cracks

0.5m
To U.S. 395

D

©2004 Maximus Press. *John Moynier Topo.*

Triple Cracks

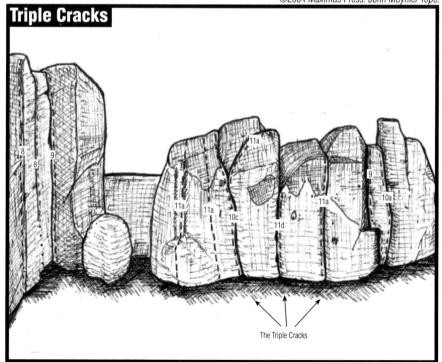

The Triple Cracks

©2004 Maximus Press.

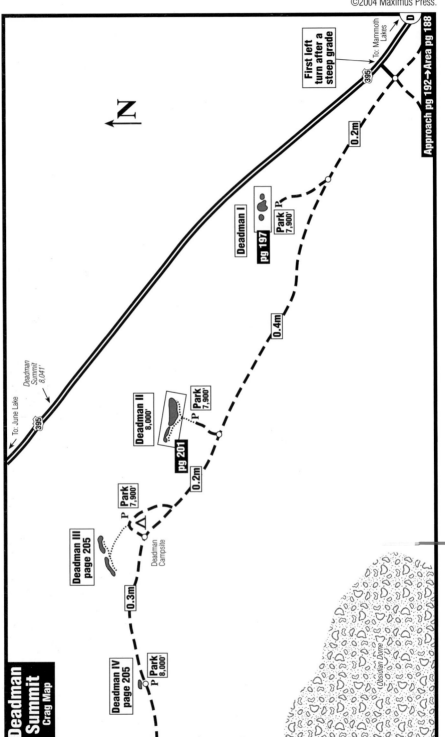

Deadman Summit Crag Map

First left turn after a steep grade

To: Mammoth Lakes

395

0.2m

Deadman I
pg 197

Park
7,900'
P

0.4m

Approach pg 192→Area pg 188

Deadman Summit 8,041'

To: June Lake

395

Deadman II
8,000'
pg 201

Park
7,900'
P

0.2m

Park
7,900'
P

Deadman Campsite

Deadman III
page 205

0.3m

Deadman IV
page 205

Park
8,000'
P

Obsidian Dome

N

Deadman Summit Bouldering

Once known for its soft pumice landings, years of high impact falls have rendered many of the landing zones at Deadmans a compressed hardpack with no give at all. In other words bring a bouldering pad! Here you will find fantastic volcanic rock littered with edges. Some of these boulder problems are quite tall! Feel free to top-rope anything that is too scary to boulder.

The Approach: Map page 192. From the U.S. 395/203 junction drive north on U.S. 395 for 10.1 miles. In the last mile you will pass a maintenance station on the right and climb a steep grade, turn left at the first left turn pocket. Immediately turn right at a "T" so that you are paralleling U.S. 395. on a pumice road. 0.2 miles past the "T" is a right turn that leads to Deadman I. 0.6 miles past the "T" is a right turn that leads to Deadman II. 0.8 miles past the "T" is a right turn that leads to Deadman III. 1.1 miles past the "T" is on the right side of the road is Deadman IV.

History: Deadman I was discovered in 1975 by Dennis Phillips. Deadman II and beyond were first climbed at by Jim Stimson and Bill Taylor. Other early activists include Vern Clevenger, Art Hanon and Kevin Leary. Developed in the late 1970s, these crags were some of the first places in the Mammoth Area to gain popularity. If they would have been discovered today some of them might have been bolted. However these are traditional cliffs that have been lead (soloed) many times.

Dave Yerian bouldering a V3 bulge at **Deadman II** (1984). ©*Errett Allen Photo.*

See Page 202

Joe Missick on the **Bachar Face** V5. ©*Dimitri Barton Photo.*

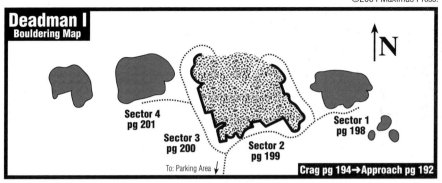

Deadman I

Deadman I is justifiably famous as a world class bouldering area. The main cliff is over 35 ft. tall and features a number of highball problems. These problems can be top-roped using large cams and trees.

Do not camp in the parking area. You will hear Jake-Braking trucks all night and when some local shows up at 7:00 AM for a workout, his dog will start licking your face. More importantly the Forest Service does not consider this spot dispersed camping.

The Approach: Map and description pages 194-195.

Deadman I Details

Environment: Jeffrey pine forest, with a lot of highway noise.
Elevation: 7,900 ft.
Season: May to mid November.
Exposure: Mostly south facing.
Rock Type: Volcanic tuff.
Bouldering: ★★★★, 40 problems.
Top-roping: Gear and tree anchors.
Drive From Mammoth: 15 minutes.
Approach: 1 minute walk.

Notable Problems

Sector 1
A. Problem V1/10d
Face climb to a committing reach.

Sector 2
B. Problem V0+/10b
Edges to a small pocket crux..

C. Bachar Face V5/12c
The Deadman I testpiece. Thin face. ➤ Photo facing page.
FA: John Bachar, early 1980s.

D. Deadman's Corner V1/10c
Fingers in a dihedral, after about 20 ft. the difficulties diminish considerably. The scene of a few ankle shattering falls. ➤ Photo page 198.

E. The Hole V3/11c
Tenuous slab climbing gets you to the hole. From here either traverse right to the corner or make a couple of sporty moves straight up, before it eases off.
➤ Photo page 186.

F. Problem V0/9
A highball classic. Face.

G. Drug Ascent V0/9
No one can remember why this easy face has this name. Also doubles as a descent route, the crux is about 10' off of the ground.

Sector 3
H. Problem V2/11a
The highball testpiece. A long reach where the angle changes is the crux.

I. Problem V1/10d
A more reasonable version of the previous problem.

J. Roof V4/12a
Face climb to a big roof, a giant exposed root makes the landing zone kind of sketchy. ➤ Photo page 200.

Sector 4
K. TV Set V1/10c
One of the best. Face.

Kevin Calder on the highball classic **Deadman's Corner** V1 (1982). ©*Marty Lewis Photo.*

©2004 Maximus Press. *John Moynier Topo.*

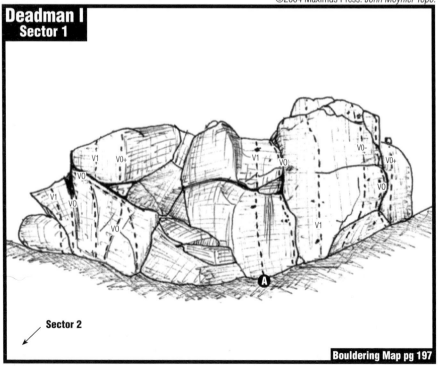

Deadman I
Sector 1

Sector 2

Bouldering Map pg 197

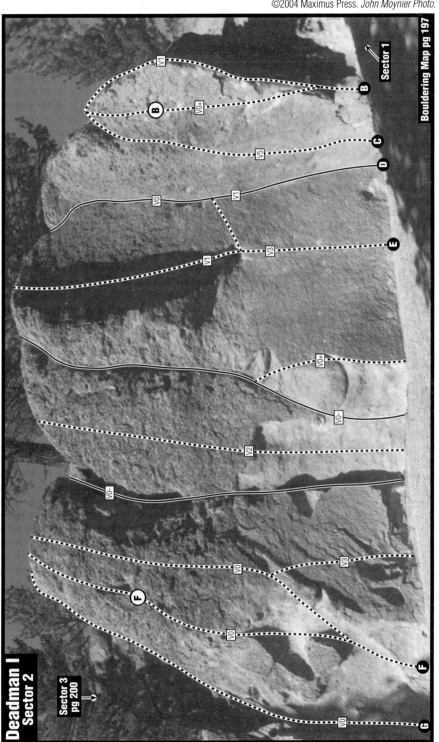

Deadman I
Sector 2

Bouldering Map pg 197

Sector 1

Sector 3
pg 200

Jim "Banny Root" May bouldering a V4 roof at **Deadman I** (1984). ©*Dimitri Barton Photo.*

©2004 Maximus Press. *John Moynier Photo.*

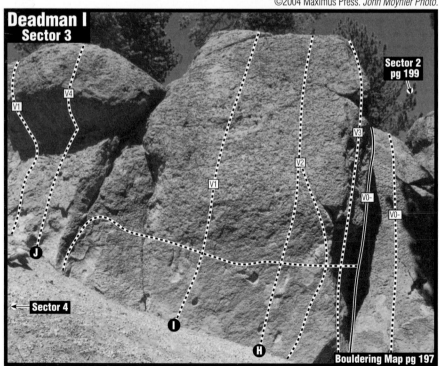

Deadman I
Sector 3

Sector 2
pg 199

V4

V1

V3

V2

V1

V0−

V0−

J

Sector 4

I

H

Bouldering Map pg 197

Deadman I
Sector 4

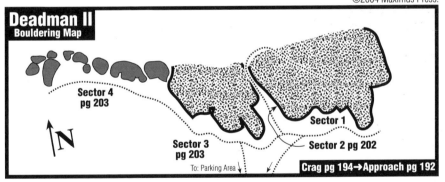

Deadman II
Bouldering Map

Sector 4
pg 203

Sector 3
pg 203

Sector 1

Sector 2 pg 202

To: Parking Area

Crag pg 194→Approach pg 192

Deadman II

Like Deadman I, Deadman II has a multitude of incredible boulder problems. Unlike Deadman I, most of the problems tend to be of a more reasonable height (20′). The boulders are on a south facing bluff and can get quite hot.

The Approach: Map and description pages 194-195.

Deadman II Details

Environment: Pumice slope on a bluff.
Elevation: 8,000 ft.
Season: May to mid November.
Exposure: South facing, very sunny.
Rock Type: Volcanic tuff.
Bouldering: ★★★★, 50 problems.
Drive From Mammoth: 15 minutes.
Approach: 5 minute pumice slope.

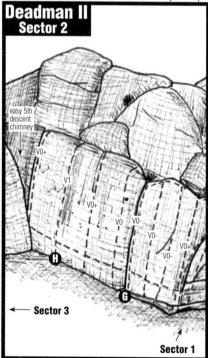

Notable Problems

Sector 1
A. Warm Up Face V0/10a
Pocketed face.
B. Problem V0-/9
Dihedral.
C. Problem V4/12a
Right face of the dihedral (the left wall is off).
Descend to the right.
D. Problem V3/11d
Powerful reach past a bulge.
E. Problem V3/11c
Undercling past the bulge. ➤ Photo page 195.
F. Problem V2/11b
Sporty seam.

Sector 2
G. Problem V0-/8
Finger crack. This is also doubles as an alternate descent for adjoining the problems.
H. Problem V1/10d
Pocketed face.

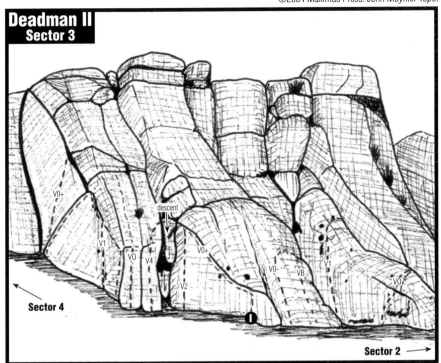

Deadman II
Sector 3

Deadman II
Sector 4

Smooth Wall

Sector 3

Bouldering Map pg 201

Sector 3
I. Problem VO+/10b
Rising hand traverse left. Descend the chimney.

Sector 4
J. Smooth Wall V4/12a
The Deadman II testpiece. Long reaches between shallow pockets lead to an exciting straight up finish.
FA: Dale Bard, late 1970s.

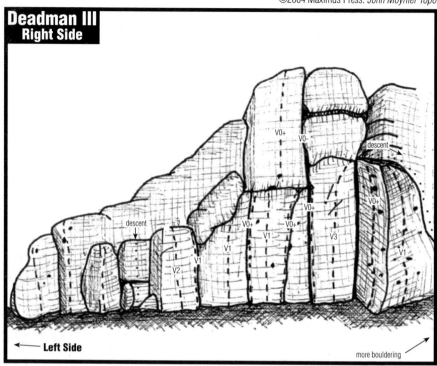

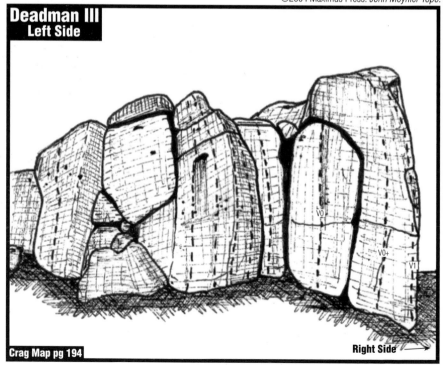

Deadman III

Not as extensive as Deadman I or II, but this crag also has many excellent problems. This spot features a number of good highball cracks on the main wall. The area is shaded most of the day by large Jeffrey pines, so it's nice even when hot.

The Approach: Map and description pages 194-195.

Deadman III Details

Environment: Jeffrey pine forest.
Elevation: 8,000 ft.
Season: May to mid November.
Exposure: Southeast facing.
Rock Type: Volcanic tuff.
Bouldering: ★★★, 40 problems.
Top-roping: Gear and tree anchors.
Drive From Mammoth: 15 minutes.
Approach: 2 minute uphill walk.

©2004 Maximus Press. *Marty Lewis Photo.*

Deadman IV

Crag Map pg 194

Deadman IV

Deadman IV is a small secluded formation with a few excellent moderate problems.

The Approach: Map and description pages 194-195.

Deadman IV Details

Environment: Jeffrey pine forest.
Elevation: 8,000 ft.
Season: May to mid November.
Exposure: South facing.
Rock Type: Volcanic tuff.
Bouldering: ★.
Top-roping: Gear and tree anchors.
Drive From Mammoth: 15 minutes.
Approach: 1 minute walk.

Adapted from the U.S.G.S. 1:24,000 Crestview and June Lake Quadrangles.

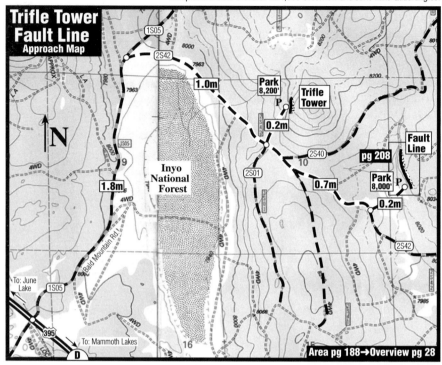

Trifle Tower

The Trifle Tower offers two quality gently overhanging sport climbs that follow cutter edges and pockets. These are easily set up as top-ropes. This crag also has some high quality bouldering on either side of the tower, some of it is quite hard, although the scope is limited.

The Approach: From the U.S. 395/203 junction drive north on U.S. 395 for 11.2 miles and turn right on Bald Mountain Rd. (1S05). Follow this gravel road for 1.8 miles to a right turn on road 2S42. Drive down this road

Trifle Tower Details

Environment: Heavily logged Jeffrey pine forest.
Elevation: 8,200 ft.
Season: June to October.
Exposure: West facing.
Rock Type: Volcanic tuff.
Top-roping: Bolt anchors.
Bouldering: ★.
Sport Climbs: 2 routes, 11d and 12a.
Drive From Mammoth: 20 minutes.
Approach: 1 minute walk.

past many logging tracks for 1 mile and turn left right before road 2S01 comes in from the right. From here drive north for 0.2 miles to a parking area below the crag. Walk up a short pumice hill.

History: Before the discovery of the Owens River Gorge and Clark Canyon, the twin Trifle Tower routes were very popular training climbs. At one point the crag even sported a belay couch. Early developers included John Bachar, Dimitri Barton, Rick Cashner, Steve Schneider and Gary Slate.

©2004 Maximus Press. *John Moynier Topo.*

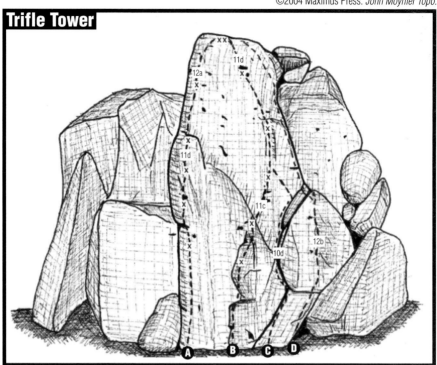

Trifle Tower

©2004 Maximus Press. *Marty Lewis Photo.*

Trifle Tower

A. Trifle Tower Left 12a**
5 bolts. Steep face. Lower off.

B. Trifle Tower Right 11d****
5 bolts. Steep face. Lower off. ☞ If this route was in Clark Canyon people would be lining up to climb it.
FA: John Bachar (free solo). Retrobolts: Steve Schneider.

C. Top-rope 10d*(tr)
Crack.

D. Top-rope 12b*(tr)
Face to crack.

Left of the tower are two difficult John Bachar boulder problems:

Lazerblade V4/12a
On the right.

Blade Runner V6/12c
On the left.

Right of the tower, a ways down, is more good bouldering.

Fault Line

The Fault Line is a long west facing bluff with lots of bouldering. The problems are generally tall with a good mixture of both crack and face problems. Sector 1 is right across a gully from the parking area, it features a swath of awesome highball moderates (➤ Photo page 14). At Sector 2 *Schneider's Roof* (V4/12a) is an amazing 135 degree hand crack that is usually top-roped. At the far north end of the crag there is a nice boulder with some shorter problems.

Fault Line Details

Environment: Jeffrey pine forest.
Elevation: 8,000 ft.
Season: June to October.
Exposure: Mostly west facing.
Rock Type: Volcanic tuff.
Bouldering: ★★★, 40 problems.
Top-roping: Bring gear and slings.
Drive From Mammoth: 25 minutes.
Approach: 1 minute walk.

The Approach: Map page 206. From the U.S. 395/203 junction drive north on U.S. 395 for 11.2 miles and turn right on Bald Mountain Rd. (1S05). Follow this gravel road for 1.8 miles to a right turn on road 2S42. Drive down this road past many logging tracks for 1.7 miles and turn left at a pumice clearing. From here drive northeast for 0.2 miles to a parking area at the crag.

Walk across the gully to reach the south end of the crag.

Fault Line
Bouldering Map

↑N

Sector 3

Fault
Line

Sector 2

0.2m
To road
2S42

P

Sector 1

Park
8,000'

D

Approach pg 206→Area pg 188

Fault Line
Sector 2

V4

©2004 Maximus Press. *John Moynier Topo.*

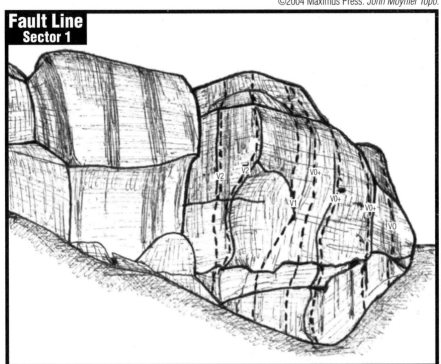

©2004 Maximus Press. *John Moynier Photo.*

See Page 212

Mike Melkonian on **Block and Tackle** 12a****. ©*Bill McChesney Photo.*

Adapted from the U.S.G.S. 1:24,000 June Lake Quadrangle. John Bachar on **Bulldog Arete** 12a**. ©*Dimitri Barton* Photo.

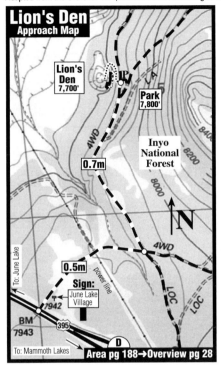

Lion's Den Approach Map

See Page 212

Lion's Den

Located in a secluded bowl this crag offers some fine technical climbs. Most of the climbs have been led, but the bolt anchors are on the almost horizontal summit of the cliff, making the crag ideal for top-roping.

The Approach: From the U.S. 395/203 junction drive north on U.S. 395 for 12.7 miles, to a point where the divided highway comes back together. Immediately turn right on a dirt road that passes behind a "June Lake Village" sign. Drive down this dirt road, (passing under a power line) for 0.5 miles. Turn left here and drive 0.7 miles to a "Y" and park.

Lion's Den Details

Environment: Forested bowl.
Elevation: 7,700 ft.
Season: May to mid November.
Exposure: West facing.
Rock Type: Volcanic Tuff.
Gear Climbs: 5 routes, 9 to 12a.
Sport Climbs: 3 routes, 11d to 12b.
Top-roping: Bolt and gear anchors, bring runners.
Drive From Mammoth: 20 minutes.
Approach: 5 minute pumice walk, with a 100 ft. descent.

From here walk northwest down the slope contouring along, then turn back left on a switchback.

History: Dennis Phillips climbed here in the late 1970s. Most of the cracks were led during the early 1980s, including Dale Bard's classic *Block and Tackle* (12a). In the 1990s a few sport climbs were added.

Lion's Den

Intro: Page 211. These routes are all in the 30 to 50 foot range. Didn't they used to be taller? You can lower off of all these routes, but you will need runners on the anchors. Whoever climbs last will have to strip the anchors and walk off.

A. Unknown 9*
Gear to 5". Offwidth crack. Bolt anchor.
FA: Doug Nidever, early 1980s.

B. Unknown 10b**(tr)
Slab. Bolt anchor.

C. Old Aid Seam 11d*(tr)
Start on the left, then cross the arete.

D. Block and Tackle 12a****
Gear to 1.5". A finger crack through a bulge, then it thins out at the top. Bolt anchor. ☞ The volcanic crack climbing testpiece of the Mammoth Area. ➤ Photo page 210.
FA: Dale Bard, early 1980s.

E. Unknown 9*
Gear to 4". Crack. Gear anchor.
FA: Doug Nidever, early 1980s.

F. Bulldog Arete 12a**
3 bolts. Arete. Lower off. ➤ Photo page 211.
FA: John Bachar, 1987.

G. Fear of Flying 10c**
Gear. Steepening dihedral. Gear anchor, walk off left.
FA: Dennis Phillips, 1980s.

H. Open Project 13?
1 bolt. Tiny edges. Bolt anchor.
P: Steve Schneider.

I. Piece of the Action 11d**
4 bolts. Arete. Bolt anchor.
FA: Steve Schneider, Kevin Calder, early 1989.

J. Classic Crack 10a***
Gear to 3.5". Hand crack. Bolt anchor.

K. Whirly Bird 12b**
5 bolts. Thin face. Bolt anchor.
FA: Steve Schneider, Kevin Calder, 1989.

Adapted from the U.S.G.S. 1:24,000 June Lake Quadrangle.   Jim May on **Like a Virgin** V3. ©*Dimitri Barton Photo.*

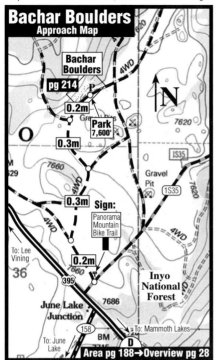

Bachar Boulders

One of the most conventional and highest quality bouldering areas around Mammoth. Many of the problems are gently overhanging on coarse pockets and edges. It can be a real pumper, finger shredding exercise. The main area at the Bachar Boulders features a high concentration of problems and a picnic table under the shade of a large pine tree. Left of here there are some great problems that are more scattered about.

Bachar Boulders Details

Environment: Jeffrey pine forest.
Elevation: 7,600 ft.
Season: May to mid November.
Exposure: Southeast facing, morning sun.
Rock Type: Volcanic tuff.
Bouldering: ★★★★★, 50 problems.
Drive From Mammoth: 20 minutes.
Approach: 1 minute walk.

The Approach: From the U.S. 395/203 junction drive north on U.S. 395 for 15 miles until reaching the June Lake Junction (Hwy. 158). Directly across the highway from the gas station is a dirt road (1S35) that heads northeast. Follow this and immediately turn left at a sign "Panorama Mountain Bike Trail". Drive on this road 0.2 miles to a "Y" and branch right. Follow this road 0.3 miles and branch left. Continue 0.5 miles to the parking area on the left beside a huge decomposing log.

From here walk west on a trail to a picnic table.

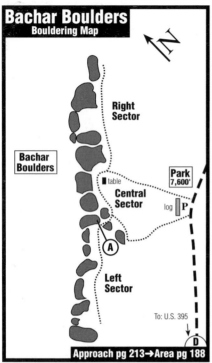

Bachar Boulders
Bouldering Map

Right
Sector

Bachar
Boulders

■ table

Park
7,600'

Central
Sector

log | P

(A)

Left
Sector

To: U.S. 395

D

Approach pg 213→Area pg 188

Jerry Moffat on **JB's Seam** V5. ©*Dimitri Barton Photo.*

History: A little bouldering went on out here during the late 1970s. In the early 1980s most every problem was either first done or repeated by John Bachar and Dave Yerian. John named this area the *"June Lake Junction Boulders"*. That name never stuck, only John and a few old dudes seem to persist in calling it that. For everyone else, it has always been the *"Bachar Boulders"*.

Notable Problems

Left Sector
A. The Dyno V7/13a
Start low matched on a big horizontal, then up to a big dyno. ➤ Photo page 216.
FA: Dimitri Barton, 1988.

Central Sector
B. Problem V2/11b
Arete.

C. Like a Virgin V3/11c
Killer finger crack. The crux is getting started, although falling off an easier reachy crux (V1/10d) towards the top has caused at least one broken back. ➤ Photo page 213.
FA: John Bachar, early 1980s.

D. Problem V7/13a
Tall desperate face, you can head up and left to avoid the upper highball crux.
FA: Dimitri Barton, early 1980s.

E. JB's Seam V5/12c
Seam. ☞ John rated this one "bouldering 12a", it seems a bit harder. A highball testpiece. ➤ Photo this page.
FA: John Bachar, early 1980s.

F. Problem V2/11a
Arete.

G. Problem V0+/10b
Optional sit down start, climb up and left up the gently overhanging face.

H. Problem V3/11d
Sit down start on pockets on left side of an arete, then climb the arete.

Right Sector
I. Problem V2/11a
Arete.

J. Problem V3/11c
Thin face leads to a finger crack.

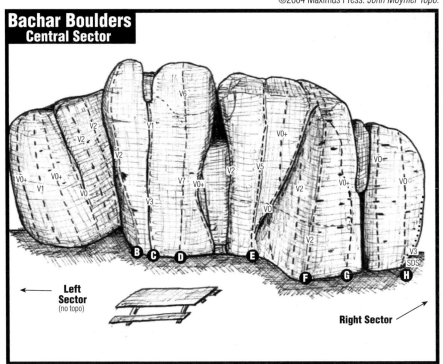

Bachar Boulders
Central Sector

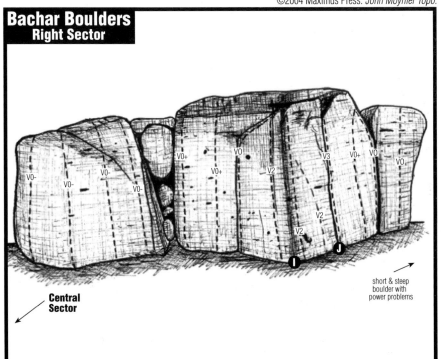

Bachar Boulders
Right Sector

See Page 214

Ron Kauk on **The Dyno** V7 at the Bachar Boulders (1987). ©*Dimitri Barton Photo.*

©2004 Maximus Press. *Marty Lewis Photo.*

Ice Cream Boulders

A small, but quality granite bouldering area right on a road.

The Approach: Map page 188. From the U.S. 395/203 junction drive north on U.S. 395 15 miles until reaching the June Lake Junction (Hwy. 158). Turn left here and drive 1.1 miles to the Oh! Ridge turnoff. Turn right here on North Shore Dr. and go another 1.1 miles, then park (well off of the pavement). The boulders are on the left side of the road.

History: When the new North Shore Dr. road was built in the late 1990s it conveniently went right past these boulders. After that it was pretty obvious what needed to be done.

Ice Cream Boulders

Environment: Roadside forest.
Elevation: 7,800 ft.
Season: May to mid November
Exposure: Varied.
Rock Type: Granite.
Bouldering: ★, 20 problems.
Drive From Mammoth: 20 minutes.
Approach: 1 minute walk.

©2004 Maximus Press.

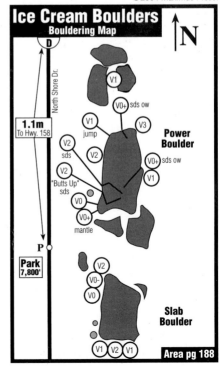

Ice Cream Boulders
Bouldering Map

Jonathon Barlev on the **Stone Crusade Boulders**. *©Kevin Calder Photo.*

Adapted from the U.S.G.S. 1:24,000 June Lake Quadrangle.

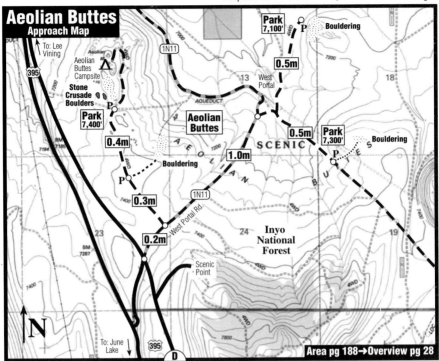

Aeolian Buttes

More of a "photo-op" than a bouldering area, this spot was featured on the cover of John Sherman's bouldering history "Stone Crusade". The two main volcanic plugs are quite tall, featuring a number of highball problems. Find the easiest line on each one—that will be the descent. There are a number of other boulderfields in the area, most of these offer better bouldering than on the plugs—consult the map for their location. The following approach instructions are for the "Stone Crusade Boulders".

The Approach: From the U.S. 395/203 junction drive north on U.S. 395 for 17.5 miles and turn right on West Portal Rd. Follow this dirt road 0.2 miles and turn left on another dirt road. Follow this 0.7 miles to a "T" and park for the main area.

Aeolian Buttes Details

Environment: High desert ridge.
Elevation: 7,400 ft.
Season: March to December.
Exposure: Varied.
Rock Type: Volcanic tuff.
Bouldering: ★★.
Drive From Mammoth: 20 minutes.
Approach: 1 minute walk.

See Page 232

John Bachar on **Gravity** 12a***** in Dexter Canyon. ©*John McDonald Photo.*

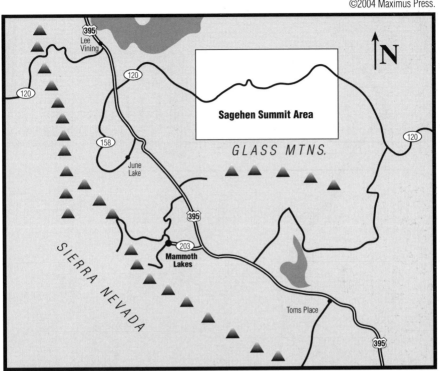

CHAPTER 9

SAGEHEN SUMMIT

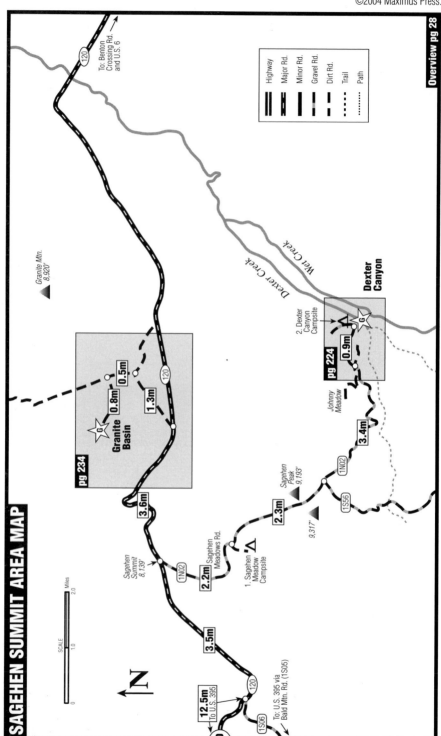

SAGEHEN SUMMIT AREA MAP

Overview pg 28

Legend:
- Highway
- Major Rd.
- Minor Rd.
- Gravel Rd.
- Dirt Rd.
- Trail
- Path

To: Benton Crossing Rd. and U.S. 6

120

Granite Mtn. 8,920'

Wet Creek

Dexter Creek

Dexter Canyon

2. Dexter Canyon Campsite

0.9m

pg 224

Johnny Meadow

3.4m

1NO2

1S56

0.5m

0.8m

1.3m

120

pg 234

Granite Basin

3.6m

Sagehen Peak 9,193'

9,317'

2.3m

1NO2

Sagehen Summit 8,139'

1NO2

Sagehen Meadows Rd.

2.2m

1. Sagehen Meadow Campsite

SCALE

Miles
0   1.0   2.0

N

3.5m

12.5m To U.S. 395

120

1S06

D

To: U.S. 395 via Bald Mtn. Rd. (1S05)

SAGEHEN SUMMIT AREA BASICS

Driving along Hwy. 120 to the east, one enters a spectacular, rarely visited landscape far removed from the hustle and bustle of Mammoth Lakes. Way off the beaten path, the Sagehen Summit Area features two crags that lie on the north side of the majestic Glass Mountains. Dexter Canyon has some of the finest traditional volcanic crack climbing in the Mammoth Area, while Granite Basin features a big granite dome with bolted face climbing and a few cracks.

Getting There

To get to the Sagehen Summit Area drive north on U.S. 395 for 20.5 miles. Turn right on Hwy. 120 and follow this for 16 miles.

Amenities

This area is very remote, the closest services will be found in the town of Lee Vining.

Primitive Camping

In this area it is possible to discretely camp for free, almost anywhere away from paved roads, as long as you are not on private property. Check with the Forest Service in Lee Vining for more information. *Please do not camp in the parking area for Granite Basin.*

1. Sagehen Meadows Campsite

Primitive camping near a meadow. No water, elev. 8,400 ft.

2. Dexter Canyon Campsite

Primitive camping on the rim of Dexter Canyon. No water, elev. 8,200 ft.

Adapted from the U.S.G.S. 1:24,000 Dexter Canyon Quadrangle.

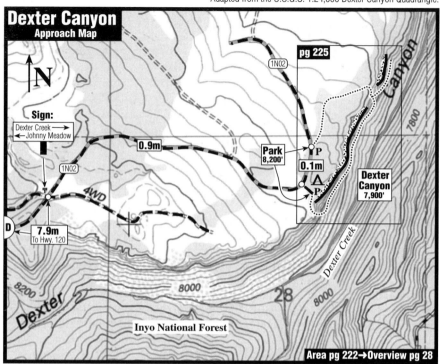

Dexter Canyon

Although Dexter Canyon has similar rock to the Deadman's and the Clark Canyon crags, the overall feel is more like the canyons of Southern Utah. Late afternoon is the best time to climb, the cliff bakes in the morning sun.

The cleanest, best formed volcanic cracks in the Mammoth Area are found here. The routes here should be treated like cracks in the southwest—place a lot of gear. Some climbers will be disappointed by the lack of fixed anchors at the top of the cracks—you

Dexter Canyon Details

Environment: Rough forested pumice slope in a canyon.
Elevation: 7,900 ft.
Season: May to mid November
Exposure: Southeast facing.
Rock Type: Volcanic tuff.
Gear Climbs: 31 routes, 5.9 to 12b.
Sport Climbs: 1 route, 12a.
Drive From Mammoth: 55 minutes.
Approach: 15 to 20 minute scramble with a 300 ft. descent.

have to do a heinous walk off after every climb. Super trad guys should be pretty psyched about this lack of bolts. There is however, an amazing pocketed section of cliff that features bolted face climbs with excellent anchors.

Dexter Canyon is definitely adventure climbing, help is a long ways off if you have any trouble.

Fred Feldman, Errett Allen and Grant Hiskes, Dexter Canyon (1985).   ©2004 Maximus Press.

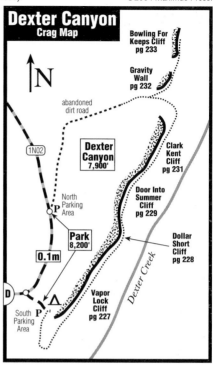

The Approach: From the U.S. 395/203 junction drive north on U.S. 395 for 20.5 miles to the Hwy. 120 East junction. From here turn right and drive 16 miles on Hwy. 120 to a pass with a "Sagehen Summit 8,139 ft." sign. Turn right here on Sagehen Meadows Rd. (1N02). Follow this road for 7.9 miles to a junction with the Johnny Meadows/Dexter Creek Rd. Continue for 0.9 miles farther to a right turn that leads to the South Parking Area and a campsite or go a bit farther to an abandoned dirt road that branches right for the North Parking Area.

From the South Parking Area hike up canyon (southwest) a few hundred yards to a rocky pumice gully. Drop down this a ways, then head left towards the crag.

From the North Parking Area hike northeast down a faint overgrown dirt road for about a quarter of a mile. From here head to the east towards a low spot and the descent gully. Angle down and left for the Gravity Wall and Bowling for Keeps. Angle down and right for the Clark Kent Cliff and the Door Into Summer Cliff.

History: Dexter Canyon was another area that was developed with an eye towards maintaining solitude and adventurous climbing. This is to be expected when you consider that the routes were pioneered by the usual suspects— Ken Yager, Gary Slate, Errett Allen, Scott Cole, Grant Hiskes and Fred Feldman—climbers who had escaped the busy confines of Yosemite.

Ken Yager on **Vapor Lock** 10d**** (1985). ©*Errett Allen Photo.*

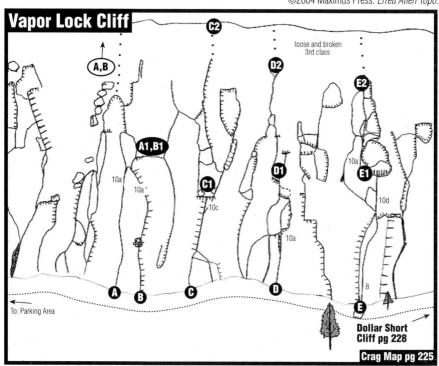

Ken Yager on **Yosemite Sam** 10b*** (1984). ©*Errett Allen Photo.*

Vapor Lock Cliff

Dexter Canyon Intro: Page 224. This is the first cliff encountered from the South Parking Area.

A. Steeplechase 10a*
Gear to 3". Crack. Walk off.
FA: Gary Slate, Errett Allen, 4/1985.

B. Sandman 10a**
Gear to 4". Crack. Walk off.
FA: Fred Feldman, Errett Allen, 4/1985.

C. Cell Block 10c**
Gear. Crack. Walk off.
FA: Errett Allen, Scott Cole, 5/1985.

D. Sandbag 10a*
Gear. Crack. Walk off.
FA: Ken Yager, Errett Allen, 8/1984.

E. Vapor Lock 10d****
Gear to 4". Dihedral. Walk off. ➤ Photo facing page.
FA: Ken Yager, Errett Allen, 4/1985.

See Page 231

Scott Cole on **Fire and Ice** 10c** (1985). ©*Errett Allen Photo.*

©2004 Maximus Press. *Gary Slate Photo.*

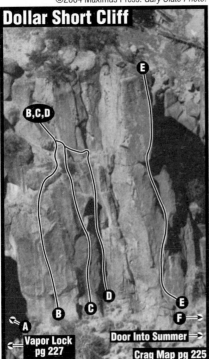

Dollar Short Cliff
Dexter Canyon Intro: Page 224.

A. Dollar Short 10b**
Gear. Climb the double cracks in the huge alcove 100' left of *Road Warrior* to a ledge. A short crack then starts off the left side of the ledge. Walk off.
FA: Gary Slate, Errett Allen, 1985.

B. Road Warrior 10b**
Gear. Thin crack. Walk off.
FA: Gary Slate, Jeff White, 1985.

C. Lizard Crack 10a*
Gear. Crack. Walk off.
FA: Gary Slate, Errett Allen, 5/1985.

D. Short Changed 9*
Gear. Right facing corner. Walk off.
FA: Gary Slate, Errett Allen, 5/1985.

E. Short Stroke 10a**
Gear. Tight hands to off-width crack. Walk off.
FA: Scott Cole, Fred Feldman, Errett Allen, 4/1985.

F. Fire and Ice 10c**
Gear. A west facing thin crack leads to a chimney. Walk off. ➤ Photo this page.
FA: Scott Cole, Grant Hiskes, Fred Feldman, Errett Allen, 4/1985.

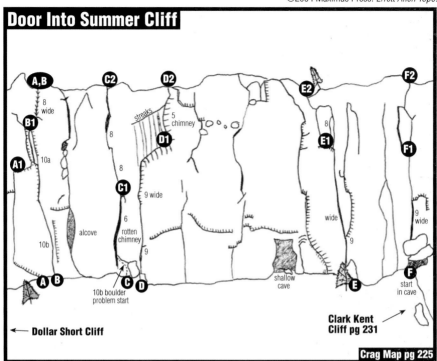

Door Into Summer Cliff

Dollar Short Cliff

Clark Kent
Cliff pg 231

Crag Map pg 225

Bob Finn on **Clark Kent** 10b****. *©Errett Allen Photo.*

See Page 231

Door Into Summer Cliff
Dexter Canyon Intro: Page 224.

A. Spring Fling 10a*
Gear. Crack. Walk off.
FA: Ken Yager, Grant Hiskes, 1985.

B. Door Into Summer 10b***
Gear. Killer lieback to a nice crack. Walk off.
FA: Errett Allen, Scott Cole, Fred Feldman, 4/1985.

C. Star Beast 10b·
Gear. Bouldery face climbing leads to a rotten chimney, then crack climbing. Walk off.
FA: Fred Feldman, Errett Allen, 4/1985.

D. Orphans of the Sky 9*
Gear. Crack. Walk off.
FA: Fred Feldman, Errett Allen, 4/1985.

E. Forbidden Planet 9**
Gear to 4". Wide crack. Walk off.
FA: Gary Slate, Errett Allen, 1985.

F. B.C. 9*
Gear to 4". Wide crack. Walk off.
FA: Fred Feldman, Errett Allen, 4/1985.

Errett Allen on **Clark Kent** 10b****. ©*Errett Allen Collection.*

©2004 Maximus Press. *Errett Allen Topo.*

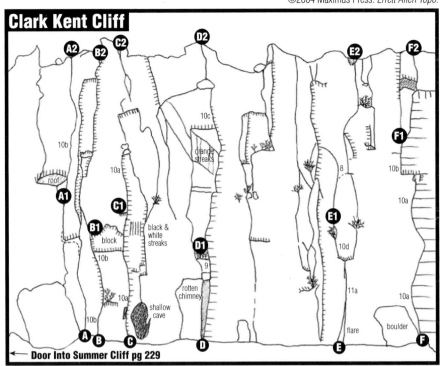

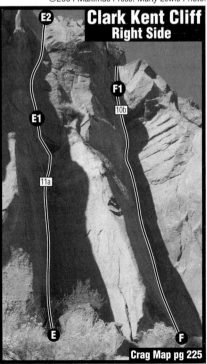

©2004 Maximus Press. *Marty Lewis Photo.*

Clark Kent Cliff
Dexter Canyon Intro: Page 224.

A. Clark Kent 10b****
Gear to 3.5". Cracks. Walk off.
➤ Photo page 229, facing page.
FA: Ken Yager, Errett Allen, 10/1984.

B. Tumbleweeds 10b**
Gear. Crack. Walk off.
FA: Ken Yager, Errett Allen, 10/1984.

C. Stalactite 10a**
Gear to 4". Dihedral. Walk off.
FA: Gary Slate, Errett Allen, 1985.

D. Foghorn Leghorn 10c*
Gear. A rotten chimney leads to cracks. Walk off.
FA: Ken Yager, Marylyn Wisner, Errett Allen, 5/1985.

E. Grandpa's Challenge 11a**
Pitch 1: 11a**. Gear. Climb a flared chimney to a thin crack, then pass a roof on the left and belay at a bush.
Pitch 2: 8**. Gear. Go up and right to the rim. Walk off.
FA: Dave Yerian, Errett Allen, 1985.

F. Yosemite Sam 10b***
Gear to 4". A huge left facing corner. ➤ Photo page 227.
FA: Ken Yager, Errett Allen, 10/1984.

G. Dagwood 9***
Gear. Climb double cracks on the right wall of a dihedral 50' right of *Yosemite Sam*.
FA: Ken Yager, Errett Allen, 10/1984.

Gravity Wall

Dexter Canyon Intro: Page 224. Best approached from the North Parking Area. This wall features some of the cleanest pocket climbing in the Mammoth Area. The John Bachar version of sport climbing—you may want supplemental gear and expect some sporty sections between bolts.

A. Crater Face 11c***
4 bolts, gear. Start in a right facing double crack, pass a ledge, then face climb. Lower off.
FA: John Bachar, Dave Schultz, 1986, GU.

B. Pocket Rocket 12b****
5 bolts, gear. Climb flakes to a face. Lower off.
FA: John Bachar, Dave Schultz, 1986, GU.

C. Gravity 12a*****
6 bolts. A bulge leads to an intimidating pocketed face. Lower off. ☞ *"Gravity—the big G—G-R-A-V-I-T-Y—gravity—say it—gotten a hold on me—heh."* —the other JB, the king of soul, James Brown. ➤ Photo page 220.
FA: John Bachar, Dave Schultz, 1986, GU.

D. Fingerprints 11a**
2 bolts, gear. Scramble up to a ledge climb past 2 bolts, then flakes lead up and left. Lower off.
FA: John Bachar, Dave Schultz, 1986, GU.

E. Big Bad Jess 10c***
6 bolts, opt. gear. Face. Lower off.
FA: John Bachar, Jessica VanBriessen, 1988, GU.

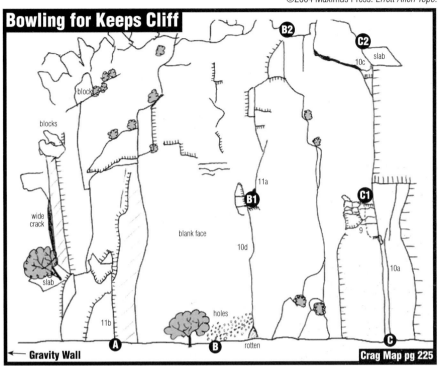

John Bachar in **Dexter Canyon**. ©*Dimitri Barton Photo.*

Bowling for Keeps Cliff
Dexter Canyon Intro: Page 224. Best approached from the North Parking Area. Drop down to the Gravity Wall and continue north down canyon.

A. Gutter Ball 11b**
Gear. A stemming corner leads to a hand crack. Walk off.
FA: Ken Yager, Al Swanson, 8/1987.

B. Bowling for Keeps 11a****
Pitch 1: 10d****. Gear. Crack to a ledge.
Pitch 2: 11a****. Gear. Face climbing along a thin crack leads to the top. Walk off.
FA: Dave Schultz, Ken Yager, Gary Slate, 5/1985.

C. Up Your Alley 10c**
Pitch 1: 10a**. Gear. Climb thin cracks to a ledge.
Pitch 2: 10c**. Gear. Climb a dihedral to a thin crack in a flare in a roof. Walk off.
FA: Ken Yager, Errett Allen, 6/1985.

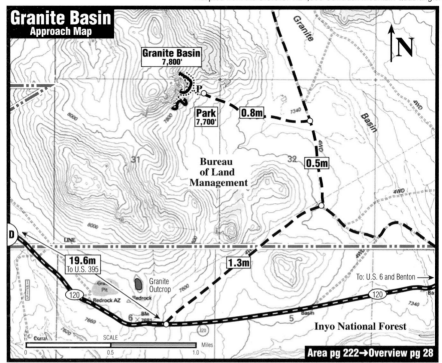

Adapted from the U.S.G.S. 1:24,000 Cowtrack Mountain Quadrangle.

Granite Basin

This crag doesn't look like much from Hwy. 120, but the scale becomes apparent as you slowly approach the base. This large granite dome has somehow escaped the confines of Yosemite National Park. The rock is a little grainy, but nonetheless, you will find enjoyable climbing in a spectacular high desert setting.

The Approach: From the U.S. 395/203 junction drive north on U.S. 395 for 20.5 miles to the Hwy. 120 East junction. Turn right here and drive 16 miles on Hwy. 120 to a "Sagehen Summit 8,139 ft." sign. From here continue on Hwy. 120 for 3.6 miles down a hill. Look for a 30 ft. granite outcrop on the left, pass this and turn left on the next dirt road. Follow this for 1.3 miles and turn left. Drive another 0.5 miles and make a left. Follow this road 0.8 miles up a hill to a loop parking area.

The crag is an easy walk from here.

Granite Basin Details

Environment: High desert, sagebrush and pinion pines.
Elevation: 7,800 ft.
Season: April to mid November.
Exposure: South and east facing.
Rock Type: Featured granite.
Gear Climbs: 12 routes, 5.7 to 10d.
Sport Climbs: 12 routes, 5.9 to 11c.
Drive From Mammoth: 50 minutes.
Approach: 5 to 15 minute walk with a 100 ft. gain.

Granite Basin
A. Hair Raiser Buttress 9*****
B. Granitology 11c*****

Northeast Face pg 241

East Face pg 239

South Face pg 237

Descent

East Tower pg 240

B

A

Waterfall Wall

History: The first climbs were done by face climbing pioneers Vern Clevenger and Tom Higgins, about the same time as they were developing the runout face routes of nearby Tuolumne Meadows. Although the style was the same (sparse protection, thin slab moves), the rock offers much more in the way of friction. The *Hair Raiser Buttress* (5.9) was a mandatory testpiece for local climbers in the late 1970s to early 1980s. It wasn't until local adventure climbers expanded the number of routes, that the crag gained broader popularity. With its combination of sporty runouts, natural gear and its off-the-beaten-track location Granite Basin still retains much of its original flavor.

Waterfall Wall
These routes are located in an alcove on the first separate formation 300 ft. south of the start of the *Hair Raiser Buttress*.

Hoot-enanny 10b**
6 bolts. 20ft. left of the waterfall. Scramble up a grainy slab and climb a steep quartz dike. Lower off.
➤ Photo page 241.
FA: Neal Satterfield, Mike Melkonian, 9/2003, TD.
Unknown 10a*(r)
4 bolts. 40 ft. right of the waterfall. Climb up huecos to a steep platey flake. Lower off.

Isabel Ledesma and Becky Hutto on the 3rd pitch of **Hair Raiser Buttress** 9*****. *©Kevin Calder Photo.*

Granite Basin - South Face

Intro: Page 234.

A. Hair Raiser Buttress 9*****

Pitch 1: 9*****. 6 bolts (if you want to use only the original bolts, clip the 1st, 3rd and 5th). A spooky, bouldery start over some blocks leads to a beautiful slab. 35m/115' lower off.

Pitch 2: 8*****. 7 bolts (if you want to use only the original bolts, clip the 2nd, 4th and 6th). Continue up the fantastic slab. 50m/165'.

Pitch 3: 9****. 4 bolts, opt. gear: small wired or TCU. Climb up the slab past a mini-dihedral on a huge dike, then continue to the top. 35m/115'.

Descent: Walk off left or do three double rope rappels.
☞ If *Hair Raiser Buttress* were in Tuolumne Meadows it would be the best slab climb of its grade! As was the style of the day this was a very bold, runout route. A few more bolts were added during the 2nd ascent. Then in the late 1990s, in a controversial move, many more bolts were added. The route is still a little sporty, but it is far from hair raising (except for the exposed start).
➤ Photo page 2, facing page, page 239.
FA: Vern Clevenger, Tom Higgins, 1975. Retrobolts: Alan Hirahara.

B. Unknown ?

Bolts, gear. Dihedral to roof, then up cracks.

C. Steppin' Stone 10d*

Gear. 2 pitch face. Gear anchor, walk off left.
FA: Mike Strassman, Chris Bishop, 1980s.

D. To Buoux or Not to Be 10c*

1 bolt, gear. 2 pitch face. Gear anchor, walk off left.
FA: Mike Strassman, Scott Ayers, 1980s.

E. Unknown ?

Bolts. Climb the blunt arete. Walk off left.

F. Spuds Gurgling Cock Holster 10c***

9 bolts, bring long runners to cut down rope drag. Climb the beautiful orange face, sporty and grainy. Climb past a hanging belay and walk off left, or do a 40m/130' rappel.
☞ A five star piece of rock with a one star bolting job. Some of the bolts are in depressions, some are sticking out of their holes and the bolts zigzag up the cliff.
FA: Mike Strassman, John Sherman, 1980s.
Variation: 10d***. Bolts, gear. About halfway up at a huge horizontal dike go up and left, past a bolt and some fixed nuts and pins.

Left of these routes on a tower there are many easy (5.6-5.8) slab options with limited protection. There is a sling belay about halfway (25m/80') up, and on top of this formation, making it ideal for top-roping.

©2004 Maximus Press. *Marty Lewis Photo.*

Granite Basin
East Face

Descent

South Face
pg 237

East Tower
pg 240

Crag Photo pg 235

Granite Basin - East Face

Intro: Page 234.

A. Mr. Brownstone 10c*

Bolts, gear to 2". Climb brown scarred rock to a roof and turn it on the left. Then continue up easy (5.8) mixed face and crack for 2 more pitches.

Descent: Walk off left.

FA: Robert Newsom, George Swiggum, 4/2002

B. Clevenger Route 9**

Pitch 1: 7**. Gear. Climb a flake to a right leaning groove to a ledge.

Pitch 2: 9**. Gear. Go up a crack, then head left to the top of a tower.

Pitch 3: 6*. Traverse a dike way left, then another one up and right following the weakness.

Descent: Walk off left.

FA: Vern Clevenger, Dennis Hennek, Galen Rowell, 1972.

C. All Along the Watchtower 10a**

Pitch 1: 10a**. 1 bolt, gear. Start up the *Clevenger Route*, then move right past a bush to a thin crack, then face climb to a ledge.

Pitch 2: 10a**. Gear. Traverse left past pitons through an airy huecoed roof, pass a flake, then up a face.

Pitch 3: 10a**. 1 bolt, gear. Face climb a waterstreak.

Descent: Traverse off left.

FA: Alex Schmauss, Malcolm Ives, Mike Strassman, 1980s.

As has happened so many times before on Eastside crags—it turns out that the following "first ascents" were probably already done in the early 1970s. This time Vern Clevenger was the climber, but the details have long since been forgotten.

D. Firefall 9**

Pitch 1: 9**. Gear. Climb a dihedral then go left to a flake and pass a roof on the left.

Pitch 2: 7**. Gear. Climb a left diagonalling dike, then go back right up a leaning crack that turns to offwidth.

Pitch 3: 7**. 1 bolt, gear. Continue up a right leaning crack to its end, then a waterstreak past a bolt.

Descent: Traverse off left.

FA: Mike Strassman, Alex Schmauss, 1980s.

E. Ordinary Route 8**

Pitch 1: 6**. Gear. Climb a dihedral then move right to a slabby crack.

Pitch 2: 6**. Gear. Flakes and huecos lead to a ledge.

Pitch 3: 8**. 1 bolt, gear. Go up a flake than some cracks and pass a bolt on a face.

Descent: Traverse off left.

FA: Mike Strassman, Alex Schmauss, 1980s.

Becky Hutto on **Hair Raiser Buttress** 9*****. ©*Kevin Calder Photo.*

See Page 237

©2004 Maximus Press. *Marty Lewis Photo.*

Granite Basin — East Tower

Northeast Face

East Face pg 238

15m/50' rappel

Crag Photo pg 235

Granite Basin - East Tower

Intro: Page 234.

A. Shaft 10b**
7 bolts. Stem up a groove to its end, then step right and climb a slab crux. 40m/130' rappel.
FA: George Swiggum, Robert Newsom, 4/2002.

B. Deadline 7*
Gear. Climb the dihedral that forms the left edge of the tower, then follow cracks up and left. 60m/200' rappel or walk off right.

C. Grape Nuts 9***
Pitch 1: 9***. 7 bolts, gear. Face climb to a crack.
Pitch 2: 9**. Gear. Face climb past horizontal cracks. 60m/200' rappel or walk off right.
FA: Mike Strassman, Craig Broderick, late 1980s.

D. Tecate Crunch 9*
Pitch 1: 8*. Bolts. Blunt arete right of roof. Belay on a flake.
Pitch 2: 9*. Bolts, gear. Climb straight up the face joining *Frosted Flakes* towards the top. 60m/200' rappel or walk off right.
FA: George Swiggum, Robert Newsom, 4/2002.

E. Frosted Flakes 7*(r)
Pitch 1: 6*(r). Gear. Traverse dike way left to a ledge. Bolt anchor.
Pitch 2: 7*. 1 bolts, gear. Face climb past horizontal cracks, go right of huge hueco past a bolt to the top. 60m/200' rappel or walk off right.
FA: Mike Strassman, Wendy Borgerd, 1980s.

F. Never Mind the Bullocks 9*(r)
4 bolts, gear. Sporty face. 60m/200' rappel or walk off right.
FA: Alan Bartlett, Mike Strassman, 1980s.

G. Post Nasal Drip 9**
1 bolt, gear. Climb a groove, then follow flakes. 60m/200' rappel or walk off right.
FA: Mike Strassman, Chris Lindell, 1980s.

The obvious water groove right of a detached pinnacle.

H. Tube 9**
5 bolts. Water groove. Lower off.
FA: Chris Lindell, 1980s.

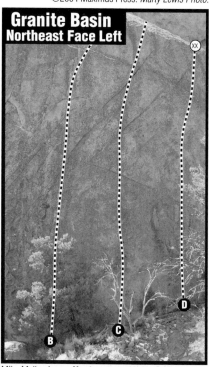

Mike Melkonian on **Hoot-enanny** 10b**. ©*Marty Lewis Photo.*

See Page 235

Granite Basin - Northeast Face Left

These routes are on a tower 100 ft. right of the *Tube*.

A. Desperado 10d*
Bolts, gear. Face climb to a crack in a bulge, then up a slab. Walk off right.
FA: Jason, George Swiggum.

B. Dick Van Dyke 8***
Bolts. Vertical dike. Walk off right.
FA: Mike Strassman, Wendy Borgerd, Scott Ayers, 1980s.

C. Unknown 10c**
Bolts. Face. Walk off right.

D. Plate of Fate 11a**
Bolts. Face. Walk off right.
FA: Jason, George Swiggum.

Northeast Face Right

E. Granitology 11c*****
19 bolts. Climb the awesome long sustained face left of a black streak. 55m/180' rappel.
FA: Mike Melkonian, Neil Satterfield, 8/2003, TD.

F. Community Service 10d****
3 bolts, gear to 2". Climb a crack then face climb left into another crack. 50m/165' rappel.

See Page 253

Roland Arsons on **Spike** 12c*** at the Tioga Cliff. ©*Greg Epperson Photo.*

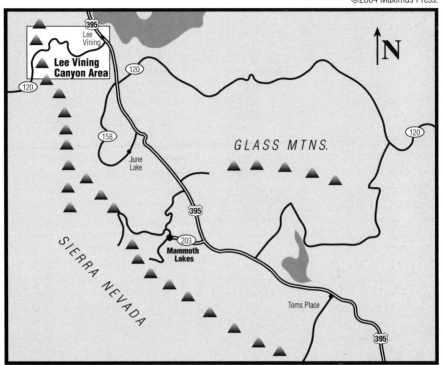

CHAPTER 10

LEE VINING CANYON

©2004 Maximus Press.

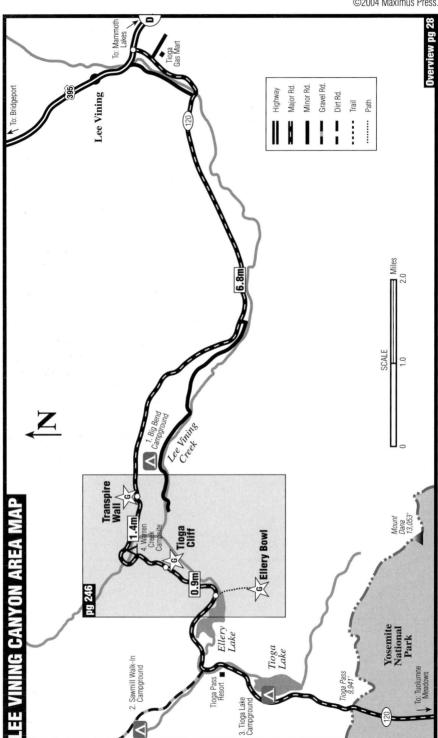

LEE VINING CANYON AREA MAP

Overview pg 28

Legend
- Highway
- Major Rd.
- Minor Rd.
- Gravel Rd.
- Dirt Rd.
- Trail
- Path

N

SCALE

Miles
0   1.0   2.0

To: Mammoth Lakes
Tioga Gas Mart
To: Bridgeport
395
Lee Vining
120
6.8m
1. Big Bend Campground
Lee Vining Creek
Transpire Wall
G
1.4m
4. Warren Creek Campsite
Tioga Cliff
G
0.9m
Ellery Bowl
G
pg 246
2. Sawmill Walk-In Campground
Tioga Pass Resort
Ellery Lake
3. Tioga Lake Campground
Tioga Lake
Tioga Pass 9,941'
Mount Dana 13,053'
Yosemite National Park
To: Tuolumne Meadows
120

LEE VINING CANYON AREA BASICS

L ee Vining Canyon is the eastern gateway to Yosemite National Park. During the winter, in this beautiful alpine area, one will find the best waterfall ice climbing in the state. Once the snow melts one will also find difficult granite face climbing and one of the best testpiece cracks in the Mammoth Area: *"Speed of Life"*. The climbs are all accessed by driving up the steep grade of Hwy. 120 as it approaches Tioga Pass and Tuolumne Meadows.

Getting There

To get to the Lee Vining Canyon Area start at the U.S. 395/203 junction and drive north on U.S. 395. After 25.5 miles turn left at the Hwy. 120 West junction. Drive into the canyon.

Amenities

Lee Vining

The town of Lee Vining has restaurants, groceries, gas and lodging.

Tioga Gas Mart

More than a gas station, there is a fantastic restaurant inside serving gourmet food. ☎ 760-647-1088.

Tioga Pass Resort

The Tioga Pass Resort offers a restaurant, general store and rental cabins. ☎ 209-372-4471. www.tiogapassresort.com

Camping

1. Big Bend Campground

Open May through mid October, the fee is $15. Picnic tables, piped water, vault toilets, elev. 7,800 ft. ☎ 760-647-3044.

2. Sawmill Walk-In Campground

Open June through mid October, the fee is $9. Picnic tables, no potable water, vault toilets, elev. 9,600 ft. ☎ 760-647-3044.

3. Tioga Lake Campground

Open June through mid October, the fee is $15. Picnic tables, piped water, vault toilets, elev. 9,700 ft. ☎ 760-647-3044.

Primitive Camping

4. Warren Creek Campsite

Primitive camping right off the highway. No potable water, elev. 8,900 ft.

Adapted from the U.S.G.S. 1:24,000 Mount Dana Quadrangle.

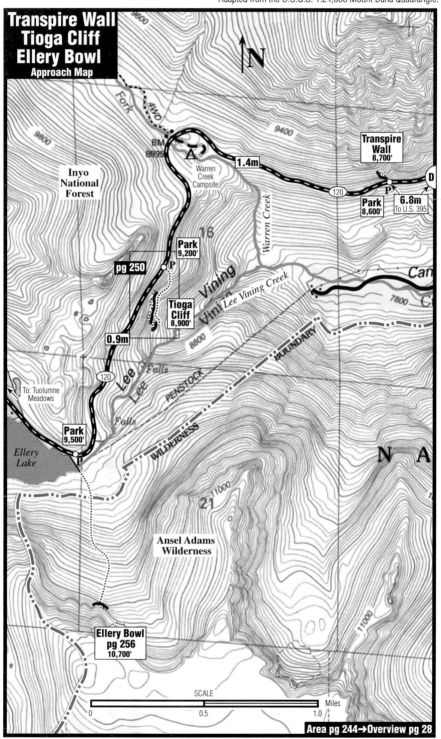

Transpire Wall
Tioga Cliff
Ellery Bowl
Approach Map

N

Inyo
National
Forest

Transpire
Wall
8,700'

1.4m

Park
8,600'

6.8m
To U.S. 395

120

BM
8999

Warren
Creek
Campsite

Warren Creek

Park
9,200'

pg 250

P

16

Vining

Lee Vining Creek

Can

7800

Tioga
Cliff
8,900'

0.9m

8800

120

Lee

Falls

Lee

PENSTOCK

BOUNDARY

To: Tuolumne
Meadows

Falls

WILDERNESS

N   A

Park
9,500'

P

Ellery
Lake

11000

21

Ansel Adams
Wilderness

11000

Ellery Bowl
pg 256
10,700'

SCALE

Miles

0   0.5   1.0

See Page 253 Bird Lew on the 1st pitch of **Titslinger** 11c** at the Tioga Cliff. ©*Andy Selters Photo.*

Transpire Wall

The Transpire Wall looks kind of scrappy from the highway, but when you get up close the quality of the rock becomes apparent. The climbing is cerebral and technical. Certain climbers will be pleased that unlike the Dike Wall and the Gong Show Crag, expect to have to place supplemental gear on these often mixed routes.

Be aware that this is a highly public and visible crag, and that your presence could be distracting for tourists not familiar with mountain driving. Rockfall is a concern, so please be careful on the talus slopes.

Transpire Wall Details

Environment: Talus slope above a busy highway.
Elevation: 8,700 ft.
Season: June to October.
Exposure: Southwest facing.
Rock Type: Impeccable granite.
Gear Climbs: 8 routes, 10a to 11d.
Sport Climbs: 7 routes, 10d to 12b.
Drive From Mammoth: 35 minutes.
Approach: 5 minute scramble, with a 100 ft. gain.

The Approach: From the U.S. 395/203 junction drive north on U.S. 395 for 25.5 miles. Turn left on Hwy. 120 West and drive 6.8 miles. Park on the left in a huge gravel pullout.

Cross Hwy. 120 then scramble up and left on talus to the cliff.

History: Developed in the late 1980s mostly by Dave Bengston and Steve Gerberding.

Tom Herbert on **Itchy Scratchy** 11d***. ©*Greg Epperson Photo.*

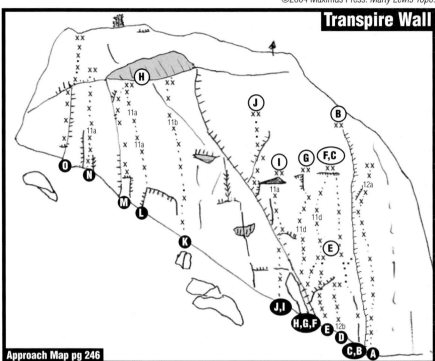

Transpire Wall

Approach Map pg 246

Transpire Wall

Intro: Page 247. It's a good idea to bring some pieces of gear for these climbs.

A. Wicked Itchy 12a★★★
11 bolts. Face. 35m/115' lower off.
FA: Steve Gerberding, Dave Bengston, late 1980s.

B. Marital Bliss 10c★★
1 bolt, gear. Start up *Fuel Pump*, then go right up a dihedral. Rappel to *Itchy Scratchy*.
FA: Steve Gerberding, Cal Gerberding, 1993.

C. Fuel Pump 10d★(r)
4 bolts, gear to 3". Face/cracks. Lower off.
FA: Dave Bengston, Steve Gerberding, late 1980s.

D. Wicked Stiffy 12b★★
3 bolts. Face. Lower off.
FA: Dave Bengston, late 1980s.

E. Red Don't Go 12b★★★
6 bolts. Face through roof. Lower off.
FA: Chris Falkenstein, late 1980s.

F. Itchy Scratchy 11d★★★
7 bolts, gear: 1.75" pieces. Face climb past the anchor of *Red Don't Go*. Lower off. ➤ Photo facing page.
FA: Dave Bengston, Steve Gerberding, late 1980s.

G. Scratch 'n Sniff 11d★★★
7 bolts, gear to 2". Face. Lower off.
FA: Dave Bengston, Mark Carpenter, late 1980s.

H. Transpire Crack 10a★
Gear. Broken left leaning crack. Lower off.
FA: Don Reid, Rick Cashner, late 1980s.

I. Walk Like an Egyptian 11a★★
5 bolts, gear to 2.5". Face. Lower off.
FA: Dan McDevitt.

J. Senoir Pappas 12a★★
7 bolts, gear. Start *Walk Like an Egyptian*, then go left up a crack to a bolted finish. Lower off.
FA: Steve Gerberding, Conrad Anker, early 1990s.

K. Rat Patrol 11b★★
7 bolts, gear. Face. Lower off.
FA: Dan McDevitt.

L. Harpole and the Hendersons 11a★★
6 bolts, gear to 1.5". Lower off.
FA: Steve Gerberding, Jim "Banny Root" May, late 1980s.

M. Unknown ?
6 bolts. Pass a small roof then face climb. Lower off.

N. Mellow Yellow 11a★★
6 bolts, gear to 2". Face. Lower off.
FA: Dan McDevitt.

O. Steely Dan 11a★★
8 bolts, gear. Dihedral to roof. Lower off.
FA: Steve Gerberding, Tracy Dorton, early 1990s.

©2004 Maximus Press.

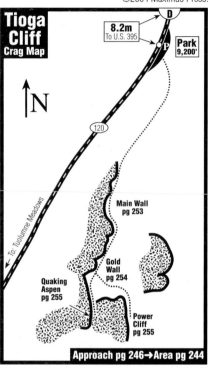

Tioga Cliff
Crag Map

8.2m
To U.S. 395

Park
9,200'

D

P

120

N

To Tuolumne Meadows

Main Wall
pg 253

Gold
Wall
pg 254

Quaking
Aspen
pg 255

Power
Cliff
pg 255

Approach pg 246→Area pg 244

Tioga Cliff Details

Environment: Scree and talus.
Elevation: 8,900 ft.
Season: July to October.
Exposure: East facing.
Rock Type: Granite.
Gear Climbs: 22 routes, 5.9 to 12c.
Sport Climbs: 13 routes, 11b to 12c.
Drive From Mammoth: 40 minutes.
Approach: 10 to 25 minute heinous scree scramble, with a 300 ft. descent.

Tioga Cliff

A fantastic expansive version of the Transpire Wall, with some formidable testpieces. The routes are below the road and as a result they are somewhat hidden from view. The approach is a bit adventurous, but the routes are certainly worth the effort.

©2004 Maximus Press. *Marty Lewis Photo.*

Tioga Cliff

Main Wall
pg 253

Gold Wall
pg 254

Quaking
Aspen
pg 255

Power Cliff
pg 255

The Approach: Map page 246. From the U.S. 395 / 203 junction drive north on U.S. 395 for 25.5 miles. Turn left on Hwy. 120 West and drive 8.2 miles. Turn left into a paved viewpoint, with an interpretive display that says "Don't Fence Me In".

Walk past the sign then go down and right (south) across unstable scree staying under any towers encountered.

History: Tuolumne Meadows climbers were looking for a place to try bolted climbing outside the prying eyes and tight regulations of Yosemite National Park. Mostly developed in the late 1980s by Dave Bengston, Steve Gerberding and Dan McDevitt. Kind of a bold traditional version of technical granite sport climbing.

See Page 253   Dave Bengston on **Jawbone Jitterbug** 11c**. ©*Greg Epperson Photo.*

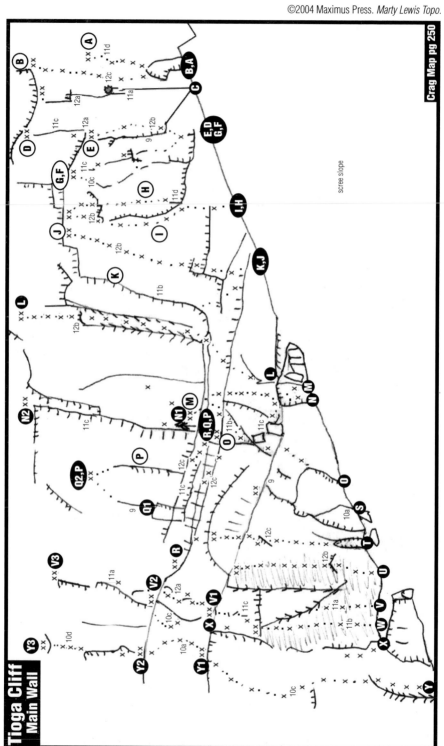

Crag Map pg 250

scree slope

Tioga Cliff
Main Wall

Tioga Cliff - Main Wall

Intro: Page 250. Supplemental gear may be required on routes that appear to be sport climbs.

A. Poindexter 11d★★
4 bolts. Scramble up a block, then climb a steep seam. Lower off.
FA: Dave Bengston, late 1980s.

B. The Finger 12c★★★
5 bolts. Scramble up a block, then climb a burly face. Lower off.
FA: Dave Bengston, late 1980s.

C. Stones Throw 12a★★★
Gear to 2.5". Follow a steep seam past a bush. Lower off.
FA: Don Reid, Rick Cashner, late 1980s.

D. Radical Left 12b★★·(r)
5 bolts, gear. Climb a mixed slab past a belay, turn a roof, then up a seam. 30m/100' lower off. Can be broken into 2 pitches.
FA: Steve Gerberding, Dave Bengston, late 1980s.

E. Stalag 13 9★
1 bolt, gear. Clip bolt then move left into a flare. Lower off.
FA: Dave Bengston, late 1980s.

F. Coq Au Vin 11c·
1 bolt, gear. Grassy crack. Lower off.

G. Golden Eagle 10c·(r)
3 bolts, gear. Clip the bolt of *Stalag 13*, then go left up a brushy face. Lower off.

H. Bag 'O Tricks 11d★★★
7 bolts (1 chain draw). Climb a series of bulges and roofs. Lower off.
FA: Dave Bengston, late 1980s.

I. Master Cylinder 12b★★★★
7 bolts. Clip the first 2 bolts of *Bag 'O Tricks*, then go left up a leaning dihedral. Lower off.
FA: Dave Bengston, late 1980s.

J. Felix 12b★★★
10 bolts, opt. gear to get started. Blocky roofs lead to a face. Lower off.
FA: Dave Bengston, late 1980s.

K. Dynomike 11b·(r)
1 bolt, gear. Clip bolt then work up and left. Lower off.
FA: Mike Forkash, late 1980s.

L. Silver Bullet 12c★★★★
13 bolts. Start on a big flat boulder, pass a small roof and enter a dihedral. 45m/150' rappel.
FA: Dan McDevitt, late 1980s.

M. Unknown 12?★★★★
7 bolts. Wild face (shares the 2nd bolt of *Titslinger*). Lower off.
FA: Dave Bengston, early 1990s.

N. Titslinger 11c★★·(r)
Pitch 1: 11c. 4 bolts, gear. Mixed climbing leads to a ledge with a tree. Climb 2nd pitch or lower off. ▶ Photo page 247.
Pitch 2: 11c. 1 bolts, gear. Dihedral. Lower off.
FA: Dave Bengston, Steve Gerberding, late 1980s.

O. Get to the Roof 11b★(r)
4 bolts, gear to 1.5". Wandering crack and face. Lower off.
FA: Ken Yager, late 1980s.

P. Earshot 12c★
3 bolts, gear to 1.5". Out a roof and up a crack. 55m/180' rappel to ground.
FA: Dave Bengston, late 1980s.

Q. Jawbone Jitterbug 11c★★
Pitch 1: 11c★★. 3 bolts, gear to 2.5". Start up *Earshot* then head left along a crack to a tower. Gear belay.
▶ Photo page 251.

R. Dangle Fest 12c★★★★
4 bolts, gear to 3.5". A wild hanging traverse left, under a big roof. 30m/100' rappel.
FA: Dave Bengston, late 1980s.

S. Invader 10a★★
Gear. A finger crack in a dihedral leads to an undercling right. Lower off.
FA: Ken Yager, Grant Hiskes.

T. Spike 12c★★★
8 bolts. Start in a dihedral, then up and right to a corner. Lower off. ▶ Photo page 242.
FA: Dave Bengston, late 1980s.

U. Iya 12b★★★
11 bolts. Pass 2 bolts then step right, pass a roof, up a face to a seam. Lower off.
FA: Chris Falkenstein, late 1980s.

V. Made for the Shade 11c★
Pitch 1: 11c. 4 bolts, gear. Face to a left leaning crack.
Pitch 2: 10c or 12a. Bolts and gear. Corners.
Pitch 3: 11a. 1 bolt, gear.
FA: Steve Gerberding, Scott Stowe, late 1980s.

W. Torqued 11b★★
6 bolts. Face climb up dark rock. Lower off.
FA: Chris Falkenstein, late 1980s.

X. Can't We Talk About This? 10?
4 bolts, gear. Face and cracks.
FA: Steve Gerberding, Kevin Carey, Carla Zezula, early 1990s.

Y. Lucky 13 10d★
Pitch 1: 10c. 12 bolts. Climb the right side of an arete.
Pitch 2: 10a. 4 bolts, gear. Face.
Pitch 3: 10d. 4 bolts, gear. Dihedral to face.
FA: Steve Gerberding, Carla Zezula, late 1980s.

©2004 Maximus Press. *Marty Lewis Photo.*

©2004 Maximus Press. *Marty Lewis Photo.*

Gold Wall

Tioga Cliff Intro: Page 250.

A. Hole in the Wall 11a**
4 bolts, gear. Climb a 5.6 corner then step right and climb cracks and seams past a hole. 50m/165' rappel.

B. Less Filling 12a**
Pitch 1: 12a**. 4 bolts, gear to 2". Climb a seam on a slab. Climb 2nd pitch or lower off.
Pitch 2: 11c**. 4 bolts, gear to 2". Face climb to a finger crack. Lower off.
FA: Dan McDevitt, late 1980s.

C. Tastes Great 10c*
4 bolts, gear to 2". Climb the finger crack just right of an arete, eventually finish up the arete. 50m/165' rappel.
FA: Dan McDevitt, late 1980s.

D. Gold Wall 10a*(r)
Gear. Start in a dihedral, then nebulous climbing leads up a beautiful gold face. 50m/165' rappel.

©2004 Maximus Press. *Marty Lewis Photo.*

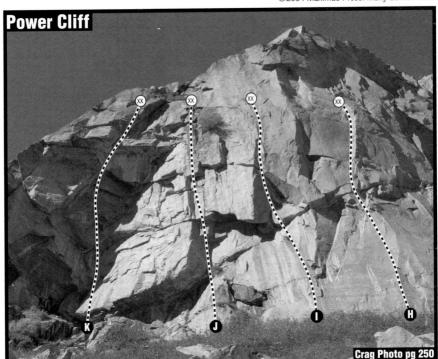

Power Cliff

Crag Photo pg 250

Quaking Aspen

Tioga Cliff Intro: Page 250. This cliff is appropriately named; all the routes start in an aspen choked area.

E. Double Cream, Double Sugar 11c**

Gear to 3.5". A short, steep handcrack on the side of the buttress. Lower off.
FA: Rick Cashner, late 1980s.

F. Quaking Aspen 9***

Gear to 3". Start on seams, then enter a beautiful handcrack. Lower off.

G. Executive Decision 11c**(r)

3 bolts, gear to 1". Slabby seams lead to a thin face. Lower off.
FA: Chris Falkenstein, late 1980s.

Power Cliff

Tioga Cliff Intro: Page 250. The Power Cliff is located down below Quaking Aspen. It is accessed via a short slippery 3rd class gully that is right against the wall.

H. Radar Detector 12a*

3 bolts, gear to 1". Starts up a seam on a slab, then climb a right leaning dihedral. Lower off. ☞ There may be a 2nd pitch.
FA: Dave Caunt, late 1980s.

I. Jaws 12a**

7 bolts. Climb a broken dihedral. Lower off.
FA: Dan McDevitt, early 1990s.

J. Unknown 12a**

6 bolts. Start in a corner, then head up seams and pass a bush on the left. Lower off.
FA: Dan McDevitt, early 1990s.

K. Gorilla Warfare 12a****

10 bolts. Climb a steep blocky face to a wide crack at a roof. Lower off.
FA: Dan McDevitt, early 1990s.

©2004 Maximus Press. *Marty Lewis Photo.*

Ellery Bowl
A. Speed of Life 11b*****

Ellery Lake

Approach Map pg 246

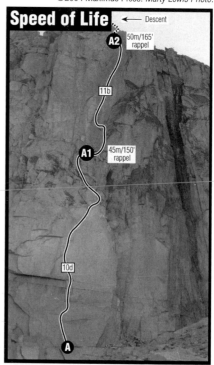

Speed of Life   ← Descent

A2 50m/165' rappel

11b

A1 45m/150' rappel

10d

A

Ellery Bowl

This alpine crag features the beautiful monolithic testpiece crack *Speed of Life*. There are a handful of other routes to the right. Please consult "Rock Climbs of Tuolumne Meadows" for information on these climbs.

Most people visit Ellery Bowl for the awesome spring skiing, especially the tight couloir to the right of the crag—known locally as "Chute Out" or "Ellery Couloir".

The Approach: Map page 246. From the U.S. 395/203 junction drive north on U.S. 395 for 25.5 miles. Turn left on Hwy. 120 West and drive 9.1 miles to Ellery Lake. Park on the left, at the east end of the lake.

Ellery Bowl Details

Environment: Alpine talus field.
Elevation: 10,700 ft.
Season: July to September.
Exposure: North facing.
Rock Type: Alpine granite.
Gear Climbs: 1 route, 11b.
Drive From Mammoth: 40 minutes.
Approach: 45 minute scramble with a 1,200 ft. gain. Kind of a grunt.
Special Concerns: Ellery Bowl is in the Ansel Adams Wilderness. Motorized drills are prohibited.

Walk across the dam, then hike south up a stable scree slope. About halfway up a low cliffband is reached, skirt this to the left past an unstable area, then continue up large talus blocks to the crag.

History: On-sighted by Don Reid in 1981.

Ellery Bowl
A. Speed of Life 11b*****
Pitch 1: 10d***. Gear to 6". Climb a seam on white granite, halfway up is a thin bouldery crux, after this climb a widening crack, then do an exciting move right to an arete, from here easy corners lead to a ledge.

Pitch 2: 11b*****. Gear to 3.5". Climb up a blocky corner, step left and enter the incredible, steep, golden, right leaning crack.

Descent: Either two 50m/165' rappels or a 4th class scramble off left (west) gets you to the base.

➤ Photo this page.

FA: Don Reid, Chris Falkenstein, 1981.

Bruce Lella on the 1st pitch of **Speed of Life** 10d***. ©*Bill McChesney Photo.*

See Page 41

Bird Lew on **Eavesdropping** 10c**** at the Gong Show Crag. ©*Andy Selters Photo.*

A Mammoth vista—the Minarets. ©*John Moynier Photo.*

CHAPTER 11

APPENDIX

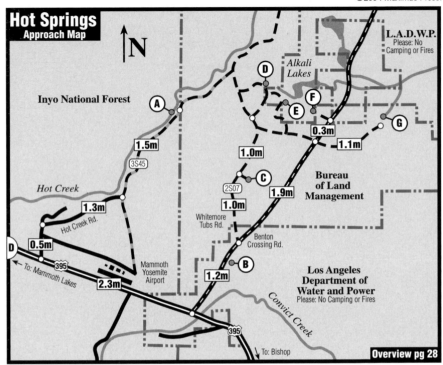

Hot Springs

This activity is included in this book because soaking in Hot Springs seems to be one of the most popular post climbing activities in the Mammoth Area.

The Eastern Sierra is a hotbed of geologic activity. The area surrounding Crowley Lake is located in a humongous crater formed by a giant volcanic eruption 760,000 years ago, and is know known as the Long Valley Caldera. There is still a pool of magma two miles down that keeps the bedrock in the area hot. When groundwater passes through these areas it is heated and forced to the surface creating hot springs. Enterprising individuals have built natural hot tubs out of rock and concrete that take advantage of these heated waters.

Access Information

Most of the Hot Springs are on public land administered by the Bureau of Land Management. The rest are on private property (with public access) that is owned by the Los Angeles Dept. of Water and Power. Hot Creek is a recreation site in the Inyo National Forest.

- ☞ Be courteous to Land Managers.
- ☞ Do not camp in the parking areas for the Hot Springs.
- ☞ Never use soap in the tubs.
- ☞ Clean up trash, even if it's not yours.
- ☞ Maintain a low profile.

Etiquette

These are busy places with a limited amount of space, so you will often have to stay back, be polite and wait your turn.

You will encounter nudity at the Hot Springs, but it is also perfectly acceptable to wear bathing suits.

Safety Concerns

☞ Always test the temperature of the water before entering.

☞ Kids and dogs should be watched closely.

☞ Alcohol and hot water can be a dangerous mix.

☞ When possible, drain the tubs and refill them before entering.

A. Hot Creek

An official Forest Service Recreation Site that is open from sunrise to sunset. Restrooms area available. A cold river crosses over some hot vents in a wild gorge. From the U.S. 395/203 junction drive 3.2 miles and turn left onto the Airport Rd. From here drive 0.5 miles and turn right on Hot Creek Rd. Follow this 2.8 miles to a paved parking area on the left. A paved trail heads down into the gorge.

The following locations are all accessed off of Benton Crossing Rd. From the U.S. 395/203 junction drive south on U.S. 395 for 5.5 miles and turn left.

B. Whitmore Hot Springs

Swimming pool, jacuzzi and restrooms. This is a public facility and there is a fee. Drive north on Benton Crossing Rd. for 1.2 miles and turn right.

C. Rock Tub

A small concrete tub. Drive north on Benton Crossing Rd. 1.2 miles. Turn left at Whitmore Tubs Rd. and drive 1.0 miles. Turn right here and park, the tub is just a short walk ahead.

D. Shepherd's Hot Spring

A concrete tub. Drive north on Benton Crossing Rd. 1.2 miles. Turn left at Whitmore Tubs Rd. and drive 2.0 miles and turn right just before a lone pine tree. Follow this for 0.5 miles, when the road forks take the left branch to a pond. The tub is in front of the pond.

E. Crab Cooker

A nice concrete tub. Drive north on Benton Crossing Rd. for 3.1 miles and turn left at a cattle guard. Follow this dirt road 0.5 miles, then turn right. Drive 0.5 miles to the tub.

F. Hilltop Hot Spring

A nice concrete pool with great views. Drive 3.4 miles north on Benton Crossing Rd. Turn left on a dirt road and drive 0.2 miles, then park. Follow a path east up a hill, and cross a stream.

G. Wild Willy's Hot Spring

A large concrete pool and a smaller tub, with awesome views. Drive 3.1 miles north on Benton Crossing Rd. Turn right at a cattle guard onto a dirt rd. Follow this for 1.1 miles to its end at a parking area. From here a short walk on a boardwalk leads to the tubs.

Warning—Frequenting hot springs is an inherently dangerous activity and the user of this book accepts a number of unavoidable risks. Hazards include: scalding water, sharp rocks, sudden volcanic activity, broken glass, arsenic, bacteria and crazed perverts.

The authors, editors, publishers, distributors and land owners accept no liability for any injuries incurred from using this book.

ROUTES BY RATING

10b***

10b****

10b*****

10c*

10c**

10c***

10c****

10d*

Further Reading

Rock & Ice #59
January/February 1994
Rock Creek Canyon
Scott Ayers
Rock & Ice Guide.
Clark Canyon
John Monyier
Rock & Ice Guide.

Rock & Ice #109
June/July 2001
Sherwin Plateau
Mick Ryan
Rock & Ice Miniguide.

Guide Services

Peter Croft
☎ 760-872-9309
595 South Barlow Lane
Bishop CA, 93514

Nidever Mountain Guides
☎ 760-648-1122
P.O. Box 446
June Lake, CA 93529
www.themountainguide.com

Sierra Mountain Center
☎ 760-873-8526
174 West Line St.
Bishop, CA 93514
sierramountaincenter.com

Sierra Mountaineering International
☎ 760-872-4929
236 North Main St.
Bishop, CA 93515-1011
www.sierramountaineering.com

Sierra Rock Climbing School
☎ 877-686-7625
SierraRockClimbingSchool.com

Mick Ryan Photo.

INDEX

H

I

J

K

L

ABOUT MARTY LEWIS

Marty Lewis grew up in the Santa Monica Mountains of Southern California, where he showed an early interest in the outdoor world. His father helped cultivate this interest by taking Marty on annual trips to the Sierra Nevada Mountains, to hike, backpack and peakbag.

The author moved to Mammoth Lakes in 1978, where he managed a successful family business. He was also a key player in the introduction of the giant afro look to the Eastern Sierra.

During the 1980s Marty dabbled in traditional rock climbing but found it a little to frightening, instead he focused mainly on bouldering and mountaineering. He soon fancied himself a fitness man, spending his time running, cycling and weight lifting.

In 1989 Marty climbed his first sport climb in the Owens River Gorge, finding it to be one of the most exhilarating, athletic things he'd ever done. From then on, he has spent his free time rock climbing, most of it in the Eastern Sierra. During this era he made a substantial contribution to the development of sport climbing in the region.

Marty has not climbed El Capitan, Mt. Everest or any 5.13's.

After twenty-two years in Mammoth, Marty has moved out of the snowbelt to a rural area near Bishop, where he lives with his wife Sharon and their dogs Blue and Joe.

ABOUT JOHN MOYNIER

John Moynier has lived in the High Sierra since 1978, working as a climbing and ski mountaineering guide for much of that time. He is a Certified Mountaineering Guide with American Mountain Guides Association and a professional member of the American Avalanche Association.

John is also a free-lance photographer and writer who has been published in numerous outdoor magazines, including <u>Rock and Ice</u>, <u>Couloir</u> and <u>Backcountry</u>. In addition, he is the author of <u>Climbing California's High Sierra</u>, <u>Backcountry Skiing California's High Sierra</u>, <u>Avalanche Aware</u>, <u>Scenic Dayhikes in the Mammoth Lakes Area</u>, <u>The Basic Essentials of Cross Country Skiing</u>, and <u>The Basic Essentials of Mountaineering</u>.

John currently lives in Bishop with his wife Rose and daughter Katie.

About Maximus Press

Maximus Press was launched in 1990 with the publication of the pamphlet "Owens River Gorge Climbs". Garage-style in appearance, this publication was nevertheless accurate, concise and easy to use. Fourteen years later after considerable improvements, Maximus Press continues to strive to produce the most useful and state-of-the-art guidebooks possible. The knowledge base of our editorial staff comes from years of experience climbing, exploring and living in the Eastern Sierra. You can count on our commitment to deliver high-quality books.

I have spent the past 26 years living in this fantastic region. The combination of spectacular natural beauty, a stable climate and an incredible diversity of climbing options, in one of the most wide open and least populated areas in California is hard to beat. Enjoy!

—Marty Lewis
Publisher

The Maximus Press editorial staff compiling a quality guidebook.

We Don't Meet the Competition. We Crush It.

Notice: Due to recent security breaches, all employees must be strip-searched before leaving the premises

Bishop, California production facilities.

Another shipment of books coming your way.

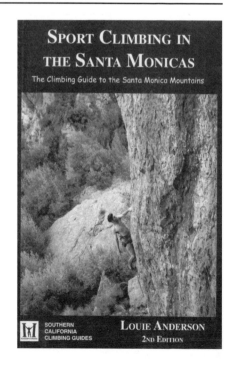

THE GOOD, THE GREAT, AND THE AWESOME

by Peter Croft

EASTERN SIERRA CLIMBING GUIDES VOL. 4

July 2002 - 1st Edition
244 pages - $30.00
ISBN 0-9676116-4-4

The Guidebook to the Top 40 High Sierra Rock Climbs

- Tricks of the Trade
- Whitney Region
- Palisades
- Bishop High Country
- Tuolumne Meadows
- Roadside Cragging

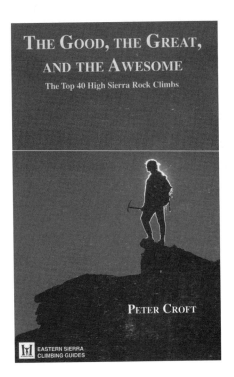

OWENS RIVER GORGE CLIMBS

by Marty Lewis

EASTERN SIERRA CLIMBING GUIDES VOL. 1

June 2000 - 9th Edition
136 pages - $19.00
ISBN 0-9676116-2-8

Featuring 600 fantastic climbs at California's premiere sport climbing area.

- Negress Wall
- Social Platform
- Great Wall of China
- Eldorado Roof
- Dilithium Crystal
- Gorgeous Towers

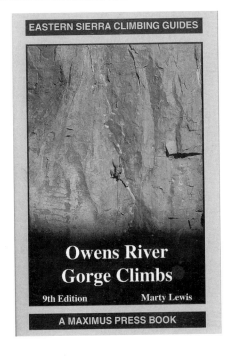